Castaway Tales

publication of this book is funded by the

BEATRICE FOX AUERBACH FOUNDATION FUND

at the Hartford Foundation for Public Giving

CHRISTOPHER PALMER

Castaway Tales

FROM *Robinson Crusoe* TO *Life of Pi*

WESLEYAN UNIVERSITY PRESS
MIDDLETOWN, CONNECTICUT

Wesleyan University Press
Middletown CT 06459
www.wesleyan.edu/wespress

Manufactured in the United States of America
Designed by Eric M. Brooks
Typeset in Quadraat by Passumpsic Publishing

publication of this book is funded by the
Beatrice Fox Auerbach Foundation Fund
at the Hartford Foundation for Public Giving

Library of Congress Cataloging-in-Publication Data
Names: Palmer, Christopher, 1948– author.
Title: Castaway tales: from *Robinson Crusoe* to *Life of Pi* /
Christopher Palmer.
Description: Middletown, Connecticut: Wesleyan University Press,
2016. | Series: The Wesleyan early classics of science fiction
series | Includes bibliographical references and index.
Identifiers: LCCN 2015037497 |
ISBN 9780819576217 (cloth: alk. paper) |
ISBN 9780819576576 (pbk.: alk. paper) |
ISBN 9780819576224 (ebook)
Subjects: LCSH: Adventure stories—History and criticism. |
Castaways in literature. | Survival in literature. | Islands in
literature. | Shipwrecks in literature. | Crusoe, Robinson
(Fictitious character)
Classification: LCC PN3448.A3 P35 2016 | DDC 809.3/87—dc23
LC record available at http://lccn.loc.gov/2015037497

5 4 3 2 1

CONTENTS

ACKNOWLEDGMENTS

Thanks to Istvan Csicsery-Ronay, Marisa Palmer, Kim Stanley Robinson, and Steve Moline for reading drafts of the book, and to Catherine Howell and Carlos Uxo for reading draft chapters. Thanks to Brian Boyd, Tania Donald, Nick Levey, and David Elliott for suggesting texts, to Parker Smathers for his support, and to Sara Evangelos for her meticulous editing. Errors and infelicities are all mine.

The website for *Castaway Tales*, including supplementary material, can be found at www.chrispalmercastaway.com.

This book is for my sons Eddie (Tokyo) and Sam (New York)—far away but not cast away.

INTRODUCTION

Castaway Tales discusses the history of the castaway tale as Daniel Defoe's *Robinson Crusoe* (1719) establishes it, with particular emphasis on the twentieth century. It's a complicated and richly varied history, and in the twentieth century it centers on revisions and critiques of the template Defoe sets out.

First, some remarks on the kind of castaway tale whose vicissitudes and variations are explored here. A castaway tale can be a tale about survivors drifting at sea or simply lost overboard in the wilds of the ocean,[1] but here, on the model of *Robinson Crusoe*, a castaway tale is defined as a tale about a castaway or a group of castaways who are isolated on an island and have to survive, to make do. The activity of making do (working, improvising, addressing practical tasks) is important because it is what distinguishes *Robinson Crusoe* from earlier tales about protagonists marooned on islands for a time, such as *The Tempest*, and because this is the kind of castaway tale adopted and adapted by a whole series of later authors, with sometimes alarming results.

Robinson Crusoe is in many ways optimistic and untroubled by worries about, for instance, the castaway's sanity during his decades of loneliness, or about his use of violence, or about his domination of others, when others do invade his solitude. The question that is pursued here is, what happens to the original as it was set forth by *Robinson Crusoe*? How does the castaway tale fare in our own age, which is uneasy about the limits of reason and of sanity, and which is troubled by violence, especially imperialist or racial violence? The short answer is that the castaway tale is subjected to many grim revisions (what will be called in a moment the phase of violence) and many sceptical ones, but that its optimism is sometimes revised, indeed, recovered, rather than discarded (this happens in what will be called in a moment the phase of reconciliation).

The clue, then, is in the nature of revision, which is pursued in this book. The revisionary tales use the traditional tale, as established by Defoe, as a frame of reference. The traditional tale is present even when it is denied. It is not missing, but denied, or overturned. In many instances we can tell this because the text in question alludes to *Robinson Crusoe*, or, in a subset of stories, to H. G. Wells's *The Island of Dr. Moreau*, and by this allusion it invites us to see what it is not doing; or it declares that it is a revision of the original by using the same characters or characters with a related name (Morel for Moreau, for instance, in Adolfo Bioy Casares's *The Invention of Morel*).

Revision involves not simply imitation but rewriting with a fresh eye, very often a skeptical or disenchanted eye. *Castaway Tales* is about the varieties of revision, and the strange and unexpected places to which it takes the castaway tale (even the strange and unexpected places to which it takes the castaway's island). The period from the twentieth century to the present has seen the most radical and challenging revisions, and *Castaway Tales* passes over the eighteenth-century successors to Crusoe,[2] only glances at those of the nineteenth century, and, regretfully, confines itself to novels and short stories, leaving out the many films and television series that present versions of the castaway tale. Utopias set on islands are likewise overlooked, because their concerns take them in different directions, their interest in the setting—the topography of the island, for instance—is much less, and their allusions to Defoe are incidental.[3]

Even with these renunciations and restrictions, a rich variety and abundance remains to be explored. There are a lot of islands in the stories discussed in this book—tropical, deserted, haunted, covered in concrete blockhouses, located in space stations that curve topology back on itself, located among freeways in central London.[4] A lot of stories are discussed in this book—a lot of trees, to borrow the metaphor of woods and trees, and among the trees some twisted shrubs (Stephen King's brutal "Survivor Type"), some strange sports (John Barth's deconstructive "Anonymiad"), even some orchids and wildflowers (Derek Walcott, "Crusoe's Island"). What of the wood—what of the overall shape and interpretation that makes sense of this mass of vegetation? This introduction highlights a couple of key terms and formal aspects, and summarizes the argument of each chapter.

The discussion stems from the influence of *Robinson Crusoe*, the influence, no doubt, of a legend or myth drawn from the novel rather than the influence of its text in all its details, but pervasive. *Robinson Crusoe* provides a template for the story of a castaway—or castaways—making do on an island. Further, as will be discussed in the first chapter, it provides a set of memorable and easily varied tropes, by which the tale can be reinvigorated or revised or parodied. *Castaway Tales* examines the interplay between features of the genre that can be varied, and the imaginative responses to history and culture that can be discerned in the revisions.

Concentrating on what has happened since the end of the nineteenth century, *Castaway Tales* identifies three broad phases in the history of the castaway tale, and these phases structure the discussion. They are labeled settlement (Chapters 1 and 2), violence (Chapters 3 and 4), and reconciliation (Chapters 5 to 7, with a reservation as to Chapter 5). Some comments on these labels: first, they stand for shifting emphases in the history of the castaway tale, not clear breaks. For instance, there is violence in many castaway tales, including *Robinson Crusoe*, but it becomes particularly prominent in a series of texts that are discussed in Chapters 3 and 4. Further, the labels stand for interdependent sets of qualities in each phase. Alter one element, whether thematic or formal, and others often alter also. If the castaways are overcome by internecine violence, the topography of the island changes too, at least as it is experienced by the castaways and as it is conveyed to the reader. If the castaway has not the competence, or lacks the will, to work on his island, then—not exactly as a consequence of this, but as an accompanying effect—the island itself will be marked with ruins or vestiges of the past. This interdependence is most striking in the phase of violence, where the sanity of the castaway is also thrown into question, and the degeneration of the castaway is accompanied by a reorientation of the shape and direction of the plot. The events of the tale—the activities of the castaway—no longer forge productively onward toward settled civilization, but turn backward to the past, or culminate in a revelation that throws all that has happened so far into doubt.

As is the case with many distinctions and categorizations, there is a core of clear and inescapable examples, surrounded by a blurred edge, consisting of texts that fit uneasily into the category into which they have been put. There are, for instance, transitional cases. Jules Verne's *The Mysterious Island* is discussed under the heading of the phase of settlement in Chapter 2, because the castaways in this novel imitate but outdo Robinson Crusoe in productivity, but the second half of the novel undermines the achievements of the castaways in the first half, and in this respect *The Mysterious Island* looks toward the period in the history of the castaway tale in which Defoe's template is radically revised. Yann Martel's *Life of Pi* is discussed under the heading of the phase of violence in Chapter 4, because of the striking glimpses into cannibal violence that feature, especially toward its end, but it is too sane and good-humored to fit easily into this category. Again, the texts discussed in Chapter 5 are important as revisions of the castaway tale but also hard to fit into a distinct phase in the modern history of the castaway tale. They range across the twentieth century; they are too skeptical to belong to the phase of settlement, and violence plays a minor role in them. Nonetheless, they do pointedly revise Defoe's template, and are in fact among the most telling and thoughtful of all twentieth-century revisions.

Some remarks on *Robinson Crusoe* and its ambivalent qualities will set the scene for the revisions. *Robinson Crusoe* celebrates the castaway's achievements: hard work, making do on his lonely island, converting and making a companion of Man Friday, and eventually proceeding from survival and settlement to rule over a small community. It's a practical, detailed, clear, and in many ways upbeat story. It has been much read; produced in simplified versions for children; often filmed. Various details are so well known as to make a kind of legend and form part of common knowledge.

Taking into account the text, the multitude of various allusions to *Robinson Crusoe*, and the many variations and revisions of the castaway story, it's fair to say that *Robinson Crusoe* exerts a continuing attraction. Much of this attraction, surely, comes from the homely, practical details of Crusoe's work. It's practical and it feels necessary, but it taps into the same fascination with play and with making a little world as do the cubbyhouse or the tree house, or camping out. It seems to have a kind of innocence. Defoe's novel thinks out what you might need to survive—then, what you might need to make a settlement—and it turns out that there is quite a lot, a kind of abundance even though it's the story of a solitary man on a small island. The abundance invites enjoyment.

Further, the castaway story seems to give us the bare elements of story: a person, the castaway, thrown back on his own resources; a basic predicament (how to survive, how to make do); and a place (an island, something that can be known, something that you can map and walk around). It's like a paradigm of story, yet it can be filled with realistic detail, and detail that has a kind of homely clarity—how to make bread, how to dry grapes. Here is another source of the attraction of the castaway tale as Defoe founds it. It seems elemental, as if stripped back to the basic constituents of any story. It seems ready to be a fable, or a myth.

So what Defoe gives us is attractive, even beguiling. Then again, the contemporary reader will likely have some reservations. Doesn't the story come untroubled from the age of confident colonialism and imperialism? Robinson Crusoe proceeds from survival to settlement to domination—rule over his island and over the others who come ashore after he has settled it, and who find themselves his subjects—Friday, Spanish sailors, ex-mutineers. And what are we to make of the fact that Crusoe has been a slave (in Morocco) and yet was on an expedition to buy slaves in Africa when he was wrecked? What are we to make of the novel's rather patronizing treatment of Friday—renamed, Christianized, rapidly shedding his own ways and culture as if they had never been, childlike in Crusoe's hands? In these aspects Defoe's novel might seem to invite, or provoke, revision; yet it does offer those attractions or enticements we have just sketched. The emphasis in the examination of *Robinson Crusoe* and its influence here is not on how *Robinson Crusoe* can be critiqued for its racism or imperialism, surely an unnecessary task now, but on how it has been adapted, revised, drastically rewritten, to express new and often disturbed or corrosive feelings about its material and themes: new feelings, not merely about the enterprise of settlement and rule, but also the faith in reason, the reliance on plain common sense, the treatment of nature as something to be used: a particular version of Western Man and his (in important ways, his) relation to the world. *That* kind of fable, or myth: not elemental, as it might have seemed, but set in ideological conditions with vast and perhaps disturbing ramifications. What is striking, nonetheless, is that a great deal of what makes *Robinson Crusoe* a beguiling book survives, if in glimpses and in very different contexts, in the revisions that are discussed in *Castaway Tales*; but what is equally striking is how elements of Defoe's novel serve as a continuing provocation to variations and revisions that turn the original on its head, and serve to express a set of doubts about and criticisms of Western Man and his behavior and subjectivity.

The focus on formal aspects of this history of revision begins from the notion of parody, as proposed by Linda Hutcheon in *A Theory of Parody* (1985). The hypothesis here is that the notion of parody is a useful starting point for understanding and tracing the process of revision that castaway tales undergo after the late nineteenth century. Parody supplies a kind of mechanism by which the castaway tale is revised, often drastically, from the late nineteenth century to the present. Beginning with the notion of parody helps focus the discussion on the mechanics of the fictions, the persistent and often very detailed interaction of revision and target text. There's an interplay between specific and easily recognizable tropes and episodes (the footprint in the sand; the castaway's failed attempt to escape from his island) and the grand concerns and implications of these narratives, about the self, civilization and barbarism, sanity, masculinity, imperialism, work, and technology. The tropes and episodes give us a grid, a set of foci, for reading the castaway novels as a richly meaningful collective text.

We begin in Chapter 1, naturally, with *Robinson Crusoe*. Chapter 1 focuses on features of Defoe's novel that both introduce a new kind of island fiction, by concentrating on how the castaway settles his island, and also challenge later revisions and parodies. Several of the memorable tropes first encountered in *Robinson Crusoe*—salvage from the wreck; the footprint on the beach—are examined, with examples of later variations. Practically all subsequent versions of the castaway story give us a revealing—and sometimes even comical—glimpse of how they are revising Defoe by the way they revise or parody these tropes. But there are broader features of the template *Robinson Crusoe* establishes, and we can list them here. There is the plain style of the narration, with its clear separation of subject and object, expressing the castaway's concentration on reasoned work on material things. There is a two-phase narrative structure: in the first phase, the castaway (or, in later tales, a group or family of castaways) works for years in isolation, and in this allowance of time—and unvisited space—achieves settlement; but in the second phase, the island is repeatedly "invaded." The castaway's island remains deserted and unvisited for decades, so that it can seem *his* island, and the visitors, when they eventually arrive, can seem invaders, even though they are often indigenes. We can, if we are inclined to, see this narrative arrangement as an evasion of the reality of colonial settlement and domination. The castaway's island really is *terra nullius*, and anyway the castaway is at first surviving, not settling. But this condition, introduced by Defoe, is better seen as a postponement, and a choice of focus. The unfolding history of the castaway tale will show how often the castaways themselves degenerate into violence and "savagery."

Robinson Crusoe and its successors in the eighteenth and nineteenth centuries, up to Jules Verne's *The Mysterious Island* (1875), which is a transitional case, detail and celebrate settlement. Chapter 2 takes a brief look at two of the many successors to *Robinson Crusoe* that keep to their model, varying rather than revising: *The Swiss Family Robinson* (Johann David and Johann Rudolf Wyss, 1812) and *Masterman Ready* (Captain Marryat, 1841). Yet even *The Swiss Family Robinson* and *Masterman Ready*, if they do not revise *Robinson Crusoe*, expand and overload it—more plants cultivated, animals domesticated; uninterrupted successes in the tasks of settlement. There are more castaways, a family—a family rather than a solitary individual, then, but in this happily cooperating unit everyone has a clear function, and the stability and practicality previously located in the lone individual is now firmly located in the family. This feature is taken even further in the third novel discussed in this chapter, *The Mysterious Island*. Verne's castaways, not literally a family, but a group of enterprising and energetic American males, undertake so much, in such orderly cooperation, and are so rapidly successful at everything they attempt, that this in itself tips the novel toward parody. Then, in the later part of the story, we have the presence of an unseen benefactor who uses mysterious powers that turn out to be based on technology beyond what the castaways have employed, and it is he who defeats the invaders when (as is common in castaway stories) they eventually arrive on the island. The effect is to undermine that success at labor and settlement that was already tending to excess. So we have reached the brink of the radical revisions of the castaway stories, brutally ushered in by H. G. Wells's *The Island of Dr. Moreau* (1896).

Chapters 3 and 4 discuss the phase of violence in the modern history of the castaway tale. These introductory comments sketch some of the complexities; "violence" is shorthand for a series of bleak developments in the castaway tale. Chapter 3 begins with *The Island of Dr. Moreau*, which is almost as important for the argument of *Castaway Tales* as *Robinson Crusoe*, because its intervention in the history of the castaway tale is so brutal and unrestrained. *Moreau* doesn't bestow specific narrative tropes on later tales as *Robinson Crusoe* did with, for instance, the discovery of the footprint; but degeneration, not a specific narrative trope, is nonetheless very common in later texts. Degeneration suggests the limits of rationality and the erasure of the distinction between civilized and primitive. *The Island of Dr. Moreau* gives us the work of Moreau, a scientist, self-exiled to his island, who is trying to turn animals into humans by means of brutal surgery. This work is seen through the eyes of Prendick, cast away on Moreau's island and struggling to comprehend what he sees. We have Moreau as a failed god and failed settler, whose work as a scientist litters the island with his unhappy subjects, and Prendick as a failed castaway, incompetent and bewildered, whose point of view subjectivizes and destabilizes the plain style of the castaway narrative.

The Island of Dr. Moreau is followed by a set of revisions picking up a variety of its features. The progeny of *Moreau* discussed in the rest of Chapter 3 are *The Monster Men* (Edgar Rice Burroughs, 1913), *The Island of Captain Sparrow* (S. Fowler Wright, 1928), *The Invention of Morel* (Adolfo Bioy Casares, 1940), *The Island of Doctor Death and Other Stories and Other Stories* (Gene Wolfe, 1980: a collection of stories of which three are variations on *Moreau*), and *Moreau's Other Island* (Brian Aldiss, 1980). Each alludes to or closely imitates *Moreau*. These stories fix sometimes on the notion of degeneration that Wells expressed both with the beast people and with what happened to Moreau and Prendick, who can also be seen as degenerating (Burroughs; Wright; Wolfe, "The Death of Doctor Island"); sometimes on Moreau's alienation from his experimental subjects and from his island (the work of Morel in Bioy Casares's novella); and sometimes on how the castaway's unreliable experience subjectivizes the narrative (Bioy Casares; Wolfe; Aldiss).

In all these cases, the pleasures, achievements, and clarities of practical work, so important in Defoe, are missing. Robinson Crusoe and the other early castaways are detached from the things and creatures of their island, which are theirs to reason about, use, and domesticate. It is this clear separation of the human being and his environment that the plain style expresses. Now, in *Moreau* and its progeny, the divisions between humans and animals are blurred (in Wells, Burroughs, Wright, and Aldiss), or humans exist in virtual form

(Bioy Casares) or emerge from the pages of a book (in the first of Wolfe's stories, "The Island of Doctor Death and Other Stories"). It seems that everything has been shaken up and put into question, even in a racist potboiler such as *The Monster Men*, where humans and orangutans exhibit the same deplorable sexual behavior. The chapter ends with discussion of William Golding's *Lord of the Flies* (1954), not a direct revision of *The Island of Dr. Moreau*, but the most powerful, and famous, rendition of degeneration in a castaway novel and the most unqualified refusal of the fantasy of children making do on a desert island, and growing up as they did so, that was behind *The Swiss Family Robinson*, *Masterman Ready*, and Golding's target text, *The Coral Island* (R. M. Ballantyne, 1858).

Chapter 4 pursues the grim themes and figures that, in the present argument, entered the castaway novel with *The Island of Dr. Moreau*. This chapter discusses *Pincher Martin* (William Golding, 1956); *Concrete Island* and "The Terminal Beach" (J. G. Ballard, 1973, 1964); *The Wasp Factory* (Iain Banks, 1984), *The Beach* (Alex Garland, 1982), and *Life of Pi* (Yann Martel, 2001). These texts return to *Robinson Crusoe*, but bring to the revision of the castaway or island novel the violence and the skepticism about Western civilized humanity that was so strong in Wells's novel. The grim nadir of the tradition is reached. Madness or delusion is frequent (in *The Wasp Factory*, *The Beach*, and *Pincher Martin*, the protagonist is mad or deluded): the plain distinction between subject and object is gone, because the subject's perception of objects is unbalanced. The island is no longer field for sober practical work. The castaway may still build, act, and explore the island, but these activities are no longer necessarily productive. The island may be repatriated (in *Concrete Island* it is in the heart of London; in *The Wasp Factory* it is off the coast of Scotland). It is often infiltrated with ruins from past wars, concrete bunkers for instance (*Concrete Island*; "The Terminal Beach"; *The Wasp Factory*), and this presence of the violent past signals the gothic, the kind of fiction that is haunted by an unresolved past.

The two-phase plot, which structured earlier castaway narratives and allowed time for the practical work of settlement, is discarded. Instead of years of undisturbed settlement, followed by a spate of "invasions," we have mystery or illusion followed by clarification or disillusionment: a very different narrative structure, and one that looks backward or inward. The invader or enemy or even cannibal is no longer an indigenous "savage" but the Western castaway or castaways (*Lord of the Flies*; Stephen King's "Survivor Type"; *The Beach*; and most startlingly in the otherwise amiable *Life of Pi*). These castaway stories begin with an uninhabited island, as did *Robinson Crusoe*, but the bringers of violence to this island, the equivalents of invaders in the structure of the story, are the castaways themselves.

Chapter 5 discusses *Suzanne and the Pacific* (*Suzanne et le Pacifique*, Jean Giraudoux, 1921), *Friday* (*Vendredi*, Michel Tournier, in two versions, 1967 and 1971), *The Year of Grace* (*El Año de Gracia*, Cristina Fernández Cubas, 1985), and *Foe* (J. M. Coetzee, 1986). Covering work from the 1920s to the 1980s, and from France, Spain, and South Africa, this chapter suggests that the literary history of the castaway tale is more complicated than the picture of a descent into violence and insanity that was traced from *The Island of Dr. Moreau* to texts such as *The Wasp Factory* in the preceding chapters. This chapter does not suggest an alternative tradition, however, but a series of interesting convergences in texts from very different times and places, all of them revising *Robinson Crusoe*.

Three important features are identified. First, *Suzanne and the Pacific* introduces a female castaway. Suzanne does not work, and the novel mocks the seriousness and emphasis on practical reason of the Defoe tradition, which is thereby, by implication, tied to the masculinity of that tradition. *Foe* centers on a female castaway who displaces Cruso (as he is called in Coetzee's novel) from the center of what had been his story, and then struggles with Foe (Coetzee's Defoe) to bring her own narrative to fruition.

Second, *Friday*, *The Year of Grace*, and *Foe* all radically revise the figure of Friday, with consequent radical changes in the figure of Crusoe. If Friday (or his equivalent in a given text) is neither biddable nor easy to know, whereas he was both in *Robinson Crusoe*, then Crusoe (or his equivalent in a given text) is the less likely to figure as sane, productive, and dominant, as he was in *Robinson Crusoe*. This revised version of Friday is no longer a servant, but is made to educate or save the novel's revised version of Robinson.

Third, the revision of both Friday and Crusoe we find in *Friday*, *The Year of Grace*, and *Foe* entails a rethinking of language and textuality in each of these novels; it opens the question of who controls the narrative and what kind of language, objective or expressive, might be appropriate to it. In Defoe there was no contrast between the language of Crusoe's first-person narration and the language of the equally sober journal that he kept for a while (initiating a practice of textuality that many later castaways follow, in varying ways).[5] Tournier's *Friday* (*Vendredi*) includes both a Robinson Crusoe and a Friday, though many details of Defoe's novel are altered; *Friday* parodies its Robinson's desire to control and systematize, and shows how his subjectivity is comically split between bureaucrat and sensualist. (Tournier's Robinson sets himself to explore his subjectivity in his philosophical "Logbook"—not a record of daily fact, as was Crusoe's journal in Defoe). The novel eventually has the natural and feckless Friday rescue him from this predicament. In Giraudoux, Suzanne, the lone castaway of the story, plays whimsical language games. Coetzee's *Foe* sidelines

Cruso's story, follows Susan's struggle to have Foe tell her story as she wants it to be told, and ends with the enigmatic Friday perhaps learning to write for himself. Defoe's Robinson Crusoe tells us his story, keeps a journal, and reads his Bible: plain and unproblematic. Matters of textuality are thematized, examined, and disseminated in the texts discussed in Chapter 5.

Chapters 6 and 7 consider some recent castaway novels for children, and some recent science fiction (sf) novels in which castaways figure. These novels are very different from those considered in the phase of violence, and, taken together, they point to a phase in the continuing history of the castaway tale that is here labeled reconciliation. They all show a revived confidence in the competence and reason of the castaway that was largely absent in the phase of violence, and irrelevant or unimportant in the more varied group of castaway tales discussed in Chapter 5. They share three further features, in varying degrees: they reimagine the castaway's relations with and place in nature; they feature an indigenous castaway, or blur the categories of indigenous and Western; and they diverge from or are indifferent to the postmodern. It seems plausible that in the contemporary, postcolonial period, these features amount to conditions for the recovery of the buoyancy and confidence of the castaway tale as Defoe established it. To make a convincing and positive castaway tale in the postcolonial, eco-aware era, you will have to incorporate—not merely acknowledge, but imagine—these features.

Why not use a term such as *revival* or *reconsideration* then, given that we should be tentative about the contemporary? The closer we are to the present, the more subjective historical assessment is. We are detecting hints of new developments, and in what is often called "genre" fiction. True, but reconciliation is a word for a more profound coming to terms with the past and its errors (or worse than errors), and behind the introduction of the indigenous castaway and the reimagining of nature in these novels there is, surely, a coming to terms of this kind, a reconsideration in order to recover.

In Chapters 6 and 7 it is suggested that the positive possibilities of the castaway tale are revived and explored in fictions belonging to literature for children and to sf. It is in recent castaway stories in these modes that we find a reconciliation with the excluded indigenous, and a reconciliation with the potentials of practical reason that were so confidently embraced in *Robinson Crusoe* and its successors in the first phase of this literary history, but then subject to corrosive questioning in the second phase. We are dealing here, not merely with somewhat different narrative forms, but with different narrative cultures (sets of attitudes and assumptions) such as join writers and readers of literature for children and join writers and readers of sf. There is space in a novel for children or in an sf novel to reexamine the castaway story in the light of contemporary thinking about females, indigenes, and nature, and thence to revive some of the optimism of early castaway narratives.

Chapter 6 discusses *Island of the Blue Dolphins* (Scott O'Dell, 1960), *To the Wild Sky* (Ivan Southall, 1967), *Kensuke's Kingdom* (Michael Morpurgo, 1999), and *Nation* (Terry Pratchett, 2008). These novels shift the center of the castaway story to the female (O'Dell; Southall; Pratchett) and the indigenous or non-Western (O'Dell; Southall; Morpurgo; Pratchett). By making these changes, these novels shake up the traditional template, and release some of the positive possibility that had figured in Defoe and earlier versions, but had been subverted or savagely rejected in much of the modern history of the castaway novel.

Chapter 7 discusses *Across the Sea of Suns* (Gregory Benford, 1984), *Teranesia* (Greg Egan, 1999), and *Second Nature* and *Signs of Life* (Cherry Wilder, 1986, 1996). All these novels, though belonging to different varieties of sf, draw on their generic resources to revise the view of nature commonly found in modern castaway narratives, and those by Benford and Egan in addition rethink the social practice of science and hence the relations of reason and nature. While *Signs of Life* and *Second Nature* revise the castaway tale to make positive parables about reason, science, and the depth of nature, *Teranesia* and *Across the Sea of Suns* are much more qualified about the scope of human reason in the face of nature, including human nature.

The castaway story seems to unfold a basic logic of survival and, eventually, mastery. Start with a castaway—an everyman, but a Western male everyman; add an island, isolation, some supplies: then various actions and events will seem to follow logically. The castaway will do such and such to subsist, find shelter and security. It's both a trick and an achievement of the realism of the genre (for instance, its plain style, its work with material things) that the narrative seems like this. Matters prove to be more complicated, however. The story indeed *seems* to spin out of the necessities and opportunities of being cast away on an island. It's an enjoyable artistic effect. But it is the changing pressures of history and culture that shape varying depictions of the single individual or isolated group in the continuing history of the castaway tale. These pressures shape views of work on nature (not just labor, but the work done by science and technology); they shape depictions of gender, race, sanity, safety, success, settlement. They help us to understand the—sometimes radical—variations and transformations that the castaway story undergoes, while attention to its basic constituents (what begins to make it a genre) enables us to observe how these pressures are given form as narratives. There's an interplay between specific and easily recognizable tropes and episodes (the footprint in the sand; the castaway's failed attempt to escape from his island) and the grand concerns and implications of these narratives. It is with the former that we begin, with discussion of *Robinson Crusoe* in the first chapter: some famous tropes, and how later versions of the tale adapt and parody them; and some broad features of the template that is established in *Robinson Crusoe*: the sanity of the protagonist, the plain style, the narrative organized into two phases.

1

Settlement

1

The Sea Captain and the Perfect Mango

Revision and Parody in Castaway Narratives

The world is full of islands, said Cruso once.
His words ring truer every day.
J. M. COETZEE, *Foe*

The castaway narrative in and after *Robinson Crusoe* is concerned with the subject's powers and frailties, with work on and domination of nature, with masculinity. So also are very many other fictions; what begins to give castaway narratives a particular character is the collection of particular tropes, features and conventions that make a genre. These are what enable a given text to express larger historical and cultural pressures in the particular form of a story about a castaway on an island, in such a way that it is recognizable as belonging to a tradition, and able to be compared to others in the series. This intertextuality is one means by which the story responds to and thinks about the larger historical and cultural pressures. We can see how the story says something about these pressures by examining how it varies or parodies or simply repeats earlier versions of the castaway story. Genre here is viewed as a kind of mechanism of refraction. It's a mechanism in that it helps to make narrative out of culture and history. It's refractive in that both history and culture, and previous versions of the story, are twisted and shifted.

Crucial to the establishment and the popularity of this genre is Defoe's *Robinson Crusoe*. In this chapter we begin by sketching the originality of Defoe's novel in comparison to the most famous and influential of earlier island narratives. It will be found to rest in the castaway's positive response to his forced sojourn on his island, and, more particularly, in his attitude to labor. From these come the direct, patient, and clear details of the castaway's making do which, in turn, create a large part of the charm of this and many later castaway novels. From this practical day-to-day work stems the achievement of settlement, and, more controversially in the subsequent history of the genre, of sovereignty over the island and later arrivals on it, such as Friday. For fifteen years Robinson Crusoe works by himself. He clothes, houses, and feeds himself; he makes chairs and bread; he fortifies his island and fences his fields and pastures. He dresses in goatskin. He makes, or remakes, civilization. He produces a new self, a religious man who is also the "governor" of his island. He thinks often and guiltily about his past, but he plans for and in many ways controls his future.

Then Robinson comes across a naked footprint on the beach, and this throws him into a turmoil of anxiety and speculation, as he realizes that cannibals are visiting his island. Eventually he encounters and defeats a party of cannibals, rescues one of them, makes an ally of him in battle with other cannibals, and receives his submission. He renames him, Friday, converts him to Christianity, and makes a servant and companion of him. Subsequent invaders —mutineers—are defeated with Friday's help; shipwrecked Spanish sailors are settled. Robinson Crusoe becomes the "governor" of his island. This is the core of the novel, the part that most readers remember, with its famous incidents such as the discovery of the naked footprint on the beach. Defoe has in fact begun with a prelude, in which Robinson runs away to sea, against the wishes of his parents, is enslaved in Morocco for a period, escapes with the help of the boy Xury, settles in Brazil as a planter and slave owner, and embarks on an expedition to buy slaves in Africa. It was this expedition that led to his shipwreck on the island, sole survivor but luckily able to salvage a variety of stores and equipment from the wrecked ship. And Defoe has prolonged the tale after the central time on the island: Robinson is rescued, returns briefly to England, then moves on to Lisbon, to discover that his partners in Brazil have protected and multiplied his fortune, and to journey with Friday through the wilds of Spain and eventually to England.[1] We even learn, in a paragraph, that he later married and became a widower (Defoe 1987, 393), and we learn of his return to his island, which continues to flourish. This before and after to Robinson Crusoe's long sojourn on his island casts many ironic reflections—his career as a slave versus his career as a slave owner and would-be slave trader; his imprudent conduct in disregarding his parents' wishes versus the prudence and discipline of his work on the island; his briefly mentioned later marriage versus his long, friendly, paternal companionship with Friday—but it is his time on the island that most counts for later renditions and revisions of the castaway tale. Here we contrast Defoe's emphases in his telling of that sojourn to famous earlier island narratives, before discussing the formal qualities of the genre that he inaugurated with this novel. We begin with a brief look at *The Odyssey* and then move on to *The Tempest*, these being arguably the most famous and influential island narratives in the Western tradition before *Robinson Crusoe*.

Odysseus wanders from island to island, encountering attractive or dangerous females (Circe, Calypso, Nausicaa, the sirens, Athena, and eventually Penelope). Odysseus as castaway does build a raft, with Calypso's help, and we learn of the work that this involves (Book V of *The Odyssey*), but during his years on Calypso's island, he mainly pines to be elsewhere, home on another island in fact, recovering his kingdom and his wife.

Prospero is different from Odysseus, and clearly *The Tempest* reverberates in island narratives even after *Robinson Crusoe* exerts its influence;[2] but Shakespeare's play takes up Prospero's story at a narrative cusp, near the end of Prospero's sojourn on his island. His own narrative to his daughter of how he came to be on the island (*The Tempest*, Act 1, Scene 2, lines 66–167) is brought forth by the chance of gaining his revenge and getting off the island, a chance that opens for him when the Neapolitan fleet comes within range of his magic. As it turns out, this involves renouncing his power over his island, and over Caliban, Ariel, and Miranda, his servants and his daughter. Nonetheless, the question of his power is an important one, as is that of his subjectivity and those of the varied personages he controls, because these personages are so diverse and elusive as to seem to allegorize a set of colonial, racial, and gendered others. This in turn throws stress on the ways in which Prospero might figure colonial domination, and as a result, in recent critical discussion, the emphasis is on the power he exerts, not on the fact that he gives it up in the course of the play. In the discussion that follows, however, it seems that the force fields of *Robinson Crusoe* and then of *The Island of Dr. Moreau* have been so strong as to demand the primary attention. *Robinson Crusoe*, *Moreau*, and their many revisions set up a complex intertextual conversation among themselves, with occasional interjections from *The Tempest*.

Prospero's island was already inhabited when he and Miranda came ashore, as Caliban protests ("This island's mine . . ." [1, 2, 331]), and like many other narratives of the contact of Europeans with indigenes, this is the context of the play's treatment of work and power. Prospero can't do without the labor that he forces Caliban to provide:

> We cannot miss him. He does make our fire,
> Fetch in our wood, and serves in offices
> That profit us. (1, 2, 310–12)

European settlers, or castaways, contrive to feel that they can or even should possess the land because it is idle, and they make the indigenes work because they are idle, and idleness is a sin. Yet the settlers want to be idle themselves, and that is actually why they force the indigenes, and later African slaves, to do the work. They want to live like gentlemen, or they simply feel that one's purpose in life is to get into a position where others work for one. Further, work is ambiguously both a duty and a curse, a consequence of the fall.

These issues and attitudes certainly shadow *Robinson Crusoe*, given that the main character is both an ex-slave (a Barbary captive) and a would-be slaver, wrecked when he was on a slaving expedition, and given that he makes Friday his servant after he has rescued him. But *Robinson Crusoe* comes as new attitudes take hold.

We can note, for instance, the different ideology of English—thence, of British—colonialism, one that is influenced by the English experience in North America, and given argumentative basis in John Locke. The English wanted to possess the land in order to work it themselves, and Locke provided a rationale for this: work on the land requires reason and labor, and is evidence of humanity; mere hunting and gathering, or reliance on the spontaneous hand of nature, is not evidence of humanity, nor of right to possess the land.[3] Robinson works himself, cultivating and enclosing and domesticating, and work is close to the center of his selfhood; nonetheless, Defoe's decision to have Robinson's island uninhabited, and unvisited for the first decades of his sojourn, shifts the emphasis. A broader shift is also, arguably, involved.

Keith Thomas discusses early modern attitudes to work, and then the emergence of a readiness to value and enjoy work for its own sake, or even for the "delight" it might bring. He quotes Defoe: "to follow a trade, and not to love and delight in it, is a slavery or bondage, not a business."[4] Robinson Crusoe does not exactly express love and delight in his work—satisfaction, perhaps—but readers do feel the attractiveness of his sober reasoning and working. According to J. M. Coetzee,

> [W]hen Crusoe has to solve the hundreds of little practical problems involved in getting the contents of the ship ashore, or in making a clay cooking pot, one can feel the writing move into a higher gear, a more intense level of engagement. For page after page—for the first time in the history of fiction—we see a minute, ordered description of how things are done. It is a matter of pure writerly attentiveness which, through being submitted to in a state so close to spiritual absorption, becomes transfigured, real. (2001, 24)

Or, as Gaston Bachelard notes, "To have an active day I keep saying to myself, 'Every morning I must give a thought to Saint Robinson'" (1969, 70).

The innovation, then, of *Robinson Crusoe* among island narratives is its positive treatment of labor. Work fills the castaway's time on his island in *Robinson Crusoe*, and because what the castaway makes of his time on the island *is* the story in this novel—not his desire to be somewhere else, as in *The Odyssey* and *The Tempest*—the novel is very largely occupied with the practical details of Robinson's work. Work is a necessity and eventually perhaps a passion for Robinson, and the novel investigates the complications of this as he moves from survival to settlement. These complications come from Robinson's own insecurity and urge to control. They don't come from the presence, let alone the claims to possession, of indigenes on the island.

An additional context for this unremitting work and self-production is arguably the emerging view of truth we can associate with seventeenth-century science. Defoe's fiction taps into the "Culture of Fact" that Barbara Shapiro (2000) has explored. Truth is something one makes by reasoned engagement with material actuality, rather than something one rediscovers by a process of anamnesis, of remembrance, or of reference to precedent and authority. About all this *Robinson Crusoe* is largely positive; it's a narrative of settlement and self-making, and it begins from work—the labor of salvaging as much as possible from the wreck, in the first instance. It will be what Robinson does from day to day, with what he brings ashore and what he finds and grows, that will make him, and the whole process is clearly caught in his plain and detailed narration. The castaway moves from survival to domination by the use of practical reason and by working. He begins from practical reason, working with things and processes—the elements, the basic groundwork, of what Denis Diderot defines in connection with the loom in the *Encylopédie*: "The loom for making stockings is one of the most complicated and rigorously logical machines that we have. [. . .] One could consider it as just one simple piece of reasoning, whose conclusion is the making of the stocking."[5]

Diderot is dealing with more complicated technology than Crusoe, however, and later texts, especially *The Island of Dr. Moreau* and *The Invention of Morel*, depict science and technology that threatens to alienate the worker from that which he is working on.

The discussion now turns to the tropes that constitute an immediately recognizable and discussible feature of the genre, and from there to broader formal features.

Illustration by Contraries

In *A Theory of Parody* (1985), Linda Hutcheon has argued that modern culture proceeds by taking some model from the past as stylistic template and then critiquing the past: the mechanism of modern innovation being, paradoxically, parodic imitation. It's a wonderful achievement, Defoe's, the founding of a modern myth, yet, being modern, parodied as soon as published—by *Gulliver's Travels*, for instance. Allusion is rife; even in *The Swiss Family Robinson* we have a little intertextual joke: "the life of Robinson Crusoe is but a finely wrought fiction" compared to what we are now reading (Wyss 1991, 38: 312). Hutcheon sees parody as a means by which modern artists acknowledge and measure the burden of the past, and establish critical and ironic distance from it. Her definition of parody is not always clear-cut, because she is determined to make it inclusive, but she emphasizes that it goes far beyond the kind of affectionate mockery of stylistic traits that makes the more genteel parody we find in, for instance, Dwight MacDonald's famous anthology (1960). Hutcheon emphasizes that parody is a textual matter; it concerns the codes and conventions of the target text. She downplays the association of parody with satire, because parody works on *representations* of reality (textual codes and conventions), whereas satire works on reality or what is taken to be reality (49, citing Ziva Ben-Porat). As a result, at times it is hard to distinguish parody, in Hutcheon's definition, from allusion or imitation. Yet this is a risk she is right to run. As John Richetti emphasizes, Robinson Crusoe is already accompanied by "the image of various anti-Crusoes," Crusoes that he might have been. Richetti sees Crusoe's saving and conversion of Friday as his conversion of his anti-type, the cannibal (1975, 49, 55). He quotes Crusoe's reflection: "Thus we never see the true state of our condition till it is illustrated to us by its contraries."

It's as if later writers can only think about Crusoes by thinking of various contraries to Crusoe; this illustration by contraries can be seen as critique or subversion, as parody in that sense, but it is also a form of thinking that begins from the inescapable presence of what is already there. From this comes the necessity, or anyway the impulse and opportunity, for a later text to define itself as alternative to the earlier one; this is where modern parody begins, in Hutcheon's account. Broader terms are then available—revisioning, appropriation, recuperation—and it is true that all the texts discussed in this book as versions of the castaway genre end as revisionings and appropriations. Parody is the starting point here; by beginning with parody, we fix upon those recurrent textual features that signal that the text is a version of a castaway narrative and are most obviously seized on and distorted (the footprint on the beach, for instance). The end result is transformation.

There are darker ambiguities to be found in *Robinson Crusoe*, but the text clearly produces a certain legend, centered on Robinson's hard work, material achievements, and plain narration, and featuring a series of moments that map the legend and stick in the reader's mind (the salvage from the wreck, the failed attempt to build a boat, the discovery of the footprint on the beach, the encounter with Friday). These are what Daniel Couégnas (2006, 321) calls "reproducible and adaptable traits," and by adapting and varying these and other features, a later text can signal its difference from *Robinson Crusoe* to anyone who knows the legend. The later text is not inventing so much as substituting: a family for a solitary castaway, a female Crusoe for a male Crusoe, Friday as central subject, a mad and violent castaway for Defoe's rational and prudent Crusoe. Or the later text is superimposing, layering more castaways, more salvages, more elaborate constructions and contrivances on the template derived from *Robinson Crusoe*.

Denis Feeney comments on the intertextual relations between Virgil and Statius in terms that apply to the relations between *Robinson Crusoe* and later castaway narratives:

> Any reading of the *Thebaid*'s engagement with the *Aeneid* will need to posit a certain way of reading the *Aeneid* itself, and this is true both of Statius and of modern readers. In both cases, that reading of the *Aeneid* will at times need to be somewhat reductive, assuming a univocal model that is good to react against, and at times more open, assuming a polyphonic model that generates possibilities for elaboration. (Feeney 2008, 27)

The univocal model can serve as template for straightforward imitations, or as provocation for revisions and parodies. The Robinson Crusoe story is at first made available for educational texts and children's stories, and this is where it flourishes in the later eighteenth and early nineteenth centuries.[6] The turn to parody and revision comes later, with Verne and Wells, and from this point violence and degeneration enter and often possess the castaway story.

The Cargo in the Wreck and the Footprint on the Beach

Robinson Crusoe stabilizes a genre and encourages routine imitations or versions, but almost every feature of its style and narrative form can also be seen as a source of instability and a provocation to later writers. The distance between the plainness of Robinson's narrative and the rich figurality of Michel Tournier's *Friday*, or between Robinson's relentless reasonableness and Frank's psychopathology in *The Wasp Factory*, or between Robinson's success as colonist and ruler and the degeneration into violence that overtakes Moreau, and also the children in *Lord of the Flies*, is very striking, but one can see the potential, or the provocation, for the second in the first. A couple of Defoe's most familiar narrative tropes can serve as examples: the salvage from the wreck; the appearance of the naked footprint. Here we concentrate on exemplifying this potential and the parody that results in later castaway tales.

Robinson Crusoe salvages everything he can from the wreck. He hardly stops until he has a hundredweight of lead, as well as gunpowder, tools, and rope (Defoe 1968, 68). The material conditions for his survival are established, and so are the conditions for the kind of survival it will be: the kind that becomes settlement, with crops, a dwelling, clothes, weapons, a fort. A later text may follow this episode of salvage closely, as does *Masterman Ready*, so as to provide the materials for the castaway's work on the island and point that work in the direction of civilization, because the salvage includes civilized things (iron tools, tables and chairs). This is the stabilizing effect of Defoe's inauguration of the genre: subsequent versions can perform a straightforward routine of salvage, survival, and settlement (see Chap. 2). Robinson gives practical reasons for his taking on what might be labeled the appurtenances of Western civilization. He needs clothes to keep off the sun, and for ventilation (171), and he tells us also how comical he looks when fully dressed and equipped, sporting his "large pair of Mahometan whiskers" (192). If clothes distinguish one from an indigene, this is only implicit at this point in the history of the castaway narrative.

Alternatively, this episode in *Robinson Crusoe* may work as a kind of challenge or provocation: for instance, the castaways salvage nothing but need nothing because the island is well stocked (*Lord of the Flies*); or the castaway salvages nothing and has practically nothing but what is in his pockets and has to improvise grittily because his island is barren, indeed is barely an island at all (*Pincher Martin*). In each case *Robinson Crusoe* asks a question that Golding answers in skeptical ways. Freed from the necessity to work, the castaways in *Lord of the Flies* fall to internecine violence; Pincher Martin's activity on his island, which seemed so tough and practical, is revealed to have been delusory. Again, in Scott O'Dell's *Island of the Blue Dolphins*, Karana laboriously digs up an iron chest, only to reject the beads and bracelets it proves to contain: "There were no iron spearheads in the chest. I closed the lid and covered it with sand" (9:53).

Karana now needs weapons, not ornaments. Alone, she is making her own home on the island, and she burns the deserted, ghostly village of her people; but she is not settling the island, which is where she was born. (Karana was left behind on the island by mischance, when the rest of her people were removed from it, to be resettled on the mainland of California.) The rejection of salvage places the story in relation to *Robinson Crusoe* with the effect of differentiating its heroine and her situation. Only some of her people's civilization is of use to her as a castaway.

What you salvage is, in effect, what you bring with you from civilization, so in revising the trope of salvage, a castaway narrative is making decisions about the importance of what comes from civilization as compared to what is to be found on the island, in nature. In Jules Verne's *The Mysterious Island*, a single grain of wheat found in one of the castaway's pockets eventually produces hundreds of thousands of bushels, so the implication is that what you bring with you is of almost inestimable value; not that Verne rests with this implication, because the island turns out to be stocked with almost everything needed for comfort and advanced technology (a substitute for tobacco; coal; clay for pottery). And having arrived with virtually nothing but that grain of wheat, because they jettisoned everything else in the effort to keep their balloon in the air, the castaways are later in various accidental ways supplied with several cargoes of materials. Verne gives us excess (totally self-sufficient settlers, very richly stocked island), but then, as we shall see, he undermines both the power of the settlers and the transparent usefulness of the island. The unseen presence of Nemo, with his advanced technology, is the cause of this change. In Ivan Southall's *To the Wild Sky*, the young castaways salvage nothing useful from the wreck of their plane—the radio is waterlogged, the empty bottle is useless. In this story, their survival will depend on what they can find on the island, and one of their number has to draw on her hitherto hidden indigenous ancestry to begin this process. Conversely, the indigenous people in Terry Pratchett's *Nation* gain valuable salvage from the English ship that was washed up (bringing with it also Mau's companion castaway, Daphne), but we see both Mau's irritated envy at how rich the "trousermen" must be, and his sadness that the ship is being dismantled, because in his culture ships have their own soul or individuality —not a thought that occurs to any European castaway.

Again, Crusoe's discovery of a naked footprint after fifteen solitary years is a famous moment (196), and one with emotional and symbolic resonances: nakedness in contrast to Crusoe's years of labor to civilize himself and develop his island; and a response of immediate fear, rather than hope for companionship after so long a solitude. To repeat the image is to recall the moment and, potentially, some of its complexities in *Robinson Crusoe*. But it can hardly be simply replicated, and this is never attempted. An example of how the moment is inverted and refunctioned, to very telling effect: most of A. D. Hope's poem "Man Friday" (1985) treats Friday in England, after his return. Crusoe has returned home from exile but plunged Friday into exile:

> Picture his situation if you can:
> The gentle savage, taught to speak and pray,
> On England's Desert Island cast away. (lines 22–24)

Try as he might, Friday's memory of his home, "the legends of his race," (50) his mother, even "the taste of human meat," (68) all fade, and he becomes acculturated, as a decorous upper servant. Then we have a big storm at Yarmouth, echo of the storm on one of Crusoe's first voyages, and in the aftermath,

> There in the sand beside him Friday saw
> A single naked footprint on the shore.
> [. . .]
> From such a footprint once he could describe
> If not the owner's name, at least his tribe,
> And tell his purpose as men read a face
> And still his skill sufficed to know the race. (lines 136–37, 142–45)

"All his years of exile fell away" (155). He is remembering how the sight of a footprint once brought knowledge, even familiarity—whereas it brought fear to Crusoe. Friday launches himself into the sea, to his death but also to freedom.[7]

In contrast, Robinson in Michel Tournier's *Friday* comes across *his own* footprint, but in the rock of the beach, as if engraved—perhaps a sign of the self-absorption of a character who spends a good deal of his time masturbating into a convenient cleft in the all-too-female body of the island. The arctic explorers in Jules Verne's *The Adventures of Captain Hatteras* (1865) are dismayed to come across footprints in the icy wastes of the unexplored north, because they would indicate that others have gotten there before them; then they are relieved to realize that these are their own footprints and they have been walking in a circle.[8] Richard, the narrator of Alex Garland's *The Beach*, plays at making his own footprint in the sand, like any kid on holidays; but here, this stands for his destructive frivolity, the decline of the Western settler into laziness and fantasy (308).[9] Finally, in *Nation*, Mau struggles ashore after a tsunami has devastated his native island, falls to the grim task of burying all his people, and sleeps, to be visited in the night by a stranger who leaves him a mango. We know this is the English girl, Daphne, also cast away by the same wave, and still decorously clad, wearing her stockings.

> He looked down at the sand. There were footprints there, not large, but they had no toes.
>
> He stood up very carefully, and looked around. The creature with no toes was watching him, he was sure. (Pratchett 2009, 35)

The variation is almost too neat, but fun. Its comedy depends on the familiarity of the image of the footprint, and its effect is to release us from many of the anxieties that shape the castaway narrative from Defoe to the modern stories of violence and degeneration, such as *The Beach*. In the film *Cast Away* (directed by Robert Zemeckis, 2000), the character played by Tom Hanks accidentally puts his handprint on the ball that is part of the miscellany of stuff he has salvaged. The print looks like a face, and the ball, trademarked Wilson, comes to serve as his companion on the island, in effect his Friday, called Wilson. The moment wraps together two familiar tropes and redirects them to underline the castaway's solitude and his talent as an improviser. He makes his own (hand)print and he makes and names his own Friday.

Other interventions can be more comical or brusque, reflecting the robustness of the tropes laid out in *Robinson Crusoe*. We can trace the variations of another set by looking at what happens to the castaway's food supply: first, a matter of survival, then a sign of abundance and achieved order, but then, with the descent into violence, the threat of cannibalism. Robinson, after much trial and error, finally attains abundance—stores of grain, flocks of goats, hundredweights of dried grapes—and the castaways in Wyss, Marryat, and Verne exceed even this, and with some ease. In *The Wasp Factory*, Frank cooks beefburgers to annoy his father who cooks vegetarian curries, but clearly both signify male—and Scottish—cooking at its worst. Robinson and the castaways in Muriel Spark's *Robinson* (1958) live off tinned food, though the island is pleasant and potentially productive. Cruso and Friday in *Foe* expend immense labor terracing the island, but have no grain to sow. The terraces wait for grain that never arrives. The sect of "Eaters" in an island castaway episode in Iain Banks's *Consider Phlebas* (1987; see Chap. 6) willfully starve off horrible scraps and offal, believing that all consumption is bad, and are ruled by a god figure in the form of a grotesque lisping pile of fat, so immense and shapeless that its gender is at first hard to discern. So much for the imperative of survival that had such productive effects in *Robinson Crusoe*, home-baked loaves and sun-dried grapes, and that allowed Robinson to settle into the kind of domestic work usually allotted to women or servants in his time. This series of variations and perversions of the basic trope of the castaway's work of subsistence in recent versions of the story suggests something comically or seriously askew about modern people's relations to food.

Conversely, in *Lord of the Flies*, the necessity of subsistence is simply sidelined: there is plenty of fruit, and all the boys need to do is pluck it from the tree. Contrivance and improvisation is from the very beginning focused on matters of social structure, order, ritual, and hierarchy: the use of the conch to summon and regulate assemblies, the election of a leader, the division into groups with functions. Jack and his tribe don't hunt pigs because the boys need meat but for reasons of ritual and politics. The final consequence is the murder of Simon, mistaken for or merged with the animal prey ("Kill the pig!"): close to the cannibalism so often associated with "savage" intruders in earlier castaway stories. ("Long pig" is the term for human flesh among Pacific Islanders, according to many tales of the South Seas.)[10] In Stephen King's "Survivor Type" and Yann Martel's *Life of Pi* (at least in one version of the tale that Pi tells after he is rescued), the cannibal impulse can no longer be seen as safely inhering in the "savage" other, as was the case in *Robinson Crusoe* and its nineteenth-century successors. The castaway is the cannibal.[11]

This sketch should not be taken as implying that the pleasures of the castaway narrative as Defoe makes them available are quite lost even in savage parodies of the story, such as *The Wasp Factory* or *Pincher Martin*. When Chantal Zabus says that rewriting authorizes as well as critiques the text that is being rewritten, this is arguably part of her meaning (Zablus 2002, 3–5). Nor should it be taken as implying that matters were stable and unproblematic in the beginning, in *Robinson Crusoe*. When Crusoe sets out the body count as a literal accounting ("2 killed by ditto [Friday], of those at first wounded," and so on [305]), his attitude to violence is shocking in its sober way, though it is still notable that he meditates several times on the rights and wrongs of killing (for instance, 219–21). This kind of moral hesitation tends to be shorn away in battles with savages and pirates in later castaway narratives.[12]

So *Robinson Crusoe* is not without its depths; the case is simply that there is an easily reproducible element in Defoe's novel that can stabilize a genre, but which also provokes parody and reversal. This element is only a part of *Robinson Crusoe*—it comes largely from the novel as made into a simplified legend in cultural memory—and is based on only the first of Defoe's three texts about Robinson's Crusoe's adventures and opinions, but the novel's attitude and procedure contains something that itself provokes dissent in later versions of the castaway story.

The Crusoe Template: Three Features

Robinson Crusoe sets forth a trajectory—from survival to domination—that can be varied and revised, and Defoe invents a series of tropes that make the castaway story recognizable and are repeatedly varied or parodied. Defoe's novel also sets forth a formal template. Three interlinked aspects of this can be identified. First is a plain descriptive style that presents material things and circumstances with sober clarity, but preserves a separation between subject and object, between the self and the world it is working on and through which it successfully expresses itself, and between writer and reader, as Defoe says in *The Complete English Tradesman*: "easy, plain and familiar language is the beauty of speech in general, and is the excellency of all writing, on whatever subject, or to whatever persons we write or speak. The end of speech is that men might understand one another's meaning; certainly that speech, or that way of speaking, which is most easily understood, is the best way of speaking."[13]

It's a style very well adapted to record contrivance, trial and error, and improvisation. Things, and even persons, are relentlessly used by the castaway, but not made into metaphors by the text. Second is a concern with the Subject—a first-person narrator who is overwhelmingly the focus of our interest, set down alone on his island as he is, realized and expressed through his engagements and observations. At this point in the history of the castaway narrative, the dark possibilities of madness and silence that might plausibly threaten someone spending decades in complete solitude are barely noticed, and not pursued. As Richetti comments, "This hysterical, formless and naturally self-destructive aspect of Crusoe is only touched on, although it is the threatening chaos implicit in his subsequent ordering of things."[14]

Linked to this is the masculinity of the castaway, which is not in itself a formal feature, but something that relates to the centering of the castaway's productivity on work and utility, and thence to the plain style that conveys this. *Robinson Crusoe* marks a departure from earlier island narratives in this respect, as we have noted, and the effect is to repress the femaleness of the island, and to make mysterious its hidden places. Not all castaways are males, but when females appear, they appear precisely in the context of a male-dominated story type, and bring other changes with them—the island is different, labor is rejected, the plain style of narration is questioned or discarded: so it is, in varying ways, in *Suzanne and the Pacific*, *Robinson*, and *Foe*.

Just as the possibilities of madness and silence are sidelined for Crusoe, the same is true of Friday, who is unfailingly good-humored and cooperative. The only time he even mildly opposes Crusoe, he does so by using his reason, questioning the logic of Crusoe's account of Christianity. Friday is in strong contrast to Caliban, who is deformed, angry, impulsive, sensuous, imaginative: a creature of the id, to borrow Stephen Greenblatt's comment on the figure of the Wild Man from which Caliban is partly derived (Greenblatt 1976, Vol. II, 567). In later depictions of Friday or his equivalent, the id that was missing in Defoe's Friday (or present only by proxy, in the other "savages" and Crusoe's fears of them) returns. The Fridays we meet in Tournier's *Friday*, Coetzee's *Foe*, and Fernández Cubas's *The Year of Grace* are elusive, impulsive, and exist partly outside language and practicality. They have the quality Greenblatt identifies in Shakespeare's Caliban, "opacity" (575). (Chapter 5 explores these revisions of Friday.)

The third foundational feature of Defoe's narrative is a basic two-phase narrative structure in which the first phase has the main character settling and developing his island in long undisturbed solitude, and the second has the island frequently visited and invaded, so that we might perhaps wonder how it escaped this for so long in the first part of the story. The narrative is episodic, therefore natural-seeming. Defoe makes adventure out of mundane, daily happenings;[15] sensation and drama are provided, but they come later in the story. We have twenty years or so of work amid unvisited isolation, then a flurry of visits and invasions—Friday, other natives, mutineers, shipwrecked Spaniards. Margaret Cohen explains the narrative rationale: "Once the island community matures, the novelist has no more story to tell, unless its harmony is disrupted" (Cohen 2006, 661).

This swerve away from the initial and prolonged state of isolation to one in which the island is visited or invaded, implausible in realist terms, no doubt suggests the new and experimental aspects of what Defoe is achieving in *Robinson Crusoe*. He founds the genre in striking and almost mesmerizing ways, but leaves loose ends—indeed, the end of Robinson's time on the island is one example, in that Robinson continues to journey and adventure after he leaves the island, but most readers forget this part of the novel or treat it as a kind of epilogue. Robinson is a wanderer, like the heroes and heroines of Defoe's other novels, and perhaps Defoe is recognizing something about modern Europeans, who are nomads, migrants as much as they are settlers; but it is the long period of settlement on his island that readers remember.[16] Later castaway stories end the narrative with the ending of the castaway's isolation on the island: the story to this point becomes what a castaway story tells. This swerve into the second phase of the story, into engagement and away from isolation, which is first seen in *Robinson Crusoe*, becomes significant because some interesting things are done later in the tradition with temporality and narrative trajectory, and because violence figures so markedly in this swerve.

With *Robinson Crusoe*, we accept the two-phase sequence of the narrative for the sake of what it yields, the magical registration of Crusoe's activity and subjectivity during his years of solitude. Similarly, we accept the limitations on his emotional range because, concentrating on what we are given, we have so much to interest us: easily comparable to Virginia Woolf's intimate registration of consciousness, says Pat Rogers in a moment of enthusiasm (1979, 125), "a state close to spiritual absorption," says J. M. Coetzee in the passage quoted earlier. These aspects of the text amount to conventions, if we bear in mind that a convention usually involves ignoring one kind of possibility for the sake of the payoff in other possibilities. Cast the convention aside, and different possibilities can be pursued.

The Plain Style

The plain style is a kind of code in that it assumes a correspondence yet separation between subject and world. The world, and activities in it, will express the subject, but he (and it is he) has the degree of separateness from it that means he can reason about it and work on it. In the heat of his combat with the cannibals, Robinson can respond to the words Friday utters: "and though I could not understand them, yet I thought they were pleasant to hear; for they were the first sound of a man's voice that I had heard, my own excepted, for about twenty-five years."

"But there was no time for such reflections now," so we rejoin the violent action, but almost at once, Robinson notes how Friday beheads one of their enemies "at one blow, cut off his head as cleverly, no executioner in Germany could have done it sooner or better; which I thought very strange for one who, I had reason to believe, never saw a sword in his life before, except their own wooden swords" (*Robinson Crusoe*, 262).

The temporal separation—narration in the past tense—is accompanied by a separation between action and reflection. Clarity of narration takes precedence over any expression of the hurly-burly of violent action.

This separation between action and reflection, and between subject and nature, is strictly maintained, as if governed by a rule; as Suzanne tartly remarks, Crusoe knows the taste of every bird on his island and the song of none (Giraudoux 1961, 9: 172). He sees his goats as "living magazines of flesh, milk, butter and cheese for me as long as I lived in the place" (*Robinson Crusoe*, 195). The result is a tension between Robinson's conscientiousness and responsiveness (as when he sees the frightened cannibals as "poor creatures") and his blunt callousness, when other humans are transformed into objects of calculation not much different from goats or baskets. With regard to his escape with Xury from Moroccan slavery earlier in the novel, he reflects, "I could have been content to have taken the Moor with me, and have drowned the boy, but there was no venturing to trust him" (27). Later, after he and Xury have been rescued by a benevolent Portuguese captain, Crusoe in effect sells Xury to the captain, though he does suffer some scruples when he does so.[17] The castaways in Verne's *The Mysterious Island* are a good deal more charitable, for instance when they encounter the wild, mute castaway Ayrton, whom they rescue from his isolation on another island, but they are similarly pragmatic in their attitudes. They recognize and name everything they come across, and they come across a lot, because Verne has stocked the island with creatures ranging from kangaroos to peccaries, as well as coal and iron, and they make use of most of it. The attitude to nature that is behind Defoe's and Verne's concentration on usefulness opens up a series of flaws and instabilities that are explored in later texts.

In the early modern period, nature is given to humans to use and dominate. Robinson Crusoe sees his goats as "living magazines." Keith Thomas gives many examples of the belief and attitude in his *Man and the Natural World*, and then traces its erosion, accompanied by "the dethronement of man." The earlier attitude emphasizes the gulf between humans and animals (soulless, lacking reason, incapable of suffering, viciously lustful or violent). As Thomas says, once the barrier is down, relations can go either way: humans in their degeneration are seen as beasts, or animals are seen as sharing qualities with humans. The difference is important, but in either case secure and confident notions of the human are disrupted. We can see the struggle played out in a series of castaway tales, especially *The Island of Dr. Moreau* (Moreau attempts to make beasts into men, while maintaining total control over his subjects as if the older attitude were still in place); *Lord of the Flies* (disturbing avatars of the pig/beast—hunted or made into a deity, or the human taken for a pig and murdered); and *Life of Pi* (Pi's relations with the tiger Richard Parker, both his companion castaway and utterly an animal). The revision is pressed further in *Teranesia*, in the humans' attempts to understand the São Paulo virus (utterly other but of mind-like powers) and in *Across the Sea of Suns*, in Warren's relations with the alien Skimmers and Swarmers, in their different imagos both violent and intelligently communicative.[18]

The earliest notable intertextual response to *Robinson Crusoe* is *Gulliver's Travels* (1726). *Gulliver's Travels* hardly follows *Robinson Crusoe* in its content: the islands and lands where Gulliver is marooned are populated and civilized. What it offers, however, is a critique of the implications of Defoe's plain style.

The plain style of *Gulliver's Travels* is perhaps even better than Defoe's at lucidly delivering the look and feel of material things and processes (a fob watch as seen by the Lilliputians; a mole on the breast of a Brobdignagian woman; how Gulliver extinguished the burning palace of Lilliput),[19] but this style also expresses Gulliver's limited attitudes and capacities, and eventually style and man painfully diverge. By the end, the style is as clear as ever, the man close to insane.[20] Clarity of style no longer connotes practical, commonsense sanity.

Robinson Crusoe is not merely a realist text but, in the way it constructs subjectivity through the world of material things, actions, and circumstances, it inaugurates realism in the novel. Yet it is also a fable. This follows from Crusoe's spiritual struggles, which suggest that he be taken as Everyman, but more fundamentally it follows from the way his island is a microcosm, the story a "drastic simplification of society and social relationships," as James Sutherland puts it (1975, 387). Crusoe is not just a man on an island, he is "*the* man on *the* island" (Richetti 1975, 55, n.20). Perhaps this combination of realism and fable is the clue to the castaway narrative's productive power—regardless, it does seem to work as an inbuilt tension or challenge, most obviously in an author like William Golding, who harbors such strong ambitions to make a fable, to see his main character not so much as an individual but as "the man," which is how he is usually named in *Pincher Martin*.

The castaway is reduced to elemental struggle, and if the work he puts in succeeds in making something like civilization, which is certainly Crusoe's achievement, then that comes to stand for Civilization in general. A desert island is something boundaried, delimited, which an individual might come to know and possess. It is in this way a little cosmos. But castaways, fugitives, recluses like Crusoe, Moreau, and their successors are not exactly dropped into a microcosm. They set themselves to make one: to civilize their island; to make men out of beasts in *The Island of Dr. Moreau*; to name, police, and control a kind of security state in *The Wasp Factory*; to introduce what they remember of the rules of adult society in the early chapters of *Lord of the Flies*. So the world is less given than made, brought into being by physical work but also by language. Because the castaway tale is a kind of fable and the castaway can stand for Western Man, the castaway tale can express a view of Western Man, sometimes by gentle parody (*Suzanne and the Pacific*), sometimes by harsh critique (*The Island of Dr. Moreau*). By the time we reach such extreme revisions of the castaway tale as *The Wasp Factory* and *The Beach*, however, this notion of the fable of Western Man is no longer relevant. The protagonists of these novels have not the depth to stand for anything so grand, even in their degeneracy; it's as if Western Man is no longer on the scene, even as a monster. And the novels we will consider in Chapters 6 and 7 are more modest in their scope. Significantly, the castaway stories in the mode of sf considered in Chapter 7 don't dwell for long on islands, so that one precondition for the castaway tale as fable, the island as microcosm, is absent.

"Our Dear-Self is, in one Respect, the End of Living"

"All Reflection is carry'd Home, and our Dear-self is, in one Respect, the End of Living."[21] The panorama that greets the character played by Tom Hanks when he struggles to the tall summit of his island in *Cast Away* precipitates a kind of vertigo for this survivor: endless sea in every direction, concentric rings of foam, ring behind ring, centered on the island, as if in mockery of the self-absorption that no castaway can avoid.[22]

Placed in isolation on an island, then, needing to bend every effort and every resource to survive, the castaway has powerful inducements to judge everything else, every circumstance and living thing, as opportunity for the self or threat to the self. The sojourn on the island has urgent positive content: it's not just an interlude in which the castaway is waiting and hoping to be somewhere else, as is the case with Odysseus on Calypso's island or Tennyson's Enoch Arden on his island.

"Enoch Arden" (1864) reflects this older view in an exacerbated form, and by doing so throws a vivid light on *Robinson Crusoe* and its successors. The only time in the poem when Enoch does *not* work is while he is cast away: much of the emotional charge of the story comes from the contrast between Enoch's productive work for his family before the time of his being cast away and his sterile work, merely for himself, after he returns and discovers he has lost his family because his wife Annie has remarried (that is, unlike Odysseus's Penelope, Annie did not wait for Enoch). And Enoch's tragic self-negation—when he returns he does not declare who he is or reveal himself to his family—is the reverse of the egotism or even megalomania that threatens the castaway in the Crusoe-Moreau tradition, as well as contrasting with Odysseus's dramatic and violent revelation of who he is when he is ready to reclaim his kingdom and his wife. "Enoch Arden" as a tale of self-negation thus reminds us how most castaway narratives involve powerfully self-assertive subjects such as Crusoe, Moreau, and Pincher Martin.

The self is the "End of Living"; other things or people are, "in one Respect," at least, means to the survival or comfort and security or fulfillment of that self. Michael Seidel cites the sea captain Robinson saves from mutineers. In the fervor of his gratitude, the captain says Robinson was placed on the island to save his life, as if, in his eyes, Robinson's more than twenty years of work and effort had their "End" in this moment.[23] Robinson, in his years of solitude, could not but see everything as revolving around himself. Here in his encounter with the sea captain, the text examines the bearings of this. If things exist to serve the (solitary) sovereign self, maybe other people do also. Each individual is the center and focus of his own life, while others are bit players, or given a role by Providence. Once the cloak of Providence is stripped away, the egotism of this attitude may appear, as it does in *Moreau* and many subsequent texts. Even Crusoe has to work hard, making lists of pros and cons for instance, to reassure himself of Providence's care for him (for instance, *Robinson Crusoe*, 83–84). He moves slowly, and with much self-mockery, toward becoming the "king," "generalissimo," and "governor" of his island (310, 344–45), but under God, who is "the Governor of nations" (221).

Giraudoux's Suzanne, for her part, finds herself on a much more benign island, with everything that a "jeune femme" could wish for, including perfect mangoes. Of the first mango that she eats, perfectly right ["juste à point"], she says, "Depuis des milliers d'années, la course entre mon destin and celui de cette mangue que je cueillis était juste à point" ["For thousands of years my destiny and that of this mango that I plucked were exactly convergent"].[24] Who could imagine that mangoes exist for the sake of the propagation of more mangoes, when they are so delicious, when our taste and their taste are so perfectly aligned? If Providence has brought her to this agreeably accommodating island, maybe it has also been preparing the mango for her, through the ages.

The parody works because Giraudoux so blithely sets himself to one side of the tradition, which is developing the possibilities of a concern with "Dear-Self" in quite other directions. Already, according to Richetti, Crusoe becomes for Friday, and later for those he rescues from the cannibals and from the mutineers, something very like the Providence that had earlier saved Crusoe (Richetti 1975, 56–59). We can recall Moreau seeing himself as God, creator, dispenser of the Law, and then watch how Giraudoux parodies Genesis as well—Moreau's reminiscence of how he labored on his first subject, a gorilla, blasphemously imitating both God's work and that of evolution, and rested afterward (*The Island of Dr. Moreau*, 14: 124)—in contrast to Suzanne's confession about her first days on her island: "Je rougis d' avouer á quoi se passa ma première semaine, quand je compare cette vie frivole á celle des naufragés classiques" ["I blush to admit how my first week passed, when I compare that frivolous life with that of the classic castaways"] (4: 67). What she is doing that makes her blush is arranging the feathers of her bed—the island, full of birds, has heaps of feathers—finding the right colors, making sure none bristle uncomfortably. It takes her almost a week, but “Après ces six jours de creation, j’étais juste arrivée á faire mon lit” [“After six days of creation, I had finally made my bed”] (68). So much for the hard practical labor of the traditional castaway; even for a teenager, six days is a long time to take to make your bed.[25]

“Now that we have instituted names as if everything belonged to us”

Naming and writing figures in the castaway narrative as both a recurrent trope (the exploration and naming of parts of the island, the keeping of a journal, the making of a calendar) and an ideological feature, in that the making of a text (a journal) can become part of the castaway’s work of settlement. The castaway does not fall silent, having no one to talk to and nothing to write on; on the contrary, he gives names to his island, he writes a journal, he makes a calendar, he writes on his island if he doesn’t happen to find or make ink and paper. He makes a mark in this as in other ways (a stockade, a fence to enclose the goats). This section examines the changes that come over this impulse of the castaway to name and record. We can ascribe some of these changes to belatedness—the consequences of telling a story that has been told many times before—but also, and increasingly, to the instability of the Subject and consequently his unreliability or reluctance as narrator. What had been taken for granted becomes problematic, complicated, something that is stumbled over.

Dr. Franklin’s Island (2001), a novel for teenagers by Ann Halam (Gwyneth Jones) shows the durability of the tradition. The novel gives us, first, an opening episode in which three young people are cast away and have to fend for themselves, with adaptations of some tropes from *Robinson Crusoe* (salvage from the wreck; disparate shoes drifting ashore). Then we have the main part of the story, an adaptation of *The Island of Dr. Moreau*, with the twist that it is told from the point of view of those being operated on, as Dr. Franklin begins to turn the children into animals. The two girls, who are more rational and constructive than the third, male castaway, begin their time as castaways by making notches on a tree to record the passing days, as Robinson Crusoe did; when they are captured by Dr. Franklin, they can’t do this, but they keep up a nightly ceremony in which they make a metaphorical notch. By this point in the story, the practice is more like that of prisoners trying to keep track of their incarceration. At the end of the story, after they have escaped, they agree that the ceremony was worth it for them, even though their count has been thrown out by all they have gone through.[26]

Enoch Arden is in this and other respects the exception, indeed the refusal.

During his time on the island, he doesn't work or talk. When he meets the sailors who will eventually rescue him, he mutters and mumbles, "idiotlike" (line 635). Once he arrives home (a word over which the poem itself stutters [664]), he works, "without hope" (816), but remains silent, repressing his cry of anguish at the sight of his happy family with their new father, and withholding his name and story till his deathbed.[27]

The silent Enoch remains outcast; one possesses by naming. This is very clear in *The Swiss Family Robinson* and *The Mysterious Island*. In the former, the father says, "Let me ask you all, if it will not be a great pleasure to converse about the country we inhabit, now that we have instituted names as if everything belonged to us?" (Wyss 1991, 13: 133) Naming and writing is from *Robinson Crusoe* onward a part of the business of knowing, controlling, and developing the island. Exacerbating or exaggerating this practice can be a way of undermining the assumptions about power and control on which it is based, as happens for instance in *Pincher Martin* ("I am netting this rock with names and taming it" [Golding 1956, 6: 86]); or pressing them to insanity, as happens for instance in *The Wasp Factory* and arguably in *Pincher Martin*; or of opening individual subjectivity to questioning, as happens in *Foe*. *Foe* is a story about the challenges of making and owning a story, in which story infiltrates experience yet experience refuses to issue in story. After an episode in which Susan Barton finds herself cast away on the island where Cruso and Friday are already living, the story moves to England and takes place between Susan, Friday, and Foe. The determinedly uncommunicative Cruso has no part in this, dying shortly after he leaves his island. Coetzee opens the question of narrative (who makes it, who figures in it) by sidelining Cruso, the person who (as Crusoe) made and controlled the narration in *Robinson Crusoe*. As intertextual awareness grows, and each succeeding text alludes to or sets itself in contrast to previous texts, then the project of writing an account of one's period on the island and/or writing oneself into the island by some inscription becomes more fraught with complexity.

Pi in *Life of Pi* is a non-European (Indian) protagonist who has already named himself (his given name was Piscine). Like Robinson, he keeps a journal until the ink runs out (Martel 2008, 208, 240), but when others—the marine investigators who interview him after he has been rescued—cast doubt on his story, he offers them an alternative version. He now emphasizes how the world is something we imagine into form. Stories depend on what the storyteller can tell—perhaps Pi was able tell us the story we have been reading, which is in most ways a positive and inspiring one, but not the more ghastly and atrocious story he now briefly offers the marine investigators (303–11). Stories equally depend on what readers or listeners can believe—the investigators have rejected the story we have been reading, so Pi offers them a different one. At the end of *Teranesia*, the point-of-view character Prabir in effect agrees to share the narrative with his sister Madhusree, who has saved him as he once saved her. In each case, this is a matter of getting safely off the island that is at the center of the story, named Teranesia by the child Prabir at the beginning of the novel. He renounces his custody of their story. After the events narrated in *Kensuke's Kingdom*, which involve both Michael and the earlier castaway Kensuke who befriended him after he was cast away on the island, we have to insert a ten-year gap. When Michael was rescued from the island by his parents, Kensuke got Michael to promise to conceal his presence on the island for ten years; we never find out what story Michael told his parents and others during this time, before he was permitted to write the account we now read.

John Barth's "Anonymiad" (1968) takes as its subject the castaway as writer. In fact, it tells of the discovery of writing itself, not to mention The Novel: a discovery that follows from the protagonist's being thrown out of epic and tragedy, both of them burlesqued in the story, and set down alone on an island, deprived of the hearers that song, drama, and (in its bardic origins) epic all need. He is a naïve minstrel, bewildered and betrayed by the dramatis personae of Aeschylus's *Agamemnon* (the betrayers are Agamemnon, Clytemnestra, and Aegisthus, with the addition of the minstrel's lover Merope). At length he is marooned on an island by the lively lecher and chancer Aegisthus. There are the usual goats already on the island, but all our anonymous narrator brings with him are nine amphorae, standing for the nine muses. As he drinks the wine out of each in succession, he fills each with his writings on goatskins, which he then launches into the ocean, to float away as the first-ever messages in a bottle, but to end up wherever they will. (One of them evidently ended up with us, because we can read his tale.) He had begun as a singer; isolated now, with no one to hear his singing, he has discovered writing itself:

> Artist through, I'd been wont since boyhood when pissing on beach or bank to make designs and clever symbols with my water. From this source, as from Pegasus's idle hooftap on Mount Helicon, sprang now a torrent of inspiration: using tanned skins in place of a sand-beach, a sea-gull feather for my tool, and a mixture of blood, wine, and squid-ink for a medium, I developed a kind of coded markings to record the utterance of mind and heart. By drawing out these chains of symbols I could so preserve and display my tale, it was unnecessary to remember it. (Barth 1968, 192)

Our narrator, now become author, works his way rapidly to prose and the novel ("long prose fictions" [194]) by the seventh amphora. He has displayed a

Crusoe-like practical ingenuity, in his use of skins, feathers, and "blood, wine, and squid-ink," but devoted this ingenuity to a recapitulation of the history of literary culture, not to the practicalities of settlement. The ninth and last amphora contains the text we have been reading, a parody of many genres, which refuses to settle into any one of them.

The first-person narrative has come to be a convention, and nowadays readers do not usually inquire how it came to be written down and published. This is clearly not the case with the "Anonymiad," belated and self-reflective, and in fact it was not the case with *Robinson Crusoe* at the beginning of the genre. Lennard Davis has traced Defoe's twists and turns as "editor" of Robinson's first-person account when he was taxed as to its truth: Defoe appealed to allegory, hinted at an underlying biography coded in the events on the island, and cheekily got Robinson Crusoe himself to swear an affidavit as to the truth of his story (Davis 1983, 158). As Neil Rennie points out, the direct, plain style as a mark of authenticity is too easily imitated; hence the confusion over travelers' narratives in the eighteenth century and beyond, up to Herman Melville's *Typee* and *Omoo* (1846, 1847): fictions taken for fact, factual narratives seen as fiction.[28] The matter becomes more disturbing in the case of *The Island of Dr. Moreau*. Prendick's narrative is published by his nephew, with disclaimers and signs of unease. ("His case," says his nephew in the introduction to the story, "was discussed among psychologists at the time as a curious instance of the lapse of memory consequent upon physical and mental stress" [79]). The extreme and bewildering qualities of Prendick's experience are discussed here, in Chapter 3. Elaine Showalter feels his whole narrative may be the account of a delusion: "The introduction, then, places the story in a psychological context, and offers an invitation to the reader to consider the tale as a hysterical hallucination, the result of a repressed trauma" (Showalter 1992, 81).

If so, *The Island of Dr. Moreau*, clearly a radical intervention in the tradition of castaway narratives, would anticipate such later texts as *Pincher Martin* and *The Wasp Factory*, whose protagonists turn out to be fundamentally deluded or deceived.

The Wasp Factory offers us a first-person narrative of a classically unstable modern kind: the insane but intelligent narrator who invites us into his abnormal world in such a way that we can't go on reading unless we join him and try to share his thoughts and desires. *The Beach* is similar: the unstable narrator is offered to us with a "what would you expect" air, as if the feckless Richard expresses the norm. Neither *The Wasp Factory* nor *The Beach* entirely abandons the plain style that was the means of expressing Robinson Crusoe's dedication to work and the use of practical reason. Both Frank and Richard, the narrators of *The Wasp Factory* and *The Beach* respectively, give us clear accounts of their daily activities and contrivances, but because these contrivances are reckless and murderous in their cases, the persistence in the plain style works as a refusal of seriousness. We didn't need to question the moral point of Robinson Crusoe's attempts to make bread: it was the practical thing to do. We do need to question the moral point of what Frank and Richard are up to, but the plain style of their narrations refuses to do so, and this refusal expresses their moral emptiness: confinement to the clear facts of actions and contrivances becomes a kind of myopia.

Robinson Crusoe: Model and Provocation

The features of the castaway narrative that Defoe puts in place are so productive that, combined, they inaugurate a genre of narrative and indeed, according to some scholars, the realist novel itself. The hypothesis on which this book is based, however, is that their dependence on certain readily accepted conventions and the likelihood that the reader is already acquainted with their outlines and tropes makes them provocations to skepticism or subversion. Later writers have to acknowledge them, for they are the presence of the past, to borrow Hutcheon's term, but later writers find they can express themselves, and express their historical situations and perceptions, by undermining them or overturning them.

This reworking and subverting can happen because the power of the narrative that Defoe inaugurates is bound up with its inner tensions: the combination of fable and realism; the interaction of free and necessitated; the ways in which the castaway is not so much set down amid a microcosm as sets himself to make one, and thus comes to express more about his self or his civilization than may be comfortable to see. Behind these tensions, surely, there is an instability and sometimes a contradiction in the enterprise of founding your self by working and surviving and thence controlling your island. This is what the revisions begin to reveal, and the revealing unleashes a lot of narrative energy.

The stronger the challenge to exert one's power and reason, the more likely it is to be put under pressure or to intensify toward insanity. The more you control, the more points at which you can see yourself as threatened: at the level of global politics, this is what may be termed the Afghanistan syndrome, but in the texts under discussion it takes the form of a supplementary island space that either threatens control or suggests how the castaway's attempts to secure it lead only to further insecurity. Again, stimulating, concrete, hands-on work with its immediate palpability and practicality can become alienated, cut off from or indifferent to the material worked on, especially when that material is human, as it is in *Moreau* and its progeny.

Castaway Tales follows Hutcheon's emphasis on textual codes and conventions as the initial targets of parody, although in practice, it proves hard to keep to this focus, because it is so often and so ferociously a general view or vision that is being pressed to extremes or exploded: the focus of discussion has to move from parody to revision. The later author of a castaway narrative doesn't so much parody the target text as grab it by the neck and throw it to the ground. In this context of increasing violence and drastic rearrangement, calmly impersonal terms such as revision, appropriation, or recuperation overlook the element of rude extremism in the intertextual relation.

Defoe inaugurates a form that binds realism and fable in a rich but unstable alliance; put pressure on that form, as later writers from Wells to Ballard and Coetzee do, and the pressure yields a series of disturbing images of humans, nature, work, knowledge, power, and the body. The tradition is tied to the business of survival and sovereignty, the work of naming, knowing, and controlling palpable material things. All this is the field of realism, but a good deal that is involved in these narratives opens questions to do with defining the human or, more precisely, Western Man. The general implications of fable (the castaway as Everyman, or every Western Man) take on a threatening edge. The microcosmic context, the restriction of space and cast list, and the concentration on a passage from nature to culture which, however, comes to have no upper limit—all these pull the castaway narrative toward fable. The castaway-become-settler reaches for sovereignty, possession, even godhead.

After *Moreau* the genre drives toward increasingly extreme exacerbations of *Robinson Crusoe*, and this throws a bleak light onto Hutcheon's sense of the importance of parody for modern art, while at the same time vindicating her thesis about the vital relation of modern art to earlier art. The more the revision refuses or distorts or writes over the top of the earlier text, the more stubbornly the earlier text haunts the later one. No doubt this bleakness is to be connected to the way the genre brings together masculinity, work on nature, and colonization: a series of cultural topics that exert a disturbing pressure when they come together. The dynamic is mostly a grim one, though it releases an often exhilarating energy—and indeed these fictions come to have a good deal to say about the pleasures of destruction.

2

The Swiss Family Robinson to The Mysterious Island

Vicissitudes of the Crusoe Template

What happiness it is to work from dawn to dusk for your family and yourself, to build a roof over their heads, to till the soil to feed them, to create your own world, like Robinson Crusoe, in imitation of the creator of the universe, and to bring forth your life, as if you were your own mother, again and again.
BORIS PASTERNAK, *Doctor Zhivago*

Dr. Zhivago's idyll does not last, and neither does the buoyant optimism of the castaway tale. This chapter, however, offers a glimpse of some nineteenth-century versions, best classified as repeating rather than revising *Robinson Crusoe*. "Does *Wilhelm Meister's Apprenticeship* 'defamiliarize' the conventions of the *Bildungsroman*? Is not the opposite the case: that with his novel Goethe founds them and makes them reproducible?" (Moretti 1983, 13).

Franco Moretti's suggestion can be applied to *Robinson Crusoe*. Looking backward, we can see Defoe's novel as defamiliarizing island narratives such as *The Odyssey* and *The Tempest*, but looking forward, we can see it as establishing a template useful for a kind of solid, routine rendition of the castaway story, as successful and influential works will often do, as part of what Moretti calls "normal literature" (1983, 15). This chapter examines two nineteenth-century castaway stories, *The Swiss Family Robinson* and *Masterman Ready*, that routinize *Robinson Crusoe*, and then discusses a third, *The Mysterious Island*, that seems to begin in the same way but swerves into a darker and more complex rendition.

Routine allows for variation, and variation, obviously, is not the same as parody or critique. Neither is exaggeration always to be seen as parody, as the example of *The Swiss Family Robinson* will make clear. Exaggeration can be homage, or competition. The Wysses and Marryat revise Defoe by exaggerating and overpopulating: more castaways cast away, more crops domesticated, more animals tamed (a flamingo, an orangutan), more technology reinvented from practically nothing. Parody makes an entrance when the variation or exaggeration has critical potential, suggesting revision, skepticism, or simply restlessness with the target text, and this is the case with *The Mysterious Island*.

The Swiss Family Robinson: The Castaway Story Regularized and Domesticated

The Swiss Family Robinson is a conscious redoing of *Robinson Crusoe*, written for children and for didactic purposes, with a family cast away rather than a single male castaway.[1] Novels in general tell either of bastards confronting the world or of foundlings fleeing it, according to Marthe Robert.[2] Castaway fictions very commonly orphan their main characters, in effect, by casting them away and requiring them to remake their lives. The presence of a functioning and paternally ordered family in *The Swiss Family Robinson* and later in *Masterman Ready* makes a contrast with most modern castaway novels, and underlines how these versions stabilize the genre for a time, though the family in *The Swiss Family Robinson* is joined near the end of the novel by Emily Montrose, who has lived as a lone castaway for three years.

The Swiss Family Robinson is quite straightforward. There are the parents, the father and head of the family a pastor, and the four sons, varying in age and therefore maturity but all of them active and helpful. They are so successful during their ten years' sojourn that, unusually in castaway stories, the parents decide to stay behind when an English ship arrives off the coast. It's very upbeat: for all the emphasis on patience and hard work, the family members succeed at everything they attempt; there are no failures, no trial and error. There's an element of competition with earlier texts, of cheerful outdoing, in the sheer variety of enterprises they undertake: dwellings they construct (at least five, several of them in a single chapter); animals they domesticate (a buffalo, a wild ass, a falcon, a flamingo, and more, joining the livestock and poultry luckily surviving on the wrecked ship); useful products they discover and exploit (flax, cotton, rubber, cassava, sago, potatoes, and more); birds, beasts, and fish they kill (any animal or bird or reptile they encounter is either killed or domesticated); and trades they master (building a boat and making beehives, a loom, a spinning wheel). The fantasy that all the world's goods and products might be brought together and used or enjoyed in one place might apply better to the imperial metropolis than to a remote island, and so might the arguably related fantasy that knowledge of all the world might be inventoried and sorted in the one place. But in *The Swiss Family Robinson*, the family directly encounters a wide variety of natural life, and the father expounds upon it, shows how it can be used, and often shows how Providence has fitted it for its place in Nature or its usefulness to Man.[3]

The Swiss Family Robinson celebrates God's Providence and offers an earthly paradise in which all good and useful things come together both for the service of the colonists and to teach the reader about nature, agriculture, and a variety of trades. The father of the family tells a religious parable that depicts all humans as "colonists of God," put on earth as the family has been put on the island (12: 126). "'Human creatures,' said I, 'are the colonists of God.'" He sums up their experience: "The ten years we had passed were but years of conquest and establishment" (60: 452). A sense of God's Providence, a sense of the patriarchal family as energetic and productive, a sense of the rightness of "conquest and establishment": these are all untroubled, if we exclude the episode in which the depredations of a band of monkeys are met by the father with a war of extermination that shocks his sons (34: 294). There is an unresting drive to more production, more activity, though it is interesting that there is much less exploration than in many castaway novels, for instance Verne's *The Mysterious Island*, which, as will be discussed, is influenced by *The Swiss Family Robinson*. Perhaps this reflects the latter novel's valuation of the domestic. Similarly, it is interesting that when the castaways here make a fortress (planting a thorny hedge, and so on [23: 203]), the gesture seems perfunctory; and when they find a grotto, which is explicitly compared to Robinson's cave, the emphasis is on how beautiful it is and on the complicated set of rooms they make within it, not on the security it might provide.

The Swiss Family Robinson is a children's book, written in brisk episodes without much regard to the steady passage of time (so it accommodates collective authorship, but throws up some continuity problems). The fact that so many chapters end with everybody going peacefully to sleep suggests the origin of the book in bedtime stories. But when Verne imitates and emulates the colonists' ceaseless activities and unbroken successes in *The Mysterious Island*, matters will become more problematic.

Masterman Ready or The Wreck of the "Pacific": Following the Template

The Swiss Family Robinson shows an energy in its excess, in the scale and variety of the family's unbroken achievements. *Masterman Ready* (1841) routinizes both *Robinson Crusoe* and *The Swiss Family Robinson*.[4] It's a careful, systematic, and somewhat bland children's book. Most of the novel details the steady, planned, successful work of the castaways under the direction of a paragon, Masterman Ready, a veteran sailor who takes the Seagrave family under his wing, while displaying the proper social deference. *Masterman Ready* is narrated in the third person, but Ready speaks so often to explain and instruct that he is virtually the voice of the text; in addition, he tells his life story over several chapters, by way of bedtime story (from Chap. 31 to Chap. 41).

The way the Seagraves and Ready come to be wrecked and marooned is perhaps the only point at which the novel diverges from the castaway template it is following. The *Pacific*, commanded by Captain Osborn, suffers a series of accidents and casualties in a storm, culminating in Osborn being stunned by falling rigging. The sailors decide to launch the remaining boat, taking the captain with them but leaving the Seagraves behind (useless mouths). Ready refuses to join the other sailors. He tells Mr. Seagrave that what the sailors did was rational ("the law of nature" [6: 30]). There is no exclaiming over the sailors' callousness, though there is a suggestion that because they want to get drunk they must be unreliable. In fact, however, the *Pacific* is not quite ready to sink, and Ready and the Seagraves manage to get it to an island and drive it ashore. And it is Captain Osborn who later comes back to rescue them, having made it eventually to Sydney. There is a little reprise of this earlier desertion, however, when the ship that the castaways sight sails away again, to their distress. Ready again says that it had to, because of the weather (44: 194), and this time it returns.

Once the castaways are ashore, however, everything happens smoothly. We have the salvage from the wreck (the castaways get a great deal out, but there is none of Robinson's excitement and relief as more and more that is of value is rescued); an early sojourn in tents; a move to an even more idyllic spot; the erection of a house; then later, the erection of a storehouse cum stockade. A well is dug, a pond for turtles, a fishpond, and a hen house. Later they discover good pasture for their goats and sheep, and—in a moment of *Swiss Family Robinson*–like overplus—nearby they come across guavas, bananas, prickly pear, yams, and eggplant growing, all at once. They find the island beautiful; they are devout and grateful to God. There are several discourses from Mr. Seagrave on how the Creator fits everything to its place and to man's use; for example, on how coral islands are formed: "Is not this wonderful, my dear boy? Is He not a great and good God who can make such minute animals as these work His pleasure, and at the time He sees fit, produce such a beautiful island as this?"[5] Mr. Seagrave argues that the most widespread animals are those best adapted to serve man, and so on.[6] Every difficulty is easily overcome with hard work and Ready's foresight:

> "But how are we to make the salt-pan, Ready?" said William. "We must cut it out of the solid rock."
>
> "Yes, William, but I have three or four of what they call cold chisels, and with one of them and a hammer we shall get on faster than you think; for the coral rock, although hard at the surface, is soft a little below it." (36: 142)

God provides. Ready foresees and plans. Mr. Seagrave occasionally adds a theological gloss. All this takes the tension out of the story and supplies reassurance and structure, supposing that the young reader is looking for these qualities. Everybody who is able to pitches in, and is given a role, and the succession of works is accomplished. Anxiety is strictly confined to Mrs. Seagrave, who often weeps, is nervous, and has vital facts withheld from her until Ready, William, and Mr. Seagrave judge she is capable of hearing them. For the rest of the time, she looks after the younger children and does the washing and cleaning. Naughtiness and failure to cooperate are equally firmly confined to little Tommy, usually described as an "urchin" and invariably silly and disobedient: he is slightly the most interesting character in the novel as a result, not exactly a savage, as savages are depicted in this period, but incapable of orderliness or understanding. When he does something silly, he is hurt or reprimanded, and says he will never do that again; but he does something else instead, and so on.

It's interesting that Tommy nearly gets taken by the sharks that are really the only natural danger the castaways encounter. There are several incidents involving sharks, and in fact everyone and everything in the text has a clear role, where possible in the work and organization of the castaways' lives on the island, but in any case, in the organization of the novel: Mrs. Seagrave is womanly sensibility; Tommy is invariable naughtiness; William, the oldest child, is enthusiasm, maturity, and intelligent curiosity; and the sharks are the dangers of the natural world. In this, *Masterman Ready* is rather slavishly following *The Swiss Family Robinson*. The family is a unit of production in which everyone has roles, whether what is being produced is settlement on the island or lessons for the reader. The text and the events the text records are transparent to each other; there is none of the ambiguity of fact and fiction that struck some early readers of *Robinson Crusoe*, and was provoked by Defoe himself, nor is there an unreliable and fallible narrator, such as we will meet with Prendick in *The Island of Dr. Moreau* and in many later castaway fictions. Authority is shared between the impersonal narration of events and the discourses of Ready and Mr. Seagrave, and all are perfectly reliable.

In Wyss, the father (the narrator of the story and leader of the colonists) goes nameless; the mother (Elizabeth) is referred to mostly in terms of her role (generous provider and so on), or as our "steward," "our good housekeeper" (45: 347). The children do have names, as well as set and reiterated characters to go with them—cute little Francis; slow, lazy, but thoughtful Ernest; lively and boastful Jack; and the more adult and brave Fritz, who also gets to be called his father's privy councilor. While he was alone, Robinson Crusoe took on roles that would otherwise be taken by a wife or servant; these later texts regularize. Specialization is the rule.

Marryat adds Juno, the family's nurse and servant from South Africa. Juno is unswervingly loyal and speaks the broken English usually given to non-Europeans in castaway and other adventure novels, but is robust and hardworking.

Masterman Ready is linear and economical, and when the family has set everything up according to Ready's plans and advice, Marryat is ready to introduce the "savages." In fact, the sailing ship that will later arrive in the nick of time to rescue the castaways from the savages, and the savages themselves (two women who are cast away on the island in their canoe, but later sneak back to their island) arrive almost on successive pages (Chap. 43, 44). This simplifies the common two-phase narrative—years of undisturbed development, then the arrivals of savages, mutineers, pirates.

The castaways have a few weeks to set up their stockade, and then the savages return in huge numbers, try to storm the stockade, and are held off by two men and a boy with muskets (loaded by Mrs. Seagrave and Juno) until things look grim. They run out of water as a result of yet another naughtiness of Tommy, and Ready is fatally speared when he ventures to the well to get some. Whereupon the men from the sailing ship arrive to the rescue, and (as the story has now passed through all the planned moves of settlement, education, and battle with savages) take the castaways on to Sydney. It seems right that the destination is this white settler colony, by this date able to be seen as ordered and even progressive, rather than, for instance, Brazil as in *Robinson Crusoe*.[7] (Mr. Seagrave gives a history of colonization from the Spanish and Portuguese to the English in Chapter 27.)

The Mysterious Island: The Template Surpassed and Subverted

Verne's *The Mysterious Island* begins by giving us a kind of fulfillment of *Robinson Crusoe* and *The Swiss Family Robinson*—the earlier texts are not so much parodied as revised and outdone. So we meet again the masculine company;[8]

the growing of wheat, domestication of animals, erection of fortifications, clash with pirates; the construction of a bridge (even more wonderful a feat here than in *The Swiss Family Robinson*); the war with the monkeys; making a boat. This last was one of Robinson's failures, at least at his first attempt. In *The Swiss Family Robinson*, there is first a pinnace put together inside the wreck from prefabricated parts, with an exit then blasted for it, and then a rather grand bark canoe, and later still a kayak. In *The Mysterious Island*, the colonists build an ocean-going yacht. It seems that earlier castaway stories exist to be pillaged for feats and motifs, which are then outdone. But Verne's novel swerves into undermining what has been so confidently built up. Andrew Martin has written of Verne's appetite for excess, for the "trop-plein," and also of his countervailing drive toward purity and reduction, and *The Mysterious Island* illustrates this.[9]

The narrative divides into two unequal phases. In the first, the settlers explore, develop, and settle their island, which they name Lincoln Island. (The settlers are a group of Americans, partisans of the Union, escaping from imprisonment in besieged Richmond by balloon, and then blown far off course and dumped near the island.) They do this with absolutely undeviating success; it's a lot of work but it's easy, really.[10] "The will to colonize meets with almost nil resistance" (Martin 1990, 101). Already in this phase, however, there are mysteriously lucky occurrences, which soon have to be seen as the interventions of some hidden person or power. In the second phase, these interventions multiply, save lives, defeat the pirates who turn up more or less on cue —this corresponds to the pattern sketched earlier in which the island is visited or invaded after a long initial period of isolation. The result of the mysterious interventions is that the settlers' achievements begin to seem rather empty, and (relative at least to the buoyancy that is normal with Verne's characters) they begin to lose heart. This is most notable in their bold and omnicompetent leader Cyrus Smith, who is reduced to advising that they do nothing but wait. Then they discover that their benefactor has been Captain Nemo of *20,000 Leagues Under the Sea*; he has been living in the *Nautilus* in solitude, the rest of his crew having died off, in a hidden cavern under the island. After this discovery Nemo dies, the island's volcano erupts, and eventually, as a result of the interaction of the cavern and the volcano, the whole island explodes and with it all their achievements, though our heroes are rescued.

Initially, then, *The Mysterious Island* can be read as a revision of *Robinson Crusoe* in stout, confident nineteenth-century terms.[11] Crusoe builds a canoe with huge effort over months, hollowing a log, and then discovers he has no way to get it to water. He builds an elaborate fortress and then, uneasy, a second, secret fortress and refuge—and then adds another. There is effort and occasional failure, for all that he benefited from what he salvaged from the shipwreck, and was given years undisturbed to do his work. In *The Mysterious Island*, by contrast, the settlers begin with virtually nothing, having thrown everything they possess overboard from their sinking balloon in the endeavor to regain height. "They lacked even the tools to make tools. [. . .] they would be forced to create with their own hands every object they might need" (Pt. 1, Chap. XIII: 137). They are left with one match and (discovered later) one grain of wheat—one grain of wheat, from which prudent cultivation yields them hundreds of thousands of bushels, outdoing Crusoe even in that respect. (His first harvest was a failure.)

It's as if Verne set out to demonstrate how much better a set of active, practical modern men would do, with their scientific and technical knowledge, than the earlier Englishman did, even though the latter had the head start of a well-equipped wreck. As Diana Loxley says, the knowledge that the castaways bring with them is enough by itself, and converts them almost at once into colonists; everything that they see, every animal or plant, they can name, and their naming has the authority of scientific knowledge. (This is the beginning of a process of abstraction that will be taken further in later fictions.)[12] The result approaches the absurd.[13] Crusoe at length has Friday; Verne's settlers bring with them a biddable Negro servant (Nab), and later they domesticate an orangutan, Joop, who is just as capable and contented.[14] (Joop, that is Jupiter, perhaps recalls Juno in Marryat.) They make a kiln, and then pottery; nitroglycerine, and then a big explosion to drain a lake. They smelt iron; they erect an 80-foot-long bridge; they tame a pair of wild asses in a matter of weeks; and so on, and on. There are no failures and scarcely any setbacks.

How is this to be assessed? Has Verne come to send himself up in his zeal to outdo Defoe and his successors? He is perfectly capable of this kind of *reductio ad absurdum*. William Butcher suggests that Verne wants "to go one better than the preceding series of Robinsonades, to sum them up but also to show them up" (Introduction to Verne 2001, xxviii).

The Mysterious Island both redoubles and undermines earlier castaway tales. There is the dramatic discovery of footprints, quite early in the story; they prove to belong to their leader Cyrus Smith himself. "I must somehow have gone blank at one point," he reflects (1, VIII: 82); this blankness stands in contrast to all that we see during the rest of the novel of the thinking and working of Smith and his companions, in which there are no blanks, and everything has a use and a name. These footprints are the first of a series of clues that the island is already inhabited—pervaded—by a mysterious other, though from very early this personage is clearly benevolent. (He rescued Cyrus Smith in the incident that left the mysterious footprints.) The result, however, is that the narrative's dealings with material things proceed on two separate tracks that surely have to meet but never quite do. One track is the narrative of work, construction, and contrivance, and here, as mentioned, *The Mysterious Island* outdoes all its predecessors. The other track is the narrative of the mysterious interventions of the benevolent other, and here material things become clues to be deciphered. For instance, "A close examination revealed it to be a shred of Ayrton's jacket, for it was a patch of felt of the kind produced exclusively by the workshops of Lincoln Island" (3, IX: 590). (At this point Ayrton, a castaway they had rescued from another island and brought to live with them, has gone missing.)

We have already learned about felting, but in that earlier passage we have clear exposition of a sequence, no mystery whatever:

> The first step would be to rid the wool of its oily, fatty substance that impregnates it, which is known as suint. This degreasing process was accomplished by soaking the wool for twenty-four hours in basins filled with water at a temperature of seventy degrees centigrade. Next they washed it thoroughly in soda baths and wrung it dry. Now it was ready to be fulled, after which [. . .] (2, XI: 372)

The novel of work, recounting challenges and tasks as they arrive and are coped with or surmounted, in an episodic fashion or in time with the passing of the months and seasons, is one thing after another; an achievement or a condition, for instance civilization, accumulates. The mystery novel, on the other hand, is surely proceeding toward a solution or explanation. How will the two tracks be brought together? First, some more details on the ways in which *The Mysterious Island* redoubles the castaway narrative.

As was mentioned, the castaways completely lack salvage, and achieve a great deal without it by the sheer power of knowledge and hard work. Then salvage comes pouring in upon them anyway: a chest, mysteriously washed ashore, full of exactly the range of tools and weapons they need; the almost intact wreckage of their balloon, providentially snagged on a tall tree and retrieved so that they can use its ropes and canvas for sails, rigging, and clothes; the wreck of the pirate ship spectacularly sunk by their mysterious benefactor, from which they salvage an abundance of equipment, timber, and metal. They explore and allot names to their island; they establish its longitude and latitude. Later, they circumnavigate it. Later still, they reexplore it, searching for traces of their hidden benefactor, but already convinced they will only find him when he wants to be found, which indeed proves to be the case. Castaways themselves, isolated and unvisited in the vast emptiness of the South Pacific, they learn of another castaway, an "outcast," on another island not too far away.

They rescue him and reclaim him for humanity from the brutish silence into which he had fallen, and eventually, when he comes to speak, learn from him of yet other castaways who had preceded him on his island. Their wonderful protector Nemo (who had made sure they learned about Ayrton, the castaway of Tabor Island) is himself an outcast, waiting death in solitude in a cavern under the island, but living in some comfort on the *Nautilus*.

Robinson Crusoe spent decades alone with only his parrot to talk to, though he could pray and in that way talk with God. To exaggerate a little, it could be said that the next step down from Ayrton, almost crazy in his isolation, is *Nostromo*'s Decoud, suiciding after a couple of weeks of loneliness in the gulf, loneliness which he has come to find intolerable (Conrad 1963, Pt. 3, Chap. 10). *The Mysterious Island* thus looks one way to Robinson's twenty-eight years of achievement, and another way, with Ayrton, to Decoud's collapse after brief isolation.

Joop the orangutan, captured by the castaways, soon becomes a member of the group, a biddable servant, human in everything but his inability to talk, and there are jokes about how useful a quality silence is in a servant. Rousseau, and after him Lord Monboddo, had argued that orangutans are human, if at a lower stage of development.[15] Verne seems to follow this, in the confident movement of the first half of the novel, in which the group of successfully cooperating companions includes a boy, a Negro, a dog, and an ape. In the later part of the text, the tendency is to draw a line around this central group and emphasize how much is left outside it: pirates, the mysterious benefactor. Ayrton is the hinge case. When Ayrton first appears, he is struggling violently with Harbert, and is mistaken for an ape (2, VI: 321; 2, XIV: 416). The humorous and positive treatment of Joop as companion is shadowed by the grimness of Ayrton as castaway. His silence is that of trauma, and takes a long time to break, though eventually he is reclaimed as human and as a companion. And there is Nemo, who saves the castaways from the pirates, former comrades of Ayrton's, and who for all his playing at Providence is as saturnine a figure as ever, and now lives solitary, cannot be named or known by the settlers for most of the text, and of course is named "No one" anyway. That is, we can see Ayrton and Nemo as shadows of the grimmer possibilities of being cast away, the negativity that Defoe's exploration of the castaway's subjectivity sets aside and that has been denied in the cheerful activism and incessant bestowing of names of Verne's castaways.[16] With *The Mysterious Island* the castaway tale thus recedes from the straightforward optimism of many earlier versions of Defoe.

Verne's castaways are inveterately social. They consult, exclaim, plan, cooperate. It sometimes appears that they don't exist when they are not with each other. The novel's complex and layered dealings with earlier castaway stories, and its shift into the mystery eventually clarified by the meeting with the dying Nemo, simultaneously outdo and undermine the tradition, and these dealings express Verne's complex feelings about the social and the solitary. Even allowing for the fact that Ayrton's brutish mutism is largely a result of his guilt for the crimes that led to his being marooned on Tabor Island, it does also suggest the fragility of the notion of the sane and productive solitary castaway that Defoe had launched upon the world. Certainly, humans in Verne's novels need companions and usually travel and work in good-humored and cooperative male teams. Yet the sociality of the castaways may not be enough, as Cyrus Smith meditates: "They were alone on this island. And it is only in society that humanity can flourish, for men need nothing so much as the aid and company of other men. Cyrus Smith knew this full well, and he sometimes wondered if they might one day meet with some circumstance that they could not overcome!" (3, VIII: 583).[17]

Yet the god of the island is Nemo, now alone, and always a figure of Byronic aloofness and disenchantment, even in *20,000 Leagues Under the Sea*, when he sailed with his crew and was observed by the usual Vernian set of travelers. Nemo's repeated rescues of Cyrus Smith and his companions set a limit to their powers and their achievements. The *Nautilus*, with its apparently perpetual supply of electricity, and the electric guns with which Nemo dispatches the pirates who were cast away on the island by the sinking of their ship (by means of a very powerful mine planted by Nemo) suggest science and technology beyond the reach of the otherwise omnicompetent and supremely confident Cyrus Smith. (No doubt if one feels that Science is progressive, then one has to admit that it will continue to progress, so Verne is being consistent in giving Nemo more advanced technology than that of the castaways; but it is notable that Nemo's technology is not explained.)

In the violence that follows the arrival of the pirates, and makes it clear to the settlers that they are not in control of their fates, the clear spatial demarcations they had imposed on the island are blurred. They have to leave their headquarters, Granite House, which they had fortified and separated from the rest of the island by a lake and a moat; they are split up. The pirates are killed, mostly by the settlers' unseen helper, in a scene that reprises the killings that often feature at a late stage in an island narrative and that are often made the subject of an arithmetical accounting.[18] The castaways explore the island again, this time trying to find the unseen benefactor who has more and more acted as Providence. This is no longer the confident and patriotic naming of parts that they indulged in on earlier expeditions (soon, with the destruction of the island, it will be "Mount Franklin" that erupts and "Lake Grant" that floods); they try to search every cranny, but they admit before they begin that the survey is futile. Their benefactor will reveal himself only when he himself chooses. The later parts of the story undo the outdoing of Crusoe in the first parts. The development and parceling of the island that had seemed to face no limits (they were starting to talk of railway lines)[19] is stymied.

When their benefactor does at length reveal himself, they are of course grateful for all his help, but he is on the point of death, and it is from his subterranean cavern that destruction comes to the whole island. In their earlier, more confident days, the settlers speculated how they might bring the island into American modernity, and as they fantasized, the reader might well have wondered at the long-term prospects of a colony consisting entirely of males. Even the dog and the orangutan are male.[20] Nemo's solitude underlines the point: the rest of his all-male crew has simply died off, and now he is dying too. The attempt to out-do Crusoe has been piled so high that it has collapsed into confusion, uncontrol, and death.

Verne doesn't kill off his heroes, and could not have done so without breaking his relationship with his readers and, no doubt, his contract with his vigilant publisher Hetzel, but he obliterates the island and all its teeming wildlife and all the settlers' constructions and arrangements. Joop perishes. Nor is this ending improvised. Verne has planned it and hinted at it almost from the beginning of the novel. The novel's go-ahead narrative of successful work and energetic exploration is punctuated by several discussions of the possibility that human affairs or the Earth itself will have an end. As the volcano begins to rumble and then erupt, Cyrus reasons out an understanding of the disaster that eventually destroys everything. It's not that his energetic rationality and the hard work and good spirit of his companions are critiqued. They are demarcated, just as the island had been mapped, measured, and subdivided. Their sphere is limited, they need Nemo's help, but within their sphere they are strong. The pull of the narrative is not so much to emphasize the limits of reasoning and hard work, "the unfailing logic of simple common sense" (3, VIII: 583) in "the domain of practical existence" (3, V: 550), as to bring intense sociality in the companions into encounter with the solitariness of the two other castaways, Ayrton and Nemo.

As far as I know, there are no direct links between *The Mysterious Island* and *The Island of Dr. Moreau*, but it does seem as if the time is ready for a more thoroughgoing assault on Defoe's model. This time, as will be seen, though Moreau and his works are first exposed as cruel and futile and then destroyed, the island and the figure of Moreau survive in a series of reiterations and variations.

2

Violence

3

Moreau and Its Progeny

Abstraction and Violence

The Island of Dr. Moreau

> When I was a kid I thought nothing could be finer or more adventurous than the Robinson Crusoe business, but that place was as monotonous as a book of sermons. I went round finding eatable things and generally thinking, but I tell you I was bored to death before the first day was out. (Wells, 1887, 266)

So speaks Butler, the narrator of H. G. Wells's story "Aepyornis Island" (1894). A fossil hunter, he has been cast away because he mistreated and quarreled with his Madagascan assistants, but he finds a companion of a kind in a giant egg that he had collected and now hatches, rears, and facetiously names Friday. The aepyornis, however, grows very tall, they quarrel, and Butler has to take refuge up a tree: "And me a human being, heir of the ages and all that" (270). Wells is clearly skeptical of the tradition of the castaway as hardworking, capable, and superior to whatever inferior types may happen along. *The Island of Dr. Moreau*, published a couple of years later, in 1896, takes this skepticism to corrosive lengths.

This chapter follows a discussion of *The Island of Dr. Moreau* with an examination of some of its successors. With *The Monster Men* (Edgar Rice Burroughs, 1913), *The Island of Captain Sparrow* (S. Fowler Wright, 1928), *The Island of Doctor Death and Other Stories and Other Stories* (Gene Wolfe, 1980), and *Moreau's Other Island* (Brian Aldiss, 1980) the variation is explicit and the theme, as in *The Island of Dr. Moreau*, is violence and degeneration. With *The Invention of Morel* (Adolfo Bioy Casares, 1940) the influence is again explicit (Moreau/Morel), but in this case it is the scientist's detachment from the realities of his island, and the point-of-view character's bewilderment that are varied. These versions of *The Island of Dr. Moreau* are arguably most interesting when they ignore the brutality of Wells's novel and fix on the possibilities of the island as laboratory, scene of experience in artifice or virtuality. It is not until we reach *Lord of the Flies* (William Golding, 1954) that a modern castaway tale really confronts the grim implications of *The Island of Dr. Moreau*. This chapter concludes with *Lord of the Flies*, a novel that is certainly comparable to *The Island of Dr. Moreau* in its depiction of the descent of humans into beastliness and in the struggle of some of the castaways to resist this descent, and whose sheer violence marks an extremity of modern castaway narrative. *Lord of the Flies* prepares us for the texts to be discussed in the following chapter, texts that share a violent and grim view of the castaway with *Lord of the Flies*, but do not directly refer to *The Island of Dr. Moreau*.

The Island of Dr. Moreau crashes brutally into the tradition of the castaway novel, which had become decorous, cheerful, and good-natured as it was adapted to children in novels such as *The Swiss Family Robinson* and *The Coral Island*. There is, in fact, violence in *Treasure Island* (a related island fiction), and, as has been argued earlier, in *The Mysterious Island* Verne carries his story of buoyant manly improvisation and settlement into uncertainty and instability. But Wells seizes the castaway novel and shakes it. *The Island of Dr. Moreau* was published in 1896, in an explosive decade in which Western imperialism reached new power and also revealed its savage side, most clearly in the Congo. The imagination of the period seethes with fictions of invasion and unnaturalness: *Dracula*, *Heart of Darkness*.[1] For the scientist Van Helsing, we have Count Dracula; for Marlow, putting his faith in rivets and efficiency, we have Kurtz; and for Prendick, struggling to keep to commonplace decency and sense, we have Dr. Moreau. The reverberations of Darwin's theories fed ideologies of power and fears of degeneration. The period was gripped by an urge to classify and label human types: criminal, cranial, ethnic, racial, psychological, and anthropological. The contributions, and very often the notoriety, of Nordau, Lombroso, Kraft-Ebbing, and Havelock Ellis testify both to the tendency and its popularity.

The novelists follow suit. Joseph Conrad, for instance, throws a net of ethnic and racial stereotypes, comparisons to animals, and summary catchphrases over his characterizations, subtle and ironic though they are.[2] It seems that there is a need to pin humans into categories in these diverse ways because the Human is in flux, because individuals and peoples are continually imagined or feared to be developing, degenerating, declining, blending, and shedding their fixed characters.[3] H. G. Wells, the pupil of T. H. Huxley, Darwin's ally and polemicist, responded in his series of scientific romances of the 1890s. *The War of the Worlds* (1898), which can be read as a comment on imperialism because its story of invasion asks, what if others did to us what we have done to others, sets the scene in the long perspective of the evolution and devolution of the technologically advanced but declining Martians, and presents in one episode the "swift liquefaction of the social body" when millions flee London (Wells 1975, 99). *The Time Machine* (1895) asks us to see the time traveler, the brutal cannibal Morlocks, and the gentle helpless Eloi as part of the one species, or what had been one species. Nothing remains fixed, not races, not civilizations, not humanity itself. *The Island of Dr. Moreau* examines Moreau's attempt to make men out of beasts, its cruelty and failure, and the beast-men's decline. If the castaway narrative up to Verne had depended on a distinction between the castaways and those who invaded their diligently developed and subdivided island, between the civilized and the violent (whether savages or pirates), then Wells throws all this into question.[4]

The moment of *Moreau* is not far removed from that of Conrad's *Nostromo* (1904) which is the novel that puts an examination of colonization and imperialism on a broad historical and social footing: the story of the silver mine is told in its involvement with the successive waves of domination that make up the colonization of Costaguana, from the Spanish to the Americans, and the novel places the exciting adventure tale (for instance, Nostromo's dramatic ride) in a context comparable in social complexity to that of a novel by Balzac or Tolstoy. In this context, the episode of Decoud's short time on the island in the gulf, his succumbing to despair and his suicide, casts multiple ironies on the castaway tale. Not only is the silver useless to Decoud, as Robinson Crusoe also reflected (*Robinson Crusoe*, 246–48)—without in the slightest being deflected from his work of survival and settlement, and without renouncing the quest for profit later, once he is off his island—but he has no will to work or survive. And the novel ends with the death of Nostromo, a death also presided over by the somber gulf. Nostromo is opposite to Decoud in most ways—extroverted, brave, and unsophisticated—but, like Decoud, he dies in solitude, cut off from the society of others, on whose admiration he depended for his sense of self (Conrad 1963, Pt. 3, Chap. 10 and 13). That solitude, which is a kind of freedom for Robinson, becomes an emptiness for Decoud and Nostromo, and the notion that a castaway might spend years in solitude without this affecting his sanity is grimly refuted.

Conrad's *Victory* (1915) is similarly in complex and skeptical relation to the castaway narrative. The scene is populated by stray Europeans, some making a living, some failing to, some vicious, none of them with much power or even disposition to settle or rule the islands where they have found themselves. The presence of Lena is crucial to the tragedy. She is rescued by Heyst and carried off to island exile, so that Heyst's impulse to chivalry and involvement is succeeded by baffled desire; but Heyst and Lena are voluntary exiles or fugitives, not castaways, except (each in very different ways) spiritually. Mr. Jones, Pedro, and Ricardo, ominous and sexually perverse villains who struggle ashore on Heyst and Lena's island as wrecked seafarers, or rather pretending to be such, are castaways, but they fill the role of the invaders or pirates in the central tradition of castaway narratives, except that they are not defeated. There are complex transpositions between the apparent castaways, who are not, and those who are apparently not castaways, yet who are, spiritually speaking. Further discussion of *Nostromo* and *Victory* would take us too far from the castaway narrative, but when associated with *The Island of Dr. Moreau*, Conrad's novels do underline that at this point in history, there is an intensity of reflection on the dangers and disenchantments of imperialism, an accumulation, in various texts, of ironies and reversals.

The castaway novel's remote, initially uninhabited island as a field for work, development, and power is reassessed. The untouched, uninhabited island can figure as a utopian opportunity. Margaret Cohen remarks, "When resourceful adventurers like Crusoe come to the island, they discover a laboratory for transforming nature into wealth and beauty" (2006, 659). This benign laboratory has become the House of Pain of the scientist Moreau, where Moreau performs surgery on animals to try to make them into humans. Labor has become Science, alienated from its (living) material and indifferent to its suffering. There is a split between Moreau's objectivity and the subjectivity of Prendick, the novel's narrator, though both fail and both tilt toward insanity. Moreau thinks only of his long-term goal—beasts made men—and is indifferent to the pain and degradation that surround him in his failed experiments; Prendick can't plan at all, and can't process or understand what is happening to him from moment to moment. What it is to be a Subject, how you live in time and perceive your surroundings, is broken open in this novel. From now on, castaway fictions will return repeatedly to this instability, oscillating between alienated abstraction and savage violence.

Prendick at times shares the beasts' irrationality, or, more precisely, their flawed and fumbling mixture of rationality and irrationality. Moreau has exiled himself from the wider human community, and sees himself as utterly separate from the beasts, and as a kind of god, but his work assumes that there is no clear dividing line between beasts and humans, so that beasts can be made human: the result is to throw the qualities of animals, humans, and God into a toxic and unstable mix.[5] The instability of relation between human and animal is very much a concern of the immediate imitations of *The Island of Dr. Moreau*, as will be seen in the discussion that follows. Later castaway fictions that take up the concern with degeneration and violence that is so strong in *The Island of Dr. Moreau* concentrate on humans.

The Island of Dr. Moreau is a "deliberately ugly book."[6] The implications of this quality for the plain style and practical orientation that Defoe establishes for the castaway narrative will be discussed later, but here we can comment on the possible relation of this deliberate ugliness to the strains and shifts of late nineteenth-century culture. The theory of evolution threatened, if not altogether destroyed, the faith in nature as harmonious and purposeful, which had sustained much of the science as well as the art of the romantic period. Kurt Bayertz summarizes one consequence: "Only an aesthetic of horror seemed possible in Darwin's day" (1990, 281). So follows, arguably, the rejection of beauty, the jagged, queasy quality of *The Island of Dr. Moreau*; and also the wastefulness of Moreau's work, insofar as Moreau is setting himself in the place of nature, which now has to be seen as hugely wasteful. He has populated his island with the beasts, or half-beasts, discarded after his operations on them. As for the bloody hands of the vivisectionist, it was Nietzsche who saw Darwinism as "a philosophy for butchers' apprentices" (qtd. in Bayertz 1990, 282). Bayertz discusses various contemporary attempts to restore beauty and spirit to nature (Ernst Haeckel, Wilhelm Bolsche—and the late writings of Alfred Russel Wallace can also be mentioned), and ends by remarking on how this enterprise was undergoing a revival at the end of the twentieth century. In Chapters 6 and 7, we will examine some recent texts that involve reconciliation with nature, part of the broad stream of ecological thinking in our own day.

In *The Island of Dr. Moreau*, the one who works on and dominates the island —or rather, the animals he has imported for his experiments, for significantly he has no real contact with the island itself—is set at a textual distance. The powerful and enigmatic Moreau is seen through the needs and errors of another white man who is not coping with island life, and who is losing his status as superior and rational. This is the castaway Prendick, author of the account we read.

Prendick is pitched out of civilization on the first page of the novel, never to return to it except as a shattered self-exile. He experiences violent deaths, near-cannibalism,[7] and near-starvation in the first couple of pages, and this is some time before he even reaches Moreau's island. His experience will shift from the "horrible" (a word frequently used in the first chapters) merely as far as "terror" (the state he remains in after escaping from the island at the end of the novel). It's not merely that he is largely passive, and usually mistaken in his inferences. It's that he is plunged from the beginning into a world of extreme sensations and overwhelming reactions and conclusions, and scarcely escapes from them or experiences relief from this state for the rest of the novel.

Here, for instance, Prendick is a drifting castaway after the shipwreck of the *Lady Vain*, about to be rescued:

> It never entered my head to attempt to attract attention, and I do not remember anything distinctly after the sight of her side, until I found myself in a little cabin aft. There is a dim half memory of being lifted up to the gangway and of a big round countenance, covered with freckles and surrounded with red hair, staring at me over the bulwarks. I also had a disconnected impression of a dark face with extraordinary eyes close to mine, but that I thought was a nightmare until I met it again. I fancy I recollect some stuff being poured in between my teeth. And that is all. (Wells 1982, 1: 82)

Prendick's experience is usually described as surreal or nightmarish, and so it is, but it also suggests what life might be like for an animal, or rather for a mixed creature in which the human and the animal each interfere with the other, which is what Moreau is making in his work on the island. Prendick's sensations come too fast for him to process, or come in too disjunct a form, unrelated, cognitively dissonant, too close to him: a glare of eyes within inches of his face; mutterings and bumpings overhead on the rescue ship; a shuffling in the dark bushes that dies away when he stops to concentrate on it; a series of screams, questions unanswered, sentences broken off (Chap. 8–10).

Prendick is again put into an open boat, after his rescue, and eventually brought to Moreau's island. He takes in the general shape of Moreau's base and fortress, of course, but without understanding its function or being allowed to penetrate the inner rooms that hold its secrets. By the time he can do so, after Moreau's death, he is to be found knocking over his lamp during a nocturnal emergency and burning down the lot, except what Moreau's former assistant Montgomery is drunkenly incinerating on the beach at the same time. Before this he finds himself in the village of the discarded beast people, narrow and close and smelly like a nineteenth-century slum, or like the standard way such "dens" were described at the time by journalists and novelists venturing into them. Then he is shut in a dark hovel within this place, taking part in a ceremony presided over by a grey-haired creature whose features he can't make out. "The voice in the dark began intoning a mad litany, line by line, and I and the rest to repeat it. As they did so, they swayed from side to side, and beat their hands upon their knees, and I followed their example. I could have imagined I was already dead and in another world" (12: 113). Then, when he flees—both from Moreau and Montgomery and from the beast people—he undergoes a kind of tour of the island in quick unconnected glimpses—thorny thickets, marshes, yellow-coated soil, boiling streams (Chap. 12). It's like a parody of the sober and purposeful survey or exploration of the island that we expect in island stories, undertaken to investigate its resources and detect possible sources of danger.[8]

The narrative is punctuated by episodes in which Prendick is running, either from a hidden but dimly perceived pursuer (or is it a companion?), or in a pursuing crowd. "The air behind me and above me was soon full of threatening cries. I heard the tumult of my pursuers in the gap up the slope, then the crashing of the reeds, and every now and then the crackling of a branch. Some of the creatures roared like excited beasts of prey. The staghound yelped to the left. I heard Moreau and Montgomery shouting in the same direction" (12: 116). These episodes all have a similar quality; once you start running and build up pace, you tend to forget whether you are pursuer or pursued—the same excitement is mixed with the same panic in either case—and the landscape, which you scarcely have time to sense as you run, becomes itself a combination of adversary and obstacle course.

Wells is ruthlessly removing any possibility of the novel settling into the practical reasoning and physical work that is a satisfying part of *Robinson Crusoe* and many of its successors. Quite late in the story, there is what amounts to a contemptuous parody of a couple of episodes from the earlier novel. This comes after Prendick has finally understood what Moreau's project is, and it has then collapsed, Moreau and Montgomery have died, and Prendick is briefly recounting for us the period of lonely sojourn that is at the heart of a novel like *Robinson Crusoe*. It is more like an aftermath in this story. Prendick makes a raft and, just like Crusoe with the piragua over which he labors for months, he can't get it to the water; but it was a wretched object anyway. He vaguely thinks of making a pot (one of Crusoe's achievements, repeated on a grander scale in *The Mysterious Island*), but there is not even any clay on the island, so he could not set to sea even if he made a raft, because he has no means of taking water with him. Moreau had developed the island before Prendick arrived, in the limited sense that he established his research station cum prison cum torture house. This was then destroyed as his power broke down, but there is no chance of Prendick doing anything similar.

Wells's registration of Prendick's subjectivity is the formal innovation of this novel in the tradition under discussion. It is not really imitated in later narratives, although we have unreliable and even pathological point-of-view characters: they all record their experiences with a degree of clarity that Wells denies Prendick. This is even the case with Golding's *Pincher Martin*, though in the end it is revealed that almost all Pincher's experiences have been delusory. The text is plunging Prendick into the condition into which Moreau has put the beast people, though without the torture and the instilled fear of pain. The central irony of the novel is this sense that no matter how often Prendick recoils from the beast people, is disgusted, horrified, scared, hostile, and so on, he is at the same time feeling roughly as they must be feeling. *Robinson Crusoe* can assume that there is a fundamental gulf between Robinson and Xury and between Robinson and Friday. By *Moreau*, this is emphatically no longer the case. In *Heart of Darkness*, Marlow worries about becoming a savage, or at least he philosophizes about how savagery calls to all of us; Prendick pretty well becomes one of the beast people, who are, however, the creations of civilization in the form of Moreau. They are not "natives." Prendick's own experience ironically contrasts with the novel's horror at the beast-men, which is being expressed through the narrator, Prendick himself. There is a resemblance to Gulliver's defensive horror at the Yahoos in Book IV of *Gulliver's Travels*. The Yahoos, if they are not human, are beast-humans. (It is perhaps because we see how Gulliver is denying this resemblance that we find his use of Yahoo skins for the sail of the boat in which he will leave the land of the Houyhnhnms and Yahoos to be atrocious.)[9] This central irony is a sign of how far the novel takes the possibilities of ironic inversion and reduction to extremity: parody.[10]

Prendick's experience of the terrors of uncontrol and immersion is arguably what causes him to submit to Moreau's account of what Moreau is really doing. He is in a condition where he will notice Moreau's detachment and persistence, because it is in such contrast to his own condition. So he will overlook Moreau's casuistry and egoism—and the degree to which the island is littered with his failures, which he terrorizes with a certain indifference. Moreau's insistence both on his orthodoxy as a scientist and on his passion as an artist, in Chapter 14, is impressive, though also a sign of his megalomania; yet there is a kind of absurdity about what he is doing. The strangely distorted and muffled creatures that Prendick notices moving the heavy loads on his arrival on the island have been made out of bulls, and this is Moreau's work, but actual bulls (oxen, say) would be better at pulling a wagon than these are (Chap. 6).

The force of the novel as deconstruction of fundamental categories is clear enough: If Moreau is God,[11] then God is not morally superior to humans or animals, and if Moreau's work is civilizing, then civilization is barbaric. If the beasts who are Moreau's victims are humanized, then humanness for them is greater capacity for suffering and fear, and lesser fitness for their environment. If Prendick is a better human being than Moreau, then he is also in the miserable subjective condition of the beast people, and Moreau's cold linear objectivity has produced the wildly unstable subjectivity of the beast people and Prendick.

Moreau's refusal of beauty and of plainness puts it in an interesting relation to the tradition of castaway tales. *Moreau* is very influential and frequently imitated, as will be seen. Defoe's founding achievement was to set self and world, subject and object, in a dynamic equilibrium. Wells wrenches them apart. No one can really put them back together again, unless it be Coetzee, with his subtle sense of how humans are isolated yet interdependent, or perhaps Egan, the first in this tradition to imagine capacity for change, and indeed a mind-like ability to plan, in nature itself: nature is emphatically no longer passive material to be worked on in *Teranesia*. Even Giraudoux's Suzanne, though she does no work and exists in harmony with her surroundings, acculturates her island, turning it into "un parc, un salon" (Giraudoux 1961,10: 201).

A key aspect of the bleak view of violence and egotism that we often meet in later versions of *Moreau* is the notion, more or less explicit, that degenerating to bestiality and violence reveals what humans are "really" like or allows the release of impulses compared to which civilized reason and restraint is a mere veneer. The more a text embraces this view, the closer it is to concluding that the problem is with nature (human nature as an aspect of animal nature) rather than civilization.[12] The distinctions are hard to draw; the very posing of something like an either/or (either nature or civilization is the source of violence) is setting our thinking on the wrong path and forcing a commitment of the kind that fiction is well equipped to avoid, but, nonetheless, the issue needs to be raised. The most interesting revisionary texts are often ones that are most skeptical of the notion that degeneration to violence reveals underlying human animality. As Genly Ai comments in *The Left Hand of Darkness*, "It is a durable, ubiquitous, specious metaphor, that one about veneer (or paint, or plioform, or whatever) hiding the nobler reality beneath. It can conceal a dozen fallacies at once. [. . .] Of course there is no veneer, the process is one of growth, and primitiveness and civilization are degrees of the same thing."[13]

The Island of Dr. Moreau can be seen, then, as a brutal intervention into the sometimes placid dialogue with Defoe that had constituted the tradition of the castaway tale. By telling the story through the point of view of the bewildered Prendick, Wells erases the distinction between subject and object, material circumstances and the activity of improvising with them or mastering them. This distinction had underpinned the plain, direct, carefully measuring style and the depiction of work, survival, and settlement in *Robinson Crusoe*. Meanwhile it is precisely the chill distance between Moreau and his objects that raises far-reaching questions about power and knowledge, science and religion. Moreau separates himself from the objects of his study: he performs the classic scientific reduction on them even though they are literally creatures of flesh and blood; but what his work underlines and Prendick's experience suggests is that the boundary between humans and animals is permeable.

Moreau prompts a raft of imitations and successors. The self-conscious intertextuality of sf, for instance the practice of "response" stories as Gary Wolfe calls them (1989, 380–87), is no doubt relevant to this, though many even of the stories that directly refer to *Moreau* are not by authors who considered themselves sf writers. Probably more important is the fact that *Moreau* taps into a series of powerful issues and anxieties, and, moreover, does this in a fashion that is challenging and brutal in formal terms because of its focus on Prendick's experience. To put the matter very roughly, it's as if one can respond to Wells's novel by embracing the darkness and insanity, even the cannibalism and bestiality, as argument about human nature, or by trying to attain intellectual distance and concentrating on the implications of *Moreau* for the sometimes dangerous way science works by abstraction from its objects.

Two early responses to *The Island of Dr. Moreau* are Edgar Rice Burroughs's *The Monster Men* and S. Fowler Wright's *The Island of Captain Sparrow*. It is interesting that they both introduce important female characters into a type of story that had been largely masculine since Defoe. Neither *The Monster Men* nor *The Island of Captain Sparrow* is successful in its handling of gender, however, or coherent in its use of *Moreau*, for all the genuine interestingness of Wright's novel. *The Monster Men* seizes on Wells's anxiety about bestiality and cannibalism, and rides it as far as it can go. *The Island of Captain Sparrow* more deliberately departs from some of Wells's emphases. In *The Monster Men*, certain elements of *Moreau*, and also of *Frankenstein*, are churned opportunistically through a pulp interest in action, fights, near-rape, and race. Professor Maxon is the Moreau/Frankenstein figure, but after some early scenes he fades from the story. His daughter, Virginia, is very important to the hectic plot, but she figures as a damsel in distress, threatened by every male on or entering the scene (an island off the coast of Borneo), from the professor's sinister white assistant through various Malays and Dyaks to a trio of orangutans.[14] As a modification of the masculinity of very many castaway narratives since *Robinson Crusoe*, this does not get us very far.

More relevant is the figure of Marcelle in Wright's *The Island of Captain Sparrow*—Ariel reintroduced in response to the way Moreau's island was given over to Calibans, as Nicolas Ruddick says (1993, 72–73). There is a beautiful and beguiling early passage in which Marcelle discloses to her future lover, who is the latest of a succession of castaways to have ended up on the island, how she has lived alone in the trees with only monkeys as companions, a solitary castaway hidden from the other castaways, living in nature. After this, however, Marcelle too is embroiled in a damsel-in-distress plot. Wright makes some ironic remarks about the conventions of this kind of plot (120), but he indulges in it just the same.

Further, while the preoccupation with degeneration was given focus in *Moreau* by Wells's sense of what was ideologically explosive in the theory of evolution, in both Burroughs and Wright this preoccupation just makes for a general racialized psychology. Characters are characterized on racial or ethnic lines—Marcelle, for instance, as a Frenchwoman ("She looked at Charlton with uncompromising Latin eyes" [241]). The notion of degeneration is used to classify the "subhuman" (199) bad guys, which is not the effect of the trope on the depiction of Prendick in *Moreau*. In addition, Wright is gripped by a kind of will to cannibalism, which issues eventually in the scene in which the rukas, hitherto depicted as wise and enigmatic birds engaged in useful horticulture, are converted in an instant to an appetite for live human flesh.[15] The novel is schematized into a contrast between Marcelle, willful, French, natural and passionate, and the degenerate castaway descendants of Captain Sparrow, so debased that they even corrupt the hitherto wise and impartial rukas, and deserve the deaths meted out to them in the denouement.

The later successors to *Moreau* may be characterized in two broad groups. The first consists of texts that make an intellectual game of *Moreau*: *The Invention of Morel*, *The Island of Doctor Death and Other Stories and Other Stories*, and also Aldiss's *Moreau's Other Island* in that it moderates as well as updates the savagery of Wells's novel. These texts also pursue the way in which the island in *Moreau* is abstracted or removed from nature. The second group of texts, to be discussed in Chapter 4, revisits the narrative of the solitary castaway making do, but develops Wells's insight that there can be depths of irrationality and even insanity in the subject who finds himself distant from civilization. The island is increasingly subjectified; to dominate one's island in Ballard's *Concrete Island* or Banks's *The Wasp Factory* is to imagine it into existence *as* island (secluded place in which actions and desires have new scope) and even as embodiment of one's own, now expanded, psyche.

The Invention of Morel: Abstraction of the Subject

An island, mapped and delimited but also porous, because large parts are invaded by the tide, and mysterious, because it is furnished with a series of deserted buildings, one of which contains a locked chamber; a magus, whose name alludes to that of Moreau; a narrator, like Prendick in being nervous and easily distracted; a quality of abstraction in that the mystery the narrator experiences is attached to a party of spectral visitors with whom he finds himself in strange disembodied contact, and whom he eventually joins: in all this Adolfo Bioy Casares's *The Invention of Morel* (1940) is comparable to *The Island of Dr. Moreau*.[16] It is very different in style, however, even given the resemblances of its panicky, moody narrator to Prendick: romantic with an ironic twist. There is no savagery, no violence; the elements are subtilized. *The Invention of Morel* is a story about virtuality. Bioy Casares was a friend and colleague of Jorge Luis Borges, and *Morel*, like Borges's stories, is a work of lucid fantasy that sets out the elements of a teasing conundrum.

Our narrator has made his way to the island because he is a fugitive, accused of some unknown and never detailed crime back in Caracas, looking for utter solitude, willing to risk the mysterious disease rumored to haunt the island. This disease attacks the senses, feeling first, and ultimately sight; it is a figure for the disembodiment that haunts the story. Being a fugitive, the narrator is nervous to the point of paranoia, and in this state, when the mystery becomes evident, he produces lots of usefully distracting theories about what is going on.

In the first phase of the story, he explores the deserted constructions that seem to furnish the island as a place for wealthy tourists. Then there appear mysterious visitors: a holiday party, carefree, dressed in the style of twenty years earlier. At first he hides from them, and then he is drawn out and tries to make contact, enticed by the beautiful Faustine, who comes each day to sit and look at the sea.

The narrator tries to approach Faustine, is totally ignored, invents elaborate ways of appealing to her (for instance, a little garden at the spot where she sits, depicting the two of them in flowers), and is still ignored. Moreover, as his behavior becomes wilder, alternating between showing himself and hiding, others among the visitors have the chance to see him but they too look right through him. Thus the mystery. Is he delirious—he was in a bad way when he arrived on the island and now lives most of the time in the swamps, not so much woken each morning as almost drowned by the incoming tide. Is he a ghost? Are they ghosts?

Finally he overhears a lecture by Morel, who explains that he has invented receiving and recording devices that can take in all of a person's life—not just sight and sound as in current (1940) devices, but all of the person's life, including consciousness. The mysterious visitors will thus find a kind of immortality, living fully, but repeatedly, but only in their lives recorded during their sojourn on the island. Beside this techno-virtuality, the narrator's romantic flower garden for Faustine looks feeble. The other visitors are understandably offended that Morel has not previously told them what he was doing with their lives, but his machines have worked, and the narrator has been experiencing the results, like one who mingles with the images in a movie but is unable to communicate with those apparently living beings—and, in this case, is driven to a kind of frenzy by their indifference, especially that of Faustine.

The narrator is trapped between the present and the eternally repeated past. His problem is that he can't be alienated enough, can be neither the operator of technology nor a figment of technology. Meanwhile he is in love with Faustine. As for Morel, the mad or at least self-willed scientist, he too was in love with Faustine and wanted this eternity with her. The narrator follows suit. He manipulates the machines and records himself into immortality with Faustine and the others, after he notes the first symptoms of the island's disease on him.

It's an island story in which the Western visitors have no contact with any indigenes—indeed, the narrator seems to be the only one who has any real experience of the life of the island, and that is an uncomfortable one. He is repeatedly almost drowned by the tides, whose function in Morel's takeover of the island is to power not only the electricity but also the recording machines that bestow immortality. The narrator reasons in a skittery, nervy fashion, and spends his ingenuity trying to communicate his love to Faustine or spying on the visitors. Science, in the form of Morel's invention, makes a substitute reality, a mediated life. If work is a matter of operating on nature, then science has become the most significant form of work, because it's the kind of work that has most transformative power. Yet Morel does not work on the material reality of the island as most castaways do; he superimposes his imagination, realized by his machines, on the island as if it were a blank space. The narrator, unhappy on the real island, unable to communicate with, or even be seen by, his beloved in Morel's superimposed world, is the victim.

And the narrator does not rebel, or try to leave the island and find the real Faustine, or sabotage the recording machines, but enters the illusion/virtuality himself. It's the development to an extreme of a tendency that is always present in island stories: the tendency to use the place as a mere stage for the working out of one's own desires. It's an allegory of an aspect of colonialism, by means of a science fictional device that also images the extremes of abstraction: the recreation of "home," the making of a Western enclave, the indifference to the life of the place itself. Yet *The Invention of Morel* is also a story about degeneration, though degeneration of a peculiarly civilized kind, in that it is about preferring a restricted and repetitive immortality as a *copy* (to use a contemporary sf term) to what life in the rest of the material world might offer. "Dear-Self" is sealed off from the world. The "actual" self of the narrator is left behind, to fade into insentience as the disease takes hold.

Gene Wolfe: Deconstruction of the Microcosm

The Island of Doctor Death and Other Stories and Other Stories is a very clever title, certainly. It advertises that the book as a whole is about stories, and gives the title of the first story, which has "and other stories" in its title. The collection shows off Wolfe's expertise with all sorts of sf subgenres (the first contact story, and so on). Included are three stories that play with *The Island of Dr. Moreau*, and here the first two are discussed, as the third is set in a prison, not on an island, and has a more indirect relation to *Moreau*. These two stories deconstruct the remoteness of the island setting and the separation from everyday society such remoteness brings about, which is traditional in the genre, though constantly undermined in recent narratives.

The first story, "The Island of Doctor Death and Other Stories," begins by commenting on the relations of real life and fiction by setting up a contrast between Settlers Island, home of the main character, the teenager Tackman Babcock, and the island of Dr. Death, location of a melodramatic story Tackie is reading, which is loosely based on *Moreau*. Settlers Island, just off the coast, is hardly an island at all, whereas the island of Dr. Death is where a series of exciting pop legends are piled on top of each other. Important members of the Settlers Island household are Tackie's needy mother, his mother's lover Jason, and his mother's fiancé Dr. Black. Jason (who drives a Jaguar, which may be a passing joke about the puma that is important in *Moreau*) buys Tackie a book, which introduces the other, fictional island and its characters. Tackie reads avidly, to escape his unhappy domestic life. Ransom, a castaway, roughly like Prendick but more of an adventurer, comes ashore on the island of Dr. Death as in *Moreau*. Ransom is threatened by Dr. Death, who is about to operate on the beautiful Talar of the Long Eyes. She escapes and takes Ransom to her secret kingdom of Lemuria; from there, he leads the Lemurians to destroy Dr. Death, in rough equivalence of the killing of Moreau. Then the contrast is erased: characters from the story turn up in Tackie's house, where a fancy dress party is in progress, so they blend in. Ransom staggers ashore from his raft onto Settlers Island, and Dr. Death simply emerges from the pages of the book that Tackie has been reading. We realize that Ransom, Dr. Death, and Talar have equivalents in Jason, Dr. Black, and Tackie's mother.

The story suggests that we read books into our lives and lives into our books. The fit is only approximate, but life is more interesting and may be somewhat more coherent when some personages intrude into it from a book, because people in books have a clearer sense of their roles, and a different being (Dr. Death in effect tells Tackie that he is immortal). But life is not much more coherent, and anyway, the characters from the story were in a sense there already on Settlers Island. It's another superimposition. The genre is feeding on its own textuality, but urbanely in this case.

"The Death of Dr. Island," Wolfe's second *Moreau* variation (first published in 1973), is more painstaking in its deconstruction of the island in question, and more radical in its implications. This time we seem to be on an island of the classical tropical kind—palm trees, beaches, monkeys; big enough to explore, yet one can probably walk around it. But the sea is fresh, not salt, and there are many other differences from a desert island. We discover them one by one as we watch the three inhabitants, marooned or imprisoned there, interact with each other and with the omnipresent Dr. Island, who is a kind of AI entity programmed as a psychiatrist. As we discover these differences, the island deconstructs: a series of expectations that seem either plausible given what we are learning, or plausible for an island story, is dismantled.

This place is not an island, though it is a body of sand and earth and vegetation surrounded by water. It is enclosed in an orb; it is a satellite hanging in space, its "sea" curving up above the land, though there is no up or down. It is a kind of prison—always a potential aspect of the island in a castaway story, as both *Robinson Crusoe* and *The Mysterious Island* acknowledge.[17] The three people marooned there, Ignacio, Diane, and Nicholas, the boy who is the point-of-view character, are mental patients. Though they are young (only Ignacio is an adult), they seem to be veterans of mental institutions of one kind or another in this story's future, and have proved stubborn, violent, and troublesome, in their own ways. Varieties of autism, solipsism, catatonia—inability to trust others or acknowledge their existence; inability to see them as persons—these are what they seem to have in common. Ironic, in the context of the tradition, that those in whom misanthropy is already extreme are marooned in something like isolation and then required to get along with each other. It does, however, appear that they are learning to do this; but then things seem to go badly wrong, only for Dr. Island to reveal that what has happened is exactly according to plan. And this revelation underlines other ways in which the island lacks the autonomy that remoteness confers on most desert islands.

At first the narrative follows Nicholas and Diane, interacting and learning about the island, coached by Dr. Island. We expect that some sort of relationship will unfold, as Nicholas seems tougher than Diane but on the other hand she is teaching him; but not so. The crucial figure in the view of Dr. Island and those who have programmed it turns out to be the third of those marooned, Ignacio, the oldest, the one who has been there longest, and the most dangerous. Ignacio is in fact murderous; reared without human contact, he cannot cope even with the direct look of another. Once Nicolas learns a little of this, however, he copes, gets Ignacio to teach him how to fish, gets Diane to share in the fish. Evidently Diane gives herself to Ignacio for the night. So it seems that the three of them are developing a sort of *modus vivendi*.

It is not so, or not as the reader might well have begun to expect. Ignacio kills Diane during the night, and then he is allowed to leave. According to Dr. Island, he is cured, the killing of Diane having been cathartic. The whole plan was to bring about the curing of Ignacio, because he is tough enough to survive in the outside world, once cured. Dr. Island has told us that in this world of the future, with its space colonies, the incidence of psychosis and collapse is much higher, so people like Ignacio can be valuable. As for Diane, she was incurable, suicidal in her hugging of her illness to herself: "Her prognosis was bad; she really wanted only death, and this was the death I chose for her," says Dr. Island (Wolfe 1980, 130). The title of the story probably refers more to the death that Dr. Island allots to Diane than to the death it suffers when Nicholas smashes it in frustration. The doctor's is a style of reasoning that either has been produced by the extreme conditions that prevail in the world of the story, which necessitate extreme calculations, or has helped to produce those conditions and, now, helps to make them worse. In either case, we have a kind of degeneration that is due to "civilization" rather than to the beast in humans.

"The Death of Dr. Island" lays bare the fact that island stories are thought experiments that use the island as microcosm to examine the status of the social, the relations of social and natural. It is set on an artificial island, planned as a controlled test of the three deliberately cast-away subjects, but one that is from our point of view ungrounded, because the world off the island does not provide anything that can we can trust as a norm by which to measure events on the island. The effect is to deconstruct the differences between the social and the natural, and abolish any third term, any theology. Prospero and Dr. Moreau, for better or worse, set themselves to improve on their societies while educating or creating social beings. Dr. Island is no Prospero, not even a Dr. Moreau, but merely the mouthpiece of Society, and a Society that doesn't really lay claim to higher purposes, either ethical or scientific.

Moreau's Other Island: The Natural Reassessed, or, "These days, you would be state-funded"

In *Moreau's Other Island* (1980),[18] Brain Aldiss updates Wells's novel and politicizes it, linking the setup on the island more directly to the rest of the world, in particular, the Cold War.[19] The result, however, is to take a great deal of the heat out of the story. It's hard to imagine that many readers would be seriously affronted or disturbed by the revision, given that its critique of US imperialism is not very surprising, though they might be piqued by the astuteness of some of the changes Aldiss has made. Mortimer Dart, the successor to Moreau, is an embittered thalidomide victim who is using genetic engineering rather than surgery, though he is almost as much a sadist as was Wells's Moreau. He has a drunken companion (Hans Maastricht) as in Wells (Montgomery), but also a sexy female assistant (Heather, who turns out to be a CIA agent). The naïve, priggish visitor who is the narrator is not an Englishman but an American, an under secretary of state named Calvert Roberts. Roberts is pompous and clumsy.

Roberts discovers that Dart is not an embittered outcast at all, but is sponsored by the US government, indeed by Roberts's own department. This sets up the revelation that Dart has developed a new race, impersonal gnomelike reptile-skinned SRSRs ("Stand-By Replacement Sub-Race"). The SRSRs are distinct from the beast-men, who are descendants of Moreau's creations, Moreau being deemed part of history in *Moreau's Other Island*. They are designed as a replacement labor force in the aftermath of nuclear massacre. The making of artificial humans has no longer a taint of blasphemy or darkness; the remote island is now little more than an efficient place to put a secret base. The rest of the world cannot be kept at a distance while a microcosm is laboriously constructed on an island; the rest of the world is already present. In a sense the island is already repatriated in *Moreau's Other Island*, before this happens literally in *Concrete Island* and *The Wasp Factory*. Eventually the beast-men are killed off, and Dart's facility is eliminated by US submariners, completing the work commenced by a rebellion of the beast-men, led by the clever Foxy, and advised in the crucial matter of burning down Dart's complex by Roberts himself.

Wells's savage attack on religion is muted in *Moreau's Other Island*. There is no equivalent to Prendick's sojourn with the beast people, his learning of their primitive theology, the roots of their own religion adapted from Moreau's. Even the attempt to give Roberts a distinctly American religious faith is low-key. Though Aldiss does effective reversions to savagery (notably, the scene on the bare top of the island in which the reclusive Warren is torn to pieces and

Roberts nearly suffers the same fate [Chap. 9]), and creates an effective faithful dog-man in Bernie, he doesn't seem interested in this side of his target text. Behind Wells's novel are ideas that no longer have force, regarding the primitiveness of non-Western people and of animals such as apes. The SRSRs in Aldiss's version are not primitive; they are civilized in a hollow way. And they are not autonomous, even in the way that Moreau's creations were, nor are they created to serve and worship their maker. No doubt the rather flat effect of the novel makes its own point, that a separate and alternative world on an island, whether a dark, savage one or an idyllic one, is becoming harder to imagine because there are no longer separate places. The narrative continually points us away from the island, to the people who have sponsored Dart but eliminate his laboratory when things get out of hand, and to the typical mediocrity of Roberts's attitudes, though it cleverly does this last by revising many aspects of Wells's Prendick.

Aldiss frames the narrative, however, with two passages about the sea that suggest a mysterious kind of unconscious that is very different from the savage or hysterical incoherence into which Prendick and the beast people are plunged in *Moreau*. In *Moreau* the sea is merely a medium on which people are cast adrift, to experience death or cannibalism; in *Moreau's Other Island* the sea is more autonomous and mysterious:

> *Another range of sounds also persisted. It issued from another order of existence entirely: from the inorganic, from the mantle of water which moved ceaselessly over the drowned landscapes of its domain. These throatless cadences had been audible almost since the beginning of time, certainly long before any stirrings of life.* (Aldiss 1982, 7; italics original)

The result in *Moreau's Other Island* is something of a split. The story retains some of Wells's sense of debased savagery, but in moderated form, with an attempt to emphasize the violence of impersonal institutions rather than that of the debased product of science or of the scientist himself; meanwhile it adds intimations of a more positive kind of unconscious. And Aldiss's other addition to Wells is also associated with the sea and placed a little away from Moreau's island. There are sensuous seal-humans living on a nearby islet. They rescue Roberts when he has to dive, from the very height to the depths, to escape the other beast people. They entertain him for a couple of days in sexual play. Unfortunately this does nothing to change his basic attitudes. In fact, he introduces the seal people to fire (bad move—the vegetation on their islet burns down) and plans to take them back to the United States with him when he is rescued by a helicopter at the end of the novel, which will also be a bad move, especially as their sexuality has involved a child, human in shape, and this is unlikely to go down well with the authorities.

Here, with the framing imagery of the sea, and the episode of the seal people, slightly to one side of the politicized revision of *Moreau* in the main part of *Moreau's Other Island*, Aldiss sets going some reverberations that do not altogether die away even in such grim revisions of the island narrative as *Concrete Island* and *The Wasp Factory*. The successors to *Moreau* discussed earlier have no sense of the unconscious or nonrational as a source of rich possibility; if you go down into the irrational, sensate depths in Wells or Wolfe, you mainly find savagery. On the other hand, whenever we have a magus figure in an island narrative, or simply one who tries to educate others as Prospero did Miranda and Caliban, then *The Tempest* becomes a point of reference. Under the sea, life seems elusive (Aldiss's "throatless cadences") and death less final (Ferdinand's transformed, supposedly drowned father in *The Tempest* will become the endlessly singing corpses in the sunken slave ship in Coetzee's *Foe*). Contemporary writers can echo *The Tempest*'s sense of marine mystery and depth and more generally of the richness of nature so as to express a changed sense of the unconscious, of nature, and of the primitive. Yet this complex of revisions of fundamental concepts is in active conflict with an intensified sense of violence and egotism, indeed, monomania: something that contemporary writers take from *Moreau* and push to extremity.

Lord of the Flies: Abstraction, Signification, Violence

Lord of the Flies has an ambiguous relation to the registration of material circumstances and difficulties that is important in the Crusoe tradition, and an ambiguous relation also to the adventure story. The novel resonates with the Veneer Theory of human nature, in which violence and cruelty is seen as waiting just beneath a veneer of civilized behavior that is easily stripped away, and this rendition compels attention by the sensational way the story fuses a reaction to Auschwitz and a reaction to Golding's experience in a boarding school for boys.

As Richard Overy shows, this view of modern life as resting on a thin crust over depths of the primitive was particularly pervasive in Britain between the wars. We can find the metaphor from Conrad to James Baldwin ("how thin is the crust of civilisation on which this generation is walking"). For understandable reasons, the attitude here summed up as Veneer Theory gained new strength in the aftermath of World War II. Edward Bond referred to "the new doctrine of natural aggression."[20]

Lord of the Flies begins when various parties of boys who have survived an air crash meet up on the beach of a desert island. They are English schoolboys; some are choirboys, and they range from little children to adolescents. They negotiate together. Two of them, Ralph and Jack, emerge as the natural leaders and then as rivals, with their allies, Piggy and Simon, and Roger, respectively. Ralph wants order maintained and rules agreed to and obeyed; he wants a fire that can serve as signal to be kept alight. He doesn't really want to enter into the life of the island, but to retain a version of the order the boys have known, and to be prepared for rescue. It is Jack who wants to enter into the life of the island, and who defines what that is to be—hunting pigs, forming a tribe. Over all this broods the idol-like pig's head on a stake (the Lord of the Flies), and also the fearful presence that is the corpse of a downed pilot ("the Beast," to the boys). Jack wins; he is joined by all except the gentle, uncannily perceptive Simon and the bumbling, intelligent Piggy. Violence follows, and by the time the Royal Navy turns up, Simon and Piggy have been murdered by Jack's tribe, Ralph is being hunted down, and the island is aflame.

We can see *Lord of the Flies* as a contribution to this debate over violence, civilization, and the primitive that had gathered intensity in the face of history and of biological theories and speculations since the 1890s. It is not, however, simply an expression of Veneer Theory, because it is also an exploration of the violence that inheres in abstraction, of the dangers of turning aside from material things and needs to the making of symbols and rituals, moving from hunting a pig to hunting a pig-idea, which could be a boy, Piggy, or Ralph—or Simon, the boy who comes to tell them that there is no beast and is then called the beast and killed. Insofar as this is what Jack does, he (and his tribe) by no means simply express the Veneer Theory of reversion to savagery or emergence of savagery from the depths; indeed, what Jack is doing is what Golding is doing in making his novel, as well as what Ralph and Piggy do also. Jack, who leads his tribe of boys toward savagery, symbolized by his demonization of the pig, and Ralph, who tries to maintain civilized rules, symbolized by keeping the fire going in the hope of signaling for rescue, have this in common. Humans, whether civilized or not, are makers of significations and symbols. Beneath civilization is violence, but violence comes in part from the abstraction and departure from the particular (and personal) that is involved in making symbols; and this is what Golding too is doing. The important distinction, it turns out, is not between civilization and savagery but between more violent or less violent ways of making things or people into symbols.

The complicated doubleness of the signification of, for instance, the fire or Piggy's specs (needed to light fire; sign of Piggy's lack of prowess; sign of his insight), and the knot of ironies around how Simon, the gentlest of the boys, is killed by being misidentified as the beast, expresses this spectrum. Simon sees that "the Beast" is an idea, or an imagination; after the killing of Simon, Jack insists that the beast lives on, because he grasps that the existence of the beast is necessary for his power. In all Golding's novels, material facts and imperatives are given as much and as mesmerizing attention as in Defoe: Barbara Everett writes of "an undiscussable whole world peculiarly substantial in itself, thingy and definite."[21] Yet a deep drive toward sign making, with its concomitant abstraction, overwhelms the often liberating sense, stemming from Defoe, that a material thing is something to be worked on and made to contribute toward survival and thence comfort.

The climactic part of the adventure story in *Lord of the Flies* is when Ralph is hunted by all the others, the Tribe as they are called by this stage, after the killings of Simon and then Piggy. The hunt is detailed in the usual fashion of such episodes—the weather, the feel and smell of the vegetation Ralph plunges through and hides in, his thinking and calculating, the sounds of the hunt that reach him and what they mean. These sounds are a code invented by Jack, whose meanings Ralph in turn decodes. As with the hunting of Prendick in *The Island of Dr. Moreau*, it's like a parody of the steady exploration of the island that we often get in castaway tales, and have indeed encountered earlier in this one. The topography of the island, previously seen as fixed and able to be mapped, is set into shifting motion and subjectified, in that we see it as Ralph's aroused senses deliver it to him (see, for instance, his awakening to the noise of the hunt, 212).

If it were not for the arrival of the British cruiser (almost too pat, too much like the last-gasp rescue of the melodramas and thrilling tales), Ralph would have been caught and killed.[22] The relentless "ululations" he hears are signs of the organized savagery Jack has brought about, and signs of the way all of the boys (except a few stray littl'uns) have become other, in their joining in a group, a mob. They have left behind any shreds of what they once were or thought they were, something underlined by the fact that young Percival Wemyss Madison can't recall his own name when the naval officer asks him.[23] This ululation is also an expression in the text of Golding's relentless plan of degeneration, which he has filled in step by step and is now consummating. Jack is practically never a point-of-view character in the novel: that role is mostly taken by Ralph, sometimes by Piggy or Simon; but Jack is the avatar of this relentlessness.

The episode of the hunt is powerful, then, and the reader has to feel with Ralph, but it is also in a sense empty. All the material details and sensations that are vital for Ralph are also futile. Something like this was always going to happen, and only intervention from outside the world of the island can stop it: which it does, but in stagy fashion. There's a consonance among Golding's plan of degeneration—his thesis, which he is demonstrating with a weight of novelistic authority and anthropological detail—the totalitarian simplicity with which Jack now controls the others, and the emblematic means to this: the masks he and others utilize to be as they now are, the equipment of spears and face-paint and chants and fortress (Castle Rock). This is what makes the novel so tight and unified, this consonance between its own undeviating trajectory and system of allegorical significations and those of Jack, the bad guy whose interiority is largely withheld from us or perhaps no longer exists, but who is a kind of ally of the novel's own formal procedures.[24]

This is a long way from *Robinson Crusoe*'s pleasure in process and improvisation and reinvention of the civilized. The crucial intermediate step is *The Island of Dr. Moreau*, with its bleak treatment of the themes of civilization and savagery. *Lord of the Flies* brings *Moreau* up to date, in the context of Auschwitz rather than Darwinian struggle and degeneration, and it is a group of castaways, children, that become beast people. *Moreau* involves several hunts, with the panic-stricken Prendick as the hunted, but the process of degeneration is less concentrated and single. Moreau is after all himself violent in a "civilized" way; some of the beasts become violent, reverting to nature as the novel's Veneer Theory sees it, but in other ways the violence passes from Moreau, whose violence is purposive, to Prendick, who is the inadvertent, inept cause of violence.

Lord of the Flies critiques *The Coral Island*, as many readers have noted. Ballantyne's novel is drawn on for the names of the main characters and mentioned by the naval officer at the end (Golding 1988, 224). Perhaps the most important feature of *The Coral Island* that Golding borrows unchanged is the fact that the place is idyllic—no need to work for survival, there's plenty of fruit, water, a mild climate. "This is a good island," says Ralph (33), and they know that if it ceases to be a good island, that's because they are spoiling it (53). Ralph fixes on a few material necessities: shelter, probably not strictly needed; a fire to signal for rescue, needed but requiring forethought, and also depending on a desire to be rescued; and also perhaps cleanliness, which he occasionally thinks about but doesn't really work at. These necessities will, however, become reified.

Ralph and Piggy are more practical than Jack and his followers, if the aim is to be rescued and return to civilized life; to be rescued, the castaways need to keep the fire alight and ready to blaze in signal, not rush off enjoying themselves hunting. But civilization is embroiled in war, and the sign of this is the corpse of the downed pilot, enigmatic deity of the island and hint that there may be no civilized life to return to. The rest of the boys are more attracted by the fact that the island frees them for play; play involves ritual, and opens the way for the tribal savagery and hunting and for the power of Jack. Jack is skilled with the noble or decisive gesture that excites or wins people over. He is learning the ways of power as he goes, and this gives him energy. He sees that violence is an effective language. He is discovering the politics of fascism all by himself. The contrast in Peter Brook's film of the novel between Jack, the tallest of the boys anyway, who usually stands, and Ralph, who sits, lost in thought and sometimes doubt, is a telling one and builds on the novel.

Struggle is not a material necessity, because the island is idyllic; struggle is for dominance, and those who give themselves to it do so because they can. The novel suggests that in being idyllic, the island can't be anything more than a scene, a backdrop to contest, for the boys.[25] Descriptions of changes in the weather and of the sea sketch something different, however:

> Somewhere over the darkened curve of the world the sun and moon were pulling; and the film of water on the earth planet was held, bulging slightly on one side while the solid core turned. The great wave of the tide moved further along the island, and the water lifted. Softly, surrounded by a fringe of inquisitive bright creatures, itself a silver shape beneath the steadfast constellations, Simon's dead body moved out towards the open sea. (170; and see 115)

It is the sea that grants Simon this calm burial, as it is imagined to do for Ferdinand's father in *The Tempest*; it is the unburied body of the pilot that broods over the island itself, until it is blown out to sea and simply disappears, as if its malign task has been completed with the murder of Simon as "the Beast." Similarly, it is the sea not the land that affords glimpses of grand ceaseless and ancient movements in *Moreau's Other Island* and *The Wasp Factory*. And it is the impersonal narrator (so far away that he speaks of "the earth planet") that opens this vista to us—no sign that the boys are aware of it. It's the "remoteness" and the "brute obtuseness" of the ocean that Ralph feels (121).

Lord of the Flies does not abandon the adventure story, in which the protagonists' engagement with things and places is dominant—making, improvising, getting from place to place[26]—but it does tend to hollow it out. This is a means to several ends: a contest between Ralph and Jack in which every clash and defeat and victory is a stage in a clear trajectory, and around which others like Piggy and Simon and Roger fall into clear places; and an allegory of civilization and savagery. In this allegory, places and artifacts come to symbolize values even for the antagonists, Jack and Ralph/Piggy, though they first enter the story as things of wonder, or of incoherent fear (when the conch is first blown [13], or the littl'uns and the beast). So it is with the pig's head, which becomes Lord of the Flies, Castle Rock, the place of the fire, the place of Assembly, the shelters, Piggy's spectacles. Only Simon confronts the pig's head, the Lord of the Flies, directly.

The novel shows how practical material things can't help but become, also or by way of substitution, symbols, shibboleths. That's how humans, civilized or savage, make meanings of things, and how they persuade to or enforce social order, which is Ralph's task in the assemblies, and Jack's when he devises rituals and chants. The novel gives us the most powerful rendition of degeneration from civilization to savagery since *The Island of Dr. Moreau*, but it also shows what civilization and savagery have in common. In that sense Jack and his tribe don't leave civilization or end up somewhere outside it. What Ralph is doing with the fire is not so different from what Jack does with the spears and the whole business of hunting. The fire goes beyond the practical and becomes an end in itself. It's as if Golding replicates, in the very process of signification that he relies on to make his story, the history by which signifiers gain a power of their own in culture or politics. Ralph so often repeats that they must keep the fire going if they are to be rescued that it starts to lose meaning even for him. Yet they do need fire; and it's the fire that Jack sets going to smoke out his last opponent, Ralph, that attracts the warship to the island at the end, just as Ralph always said it would. By this point, the uses of fire have got thoroughly disseminated, and it is hard to say whether this signifies a descent into savagery or the arrival of a species of abstraction and nihilism that is most familiar to us from "civilized" warfare—destroying the village in order to save it. Jack steals Piggy's spectacles so as to possess the power to light fire, though according to Ralph, he could have borrowed them; the fire Jack lights to capture Ralph is likely to burn out the whole island, and real premodern humans (those who are usually called "savages" in castaway novels) would practice a more rationally limited form of warfare.[27] Like Wells, Golding simultaneously expresses the idea that humans are savages or animals, violent and irrational at heart, and gives us a critique of civilization. This is done with a twist—it's not just the idea that Ralph and Piggy are weak beside the raw power of violence represented by Jack and his followers, and not just the way in which Jack is a fascist or tyrant (as much as a savage chief) in his resort to violence, his will that violence be the only language permitted, but that Ralph, Piggy, and Jack share a common process of meaning-making. Then again, Simon is different; his confrontation with meaning or his intuition of meaning is more direct, and this is seized on by Brook, who makes us watch each of Simon's interventions between Jack and Ralph or Jack and Piggy.

Lord of the Flies makes us think in terms of the elements of the religious (the Beast, the Lord of the Flies, Simon's visions) in a way that no other castaway tale does. There is a suggestion in Simon's fate as messenger and victim that he is a kind of sacrifice. If so, *Lord of the Flies* touches on the notion of Sacrifice as the truth of social life and renewal that is a preoccupation of one strand of twentieth-century culture. But Simon does not offer himself for sacrifice, as did the maiden in Stravinsky's *Rite of Spring*, the work that introduced the idea to modern culture; the manner of his killing associates sacrifice more with fascism. The effect is ambiguous: Simon was murdered, yet the triangle of Beast, Lord of the Flies, and Simon—the dark side of the island itself—might seem to make this fated.[28]

The novel's aliveness to the way in which things or processes become symbols is not just how the text works, but how the characters come to live and think; and it is not just savage or primitive, a matter of taboos and rituals, but relates to how signs have to be different from things. Further, it is connected to the novel's depiction of schoolboys. These boys already live by rituals, chanting, bullying, and they already expect authority and power: who is to be leader and give the orders, who is to be the one mocked and derided. Piggy, who is the obvious candidate for the role of being mocked and derided, nonetheless has mocked Simon.[29] The violence in *Lord of the Flies* is like the sometimes nasty but not-too-grim behavior of school kids, *and* like the violence of mobs. Boys fighting can't hurt each other too badly, yet boys with spears or heaving a rock or in a mob can kill.[30] Golding underlines the point with the shift from merely throwing stones at Piggy to killing him with a rock.[31] It is Roger who heaves the rock that kills Piggy, and Roger is both a creepy little boy who likes throwing stones and a torturer and executioner, appropriate sidekick to Jack as tyrant. Similarly, the antagonism of Ralph and Jack is for most of the novel that of two big boys—arguing, contesting, fascinated with each other, making up. Some boundary is crossed, and it all becomes radical. Golding doesn't really examine this in Jack, who is scarcely ever a point-of-view character. In Ralph, the antagonism concerns the desperation of his sense of civilization, the necessity of maintaining fire and of rules. Perhaps, in the way that Golding's dualism works, Ralph comes to stand for civilization, being capable of thinking and wavering and resolving, whereas Jack, frustrated from early in the novel, is almost driven to occupy the opposite condition, to become a pure will to violence and power that can know no limits and coolly plan a hunt that, because of the fire, can also destroy the island itself. Certainly, Jack in his way is as English as Ralph is, and the British Empire was made by Jacks as well as Ralphs.

So the antagonists are interdependent, just as Jack's descent into savagery is by no means a movement away from ritual and sign making into some insensate or purely instinctual realm. Neither of them really arrives at any positive attitude to or acceptance of the island, even though it is Jack who doesn't care about keeping the fire going as a rescue beacon, and probably simply wants to stay on the island. Jack does not see that he won't be a boy forever, though the ferocity of his desire to eliminate Ralph, who stands for getting off the island and moving into the future, as well as for the orderly genteel ways of their past, might signify unacknowledged awareness of this.

When the novel is working well, this habit of abstraction—a simplifying but perhaps inevitable abstraction making—is explored by *Lord of the Flies* itself, because it shifts between making abstractions and observing, sometimes sympathetically, sometimes anthropologically, how the characters in the novel find themselves making abstractions. When the novel is not working well, this abstraction becomes a kind of destination that it can march toward single-mindedly as if it explained everything.

This chapter has perhaps given more attention to the impact and shock of *The Island of Dr. Moreau* in its moment and later, than to the impact and shock of *Lord of the Flies* in its moment. But this latter was intense, amounted to a recovery and concentration of the power of *The Island of Dr. Moreau*, and can be seen in the series of castaway fictions that is discussed in the next chapter.

4

Successors of *Moreau*

Madness and Cannibalism

This chapter discusses texts from the later twentieth century that take the castaway narrative into madness and violence that is yet more extreme than was the case with the immediate progeny of *Moreau*: William Golding's *Pincher Martin* (1956); J. G. Ballard's *Concrete Island* (1973) and "The Terminal Beach" (1964); Iain Banks's *The Wasp Factory* (1984); Alex Garland's *The Beach* (1996); and Yann Martel's *Life of Pi* (2001). In being at once extreme and intertextual, these revisions of the castaway tale show the typical signs of belatedness: what had been diffused and perhaps inexplicit is spelled out and crystallized. For instance, the treatment of the castaway's or settler's drive to name his island is explicit in *Pincher Martin*, *Concrete Island*, and *The Wasp Factory*, although the island is now both grimmer and disturbingly subjectivized: a barren harsh rock, hallucinated by the castaway who seems to struggle to make it yield his survival; a patch of urban wasteland hemmed by roaring traffic, which then grows internal dimensions that do not fit its external dimensions; a muddy area off the Scottish coast, close enough to the mainland to be connected by a bridge, the scene of psychopathic play. What is being named is emphatically not tropical or undiscovered. The naming thus takes on a more extreme quality. The namer is unreliable: his history and his grittily material experiences on his rock are a kind of willed illusion in *Pincher Martin*; his behavior is cheerfully murderous in *The Wasp Factory*; drifting toward extinction in "The Terminal Beach"; aimless, feckless, and subject to hallucinations in *The Beach*. Neither the island nor the castaway now has much purchase on the rationally calculable, though the preoccupation not only with naming but with working material things and with calculating and controlling remains. This preoccupation is now stark and willed because stripped of its bases in rationality.

In their extremity these texts recall *The Island of Dr. Moreau*, but only *The Wasp*

Factory alludes to Moreau, the scientist as would-be god. *Robinson Crusoe* reappears as the more important target text. *Pincher Martin* and *The Wasp Factory* are structured from page to page with the same careful recording of the negotiations of subject and material world that predominates in *Robinson Crusoe*, even if this is taken to extremes of self-alienation and insanity, respectively. But each ends with a stunning revelation in the last pages that may well have the effect of inverting all the reader's understanding of what has happened. The two-phase narrative structure that we identified in earlier castaway stories is no longer prominent. *Life of Pi* is similar in this respect: Pi responds to the skepticism of the listeners about the extraordinary story of his time on the drifting lifeboat with a tiger as companion by a defense of the imagination's construction of reality. He proceeds to offer an alternative story, one much grimmer than the story we have just read. Circumstantial material reality is no longer to be relied on. *Robinson Crusoe*'s contract between text and reader, which says that clear description of the surface of things will give us all we need to establish a trustworthy reality, is annulled.

In what follows, these variations are traced in more detail. It is impossible to explain in a formula what it is that impels them, and thereby gives such dark energy to the tradition in its twentieth-century forms. Indeed, the potential of the central tension between realism and fable that we noted as present in *Robinson Crusoe* and pressing in *Lord of the Flies* is demonstrated by the fact that the castaway story can respond to so much: the decline of imperialism, realignments in gender, the Cold War and the Nuclear Age, the putting into question of Western humanism itself. The discussion that follows notes symptoms of these forces without offering a general theory. It is worth recalling, however, that the real history of remote islands in the twentieth century must be affecting the fiction, even as the fiction becomes, in many cases, more explicitly intertextual: prison islands; test site islands; phosphate islands and other islands of extraction;[1] tourist islands; islands whose inhabitants have been immiserated or deported so that the site can become an air base: Robben Island, Eniwetok and Mururoa, Nauru, Hashima, Iwojima, Diego Garcia.[2] Islands are no longer idyllic. The longer the castaway story is pursued, the greater the need to revise or subvert it in changed times. As postimperial becomes postmodern, authors' awareness of fictionality ramifies, taking sometimes dismaying and sometimes exciting forms. We glanced at this with Barth's "Anonymiad" in Chapter 1; examples to be discussed in this chapter are less playful.

Can these revisions usefully be described as parodies? The combination of self-conscious, allusive intertextuality and the impulse to press the possibilities even of so extreme a text as *Moreau* to yet further extremes would suggest so.

The discussion that follows sets out to explore how well the notion of parody serves, by concentrating on what these texts do with certain tropes (for instance, the naming of the island), and certain features of style (for instance, the plain descriptive style and, in tandem with this, the account of the castaway's work and improvisation). Ballard begins *Concrete Island* by reminding us of the sober informative style of the traditional account: "Soon after three o'clock on the afternoon of April 22nd 1973, a 35-year-old architect named Robert Maitland was driving down the high-speed exit lane of the Westway interchange, in central London" (Ballard 1974, 7). This style is set before us only to be replaced by resonances, for instance, "The atlas of wounds into which his body had been transformed went out like a dead sky" (27).

Insofar as these tropes and features of style are put under extreme pressure, then parody is a useful description. It helps to control and focus the larger issues surrounding the depiction of science and reason, and of the subject. But the underlying theme in very many of these texts is how isolation on an island leads the subject through—or past—an engagement with material circumstances and as far as insanity. In this respect, these most skeptical and brutal of castaway novels remain true to the modern origins of the genre in *Robinson Crusoe*, in that it is what happens to the castaway that is the focus, not what he does to any indigenes. This is not surprising, though it is striking in the texts under discussion; the focus of *Heart of Darkness*, one of the classic texts about imperialism, is on Kurtz's madness and Marlow's breakdown, after all, and it is the Europeans who are the problem in the Congo of the novella, not the Africans. Contemporary castaway narratives accept the logic of the genre's concern with Western subjectivity when they revise the exotic setting of the story, seemingly so important and attractive in traditional castaway tales, and bring the island back to the metropolis.

Pincher Martin: Paradoxes of Survival

William Golding's *Pincher Martin* (1956) is as bleak about the attitudes and behavior of the castaway as any of the island narratives that come after *Moreau*. As the story unfolds, it appears that Martin has been cast away from a sinking British destroyer in World War II. The setting is the barren and cold Atlantic. Martin struggles onto an island that is little more than a big rock, and with effort and a lot of hard thought strives to secure his survival. He becomes delirious, suffering memories and flashbacks of his past, that of a harsh go-getter and rapist, of his treacherous relations with his friend on the ship, and eventually has a vision of an angry god.

Material reality certainly seems to be present in many of these details of survival and self-assertion; it is not something Pincher works with so much as something he sets himself to master by force of will. The work of survival does not achieve a balance between the subject and the world; instead, the subject struggles with the world and expands until he bursts. At that point we discover that Martin has actually been dead since shortly after he hit the water. In the short interval before he perished, he has been constructing not only the means of his survival and potential rescue, but the island itself, out of memory powered by will and denial. Critical discussion of the novel in the 1950s and 1960s accepted Golding's intentions here, and set itself to reread, noting the clues in the text to Pincher's real state, and endorsing the idea that to refuse to accept one's death is somehow contemptible, especially in someone flashbacks reveal to have been "ugly," "filthy"[3] in his former life, a monstrous egotist and a rapist. Only V. S. Pritchett among earlier critics suggests that the passages about Pincher's earlier life are not particularly successful, even if one grants that they are data that can't be ignored.[4]

The present discussion reassesses Pincher's struggle to survive, which, in the context set up in this book, represents a return to the fascination with material detail, work, and improvisation that *Robinson Crusoe* brings so vividly to our attention. It's not that *Pincher Martin* embraces Defoe's buoyancy and confidence—this is still a very grim novel; it's that there is a tension between Pincher's struggle to survive and his egoistic desire to dominate. This tension is what makes the novel gripping.

> I am netting down this rock with names and taming it. Some people would be incapable of understanding the importance of that. [. . .] I will tie it down with names. If it tries to annihilate me with blotting-paper, then I will speak here where my words resound and significant sounds assure me of my own identity.[5] I will trap rain-water and add it to this pool. I will use my brain as a delicate machine-tool to produce the results I want. Comfort. Safety. Rescue. (Golding 1956, 6: 86–87)

Pincher's island is a rough pinnacle of rock reaching down thousands of feet into the cold and stormy Atlantic. This is not a comfortable tropical island, so it is plausible that he will have to struggle and fight rather than cooperate with material circumstances. But even so, this passage lays bare the concerns of the island narrative since Defoe. We have the struggle not merely for survival but control and comfort; the instrumental use of reason that technologizes the island, or the self (the mind as a "delicate machine-tool"); the struggle to survive and control as an assertion of self, and even a definition of the self (in *Pincher*

Martin, the self is defined as centered on knowledge, intelligence, thought); the use of language and in particular naming to assert the self and subdue the island. In *Pincher Martin* these features are no longer potential or implicit. Pincher formulates them and embraces them. Castaways in this tradition commonly name their island and its features, make marks, make an inscription,[6] but in seeing this as tying the island down, chaining it, Pincher puts the matter very starkly.

At first he is in the water, struggling to get his sea boots off (later we will be told that he died before he could do so); then washed up against the rock looming out of the endless waves. He scrambles higher, finds some shelter and rest. His time of being cast away begins. There are flashbacks to his earlier life and his last hours on the destroyer, which make clear that when the torpedo hit, he was planning to pitch his virtuous and envied friend Nat overboard with a sudden change of course. He starts to differentiate the island and its possibilities, resources even. He is reduced to an awkward body, weighed down as much as protected by his life jacket, oilskins, and so on. His consciousness fluctuates. Sometimes it is disoriented and disintegrated, a self looking out of openings, windows, with a hole below them from which sounds come, the parts of this body seeming not a part of his self; but sometimes it is observing, surveying, resolving.

Pincher finds a hollow that he can wedge himself into and sleep, more or less sheltered; he finds a cave where fresh water has collected, somehow dammed and held in place by a mysterious red weed, which makes the place like an image of a mouth or a vagina. He forces himself to eat mussels and some other life form described as red jelly. Not surprisingly, he becomes ill and constipated, but then, very ingeniously, he makes the remains of his life jacket into an instrument for administering an enema, and relieves himself.

> He hutched himself back against a rock with his legs sprawled apart. The music rose, the sea played and the sun. The universe held its breath. Grunting and groaning he began to work the rubber tube into his backside. [. . .] He began to work at the bladder with both hands, squeezing and massaging. He felt the cold trickle of the sea water in his bowels. He pumped and squeezed until the bladder was squashily flat. He extracted the tube and crept carefully to the edge of the rock while the orchestra thundered to a pause. (II: 165)

Here we can talk of parody in Hutcheon's sense. We have the grand orchestra and the squashy bodily task. Yet we also have a powerful and stubborn rethinking of the business of material survival. Pincher plans. He must try to trap more water. He must set aside a day for thinking. He must believe he will be rescued. He must work to retain his identity. He knows that this care of his self is care of his personality, his sanity even, as well as care of his body.

He must make his presence legible to passing ships: "I must make a man to stand here for me" (4: 61). He improvises a kind of scarecrow out of round rocks, crowned with silver paper that had been wrapping for chocolate. He must also make a sign visible from the air: "Men make patterns and superimpose them on nature" (7: 108). He is right: a divergence from nature is the only thing that men will recognize as the sign that a man is on this rock. He tries to arrange seaweed in "a single indisputable line" (8: 109).

All this work does revive the concern with material necessity that energized Crusoe. Martin has to work at survival, and his perceptions of what has to be done come to him as resolutions, spoken out loud: "I must make it at least a yard wide and it must be geometrically straight" (8: 109). There's a kind of liberation in all this, important to the castaway narrative as a story of survival. Pincher Martin has become man in essence or reduction, grateful for rainwater, lucky to have red blobs to eat, speaking only of necessities, struggling to assert control and even identity:

> He had a valuable thought, not because it was of immediate physical value but because it gave him back a bit of his personality. He made words to express this thought, though they did not pass the barrier of his teeth.
>
> "I should be about as heavy as this on Jupiter."
>
> At once he was master. He knew that his body weighed no more than it had always done, that it was exhausted, that he was trying to crawl up a little pebble slope. (2: 27)

We are very aware that Pincher Martin is Western Man, his identity reliant on control and assertion, on the power of naming, but his efforts and successes are still compelling, because of this reduced, essential aspect of what he is doing. The paradox is that the selfishness and willfulness that made him so obnoxious (and unhappy) in his past life serve him well in the task of survival, where there is only his self to save and only his mind and his body to do it with. This paradox bears on the absolute subjectivity (the phrase is Ballard's) that is at the heart of the castaway narrative, allowable and even creative in *Robinson Crusoe*, destructive in *Moreau*, insane and self-deluding in *The Wasp Factory*. It is confronting—this absolute subjectivity of Pincher's is tough even if destructive. The force of the confrontation is evaded if the struggle to survive is stigmatized as perverse, unregenerate, and so forth.

What follows is that Pincher loses his grip, and his sense of his own distinctness erodes in a spectacular *Lear*-like storm that culminates in a confrontation with a dark deity, and the death he had denied is accepted. He has never been without an unconscious and a troubled memory. His strong and energized consciousness clings uneasily and with effort to the surface of this other self in a way that is clearly expressed by the topography of the story—the man on a rock, with its cavities and trenches and weed, which reaches down thousands of feet to the bottom of the sea, and is surrounded by thousands of miles of restless formless coldness. The structure of the fable, the image of a man on a harsh rock in the midst of a vast sea, overshadows anything Pincher does or says. It's not going to make all that much difference if he names various features of the rock Piccadilly or Leicester Square, as soldiers did in the trenches. The terrifying cold depth of this sea is felt here as it never is with the tropical islands on which most castaway stories happen. Further, as the story goes on, the rock comes to seem more allegorical and less material, with its cavities into which he crawls, its primitive life forms, its seagulls usually called "feathered reptiles." Pincher has nightmares. He remembers when he had mirrors, photos, others, from which or whom to gain a sense of self: "I could find assurance of my solidity in the bodies of other people by warmth and caresses and triumphant flesh. I could be a character in a body. But now I am this thing in here, a great many acres of bruised flesh, a bundle of rags and these lobsters on the rock" (9: 132). ("These lobsters" are his hands.) He is broken down to almost nothing.

Whether this process, ending in his acceptance of death, exhibits the cruel mercy of God, is not a question that will be pursued here. There is, however, something else, which emerges strongly when this narrative is put in context with other island narratives.[7] Novels about castaways may well assert the necessity and also the pleasures and opportunities of taking care of one's own survival, but they tend to be haunted by death. The others who were with the castaway have mostly died, and more deaths will probably follow later in the story, for instance when the island is invaded. *Pincher Martin* takes place during World War II, and it begins to seem ironic, if not an evasion, to single out the lone survivor when there are so many missing; so the novel reveals that Pincher has been dead from the beginning, and the two-phase narrative structure is itself less important to the effect of the novel than the structure of delusion (Pincher is successfully surviving) followed by abrupt revelation a few pages from the end (Pincher has been dead all along). When his corpse is found, he rejoins the nameless masses of the war dead. His egotism as an individual no longer matters. *The Wasp Factory* will follow this structure too, though here the revelation concerns the gender not the ontological status of the main character.

This narrative structure—reportage followed by revelation—occurring in such otherwise different texts, suggests the growing instability of the castaway story. It hasn't abandoned the practical materiality of *Robinson Crusoe*, but in its last pages it reaches for a sensational underlining of the subjectivity and ontological instability of the whole thing.

"The Terminal Beach"

This island was a fossil of time future.

J. G. BALLARD, "The Terminal Beach"

J. G. Ballard's "The Terminal Beach," however, abandons sequential narrative altogether, in the attempt to respond to what the Nuclear Age has done to the relations of past, present, and future. This is the new temporality of what the main character Traven calls "the pre-Third."[8] The story narrates Traven's physical decline, his refusal to do anything to ensure his survival on Eniwetok, but this in a landscape where nature has been overlaid with culture, and the culture is a culture of death. In fact, in the kind of temporality that Ballard explores in the text, nuclear annihilation is present as if it had already happened, or at least as if it had sucked Traven and the island into a zone in which the future and the archaic past are fused. If the emphasis of *Pincher Martin* is on Pincher's refusal to accept his death, the emphasis of "The Terminal Beach" is on Traven's awareness that death—a new kind of death—is as if it has already happened. In both cases this outcome is striking in a genre that had paid so much attention to the struggle to survive and indeed to transform survival into domination.

Traven has come ashore on Eniwetok, the now-deserted site of atomic testing, littered with concrete bunkers and other vestiges (abandoned warplanes, for instance); here he has settled, wandering and musing, avoiding other visitors to the island who might have helped him to leave it. But it is the place and the time that we notice, more than the actions of the castaway. The imagery is of the archaic, in particular of the massive blankness of ancient civilizations and ancient ruins, Stone Age or Egyptian (and Assyria and Babylon [Ballard 1966, 139]), and the way they suggest death—mausoleums, megaliths, obelisks, tomb-booths, runic inscriptions, "Eniwetok Man" (150).[9] The constructions that overlay the island are signs, or codes. The word "cipher" is used several times; also "runes" and "runic ideograms" (141). In turn the signs or codes can be connected to the archaic, as a term like *runes* suggests. The suggestion is of a meeting point of the far past and the future: an ancient, dead, enigmatic but long surviving past (such as that of the pyramids) is emplaced in seconds. The nuclear explosion creates strata of fused rock in a microsecond, though this would usually take ages of geological time. But the place has two other aspects: it is a modern construction of concrete blocks, bunkers, and blockhouses arranged in rings and grids, with the rough unlovely features of such artifacts (for instance, "exit grilles" [139]); and it is geometrical, "Cartesian," abstract, as if it were a concept made solid and permanent, replacing and obliterating most of the landscape. Thence Traven's reflection, "If primeval man felt the need to assimilate events in the external world to his own psyche, twentieth-century man had reversed this process; by this Cartesian yardstick, the island at least *existed*, in a sense true of few other places" (138).

The constructions and ruins have superimposed themselves on the landscape so thoroughly as to have obliterated what was there before. Traven forgets where the sea is, though he has dealings with the target basins that are part of the artificial topography of the tests; the dunes just beyond the dead city of the blocks signify only by way of their moving, sickle-shaped shadow, like a piece of geometry or a measuring apparatus, not a natural form. An effect of this conjunction of images and interpretations is that things seem utterly closed: the future meets the deep past—not only that of ancient civilization and stone age humans, but that of ancient saurians (136), and "dead reptile birds," which is how the carcasses of B-29s are seen (140). The modern present of Cartesian geometry and organization meets the past of megalomaniac projects to commemorate sacred kings; and the future encroaches on and occupies the present, as well as fusing the extermination camps of the recent past and the exterminations to come: "an Auschwitz of the soul whose mausoleums contained the mass-graves of the still undead" (138).

The nuclear is here seen as making a new kind of time—stalled, quantal; that is, not progressing by unbroken flow but in unconnected and impossible-to-relate jumps. Traven's moods of passivity, aimlessness, and hopelessness express this condition. This is one way in which the story intervenes in and overturns the rules of the castaway narrative. Traven does not record his stay or mark the passing of time with some sort of calendar, because time is not like that anymore and never will be again. The narrative is only loosely consecutive. It takes the form of blocks of prose with headings; it ends with a partial repetition of the phrases with which it began. The text doesn't begin with Traven's arrival on the island: that is told to us five sections in. Nor does it end either with Traven's departure (he eludes several opportunities to be rescued) or his death, or his reunion with his lost wife and son who haunt his days on the island and are gradually coming closer to him.

The recurring visions of his wife and son are very poignant, the more poignant for the coolness of Ballard's usual tone and vocabulary ("inventory," "incentive," and so on). There is something about the personalness of the ghosts and their deaths that makes a rift in the bleak, cool impersonality of the story's attempt to imagine an individual attuning himself to the utterly indifferent time and place of the nuclear, fossicking among charts of mutated chromosomes (146).[10]

Concrete Island: The Castaway as Tramp

This is a desert island novel with a difference. Here the island is a forgotten and disregarded segment of waste ground (Ballard, 1974, 9: 69), cut off from the rest of London by elevated freeways, roaring with packed and dangerous traffic, but perhaps only an island if one regards it as such: "The 'island'—is that what you call it?"—Jane's question to Maitland (Ballard 1974, 11: 84).

The main character, Richard Maitland, is an architect, appropriately, because this place is a side effect of planning and construction at its most brutal and indifferent. He crashes onto the island in his Jaguar, receiving minor injuries, and then, when he tries to cross the freeway, receives a major injury and becomes marooned. He finds himself with two others who stay by choice: Jane, who slips out from time to time to work as a prostitute, and Proctor, a mentally handicapped man who has taken refuge on the island to escape from a society that has abused him. Proctor is innocent and harmless, though Maitland corrupts him with drink (he had half a dozen bottles of Burgundy in the back of his Jaguar). This reminds us of a colonial practice, but more particularly of Caliban, as also do Maitland's dealings with Proctor's illiteracy. He teaches Proctor to write but tricks him into copying his, Maitland's, own name, so as to attract rescuers.[11] (Proctor had earlier erased the messages that Maitland himself wrote, because he was afraid that anyone who came to the island would harm him.) The trick doesn't work: Maitland's name is garbled. This combination of two traditional gestures—teaching language to the savage and naming the island after oneself—fails in both.

In fact, Maitland's attempts at making do are usually ineffective. For instance, he works out an ingenious way of setting fire to his car, to provide the signal flare that is standard castaway practice, but the car has served him as shelter, so it is not very sensible to set it on fire. Anyway, the resultant fire is not bright enough, and he realizes that from the freeways it probably looks just like "part of some tramp's celebration" (7: 51–54). Maitland is Crusoe/Prospero stripped of survivalist ingenuity and capacity to change others, but left with the drive to dominate. He is not only self-destructive or apathetic much of the time, but actively obnoxious, selfish, and violent toward Proctor and, to a lesser degree, Jane.

A Crusoe figure will end up bearded, tanned, dressed in skins or rags, and festooned or surrounded with all the bits and pieces he has scrounged and turned to new and often more basic uses, that is, uses concerned with the struggle to survive. The outcome will be a primitive dignity and a recontacting with what we recognize as basic reality. The film *Cast Away* (Zemeckis 2000) is a good example, because the character played by Tom Hanks becomes well muscled and fit-looking, rather than weathered and scrawny, which would seem a bit more likely; he displays material ingenuity with the ice skates he has found among his salvage (he uses the blades as knives and saws), and social ingenuity with the basketball that he turns into a companion, thereby avoiding the slightest taint of Friday-ism. The way down, the reduction to the primitive and physical, is also the way up, to dignity and a kind of power—lordship over the island as well as practical capacity and self-sufficiency. A tramp or derelict person, however—dirty, shambling, dragging maybe a loaded shopping trolley or scrounged remnants—is a figure without dignity. *Concrete Island* presents the castaway Maitland as in many ways just a tramp: degraded, scarred, messy. This is how anyone who came across him would classify him. In modern urban life, it seems, the way down is easily available but it is not also the way up: a harsh rendition of degeneration. "Derelicts slept in the rusting cars, and the occasional tramp wandered like a schizophrenic Crusoe among the wild palms and tamarinds" (Ballard 1999, 21). This is from Ballard's "Myths of the Near Future," set in a world in which both social organization and individual psyches have collapsed: Crusoes are plentiful, and there is no island, though the tropical setting might remind us of one: everyone is in effect marooned.

So far, Ballard's move in *Concrete Island* in transferring the desert island to the metropolis, and retaining enough of the cast and actions of castaway narratives to underline how unpleasant and unconstructive the central figure is, might seem pure parody: a revision that inverts everything, taking away the romance. In his earlier fiction, Ballard explored the possibility that leaving the world of Western rationality and linear time would bring a new and rich subjectivity and temporality.[12] *Concrete Island* foreshadows Ballard's later series of novels of urban or suburban breakdown and violence (*Crash*, which appeared the same year; *High Rise*, *Super-Cannes*, *Millennium People*).

But the division of Ballard's work into phases is not so clear-cut, and there is more to *Concrete Island* than this. To define it, we need to look again at the depiction of the island. It is torn away from distant seas and plonked down in urban mess, but a touch of the exotic seeps back. At first, the emphasis is on what surrounds the island, and on the newness of the place, the earth still loose, the "compulsory landscaping" not yet supplied (Ballard 1974, 2: 17). Then it begins to seem larger, richer, and older, with its waving grass, its remains of a cinema, an air raid shelter, a graveyard; Maitland's relations with the island and with his own body take on a new depth.

The "sea," which in its usual form can be dangerous and desolating but also beautiful and a place to swim and a source of fish, is transformed into something constructed. The island is surrounded by freeways and all their industrial fittings: culverts, caissons, grilles, barriers, and overpasses. Ballard has a good sense of the flat, merely denotative vocabulary of construction such as this. That which surrounds the island, then, is more obviously concrete than the island itself.

The island has a few structures on it, as well as the carcasses of cars, but is mostly overgrown with grass. This grass is evoked in unexpectedly lyrical and tender fashion. It's as if the island is flooded with grass, which has the changeable indefiniteness of a liquid. The land becomes like the sea, while the "sea" that surrounds it is harsh and unyielding. There are nettles, there are rats, but the island is covered with waving, tall, "seething" grass, and it seems alive: "The long grass seethed around his legs, greeting him like an affectionate dog" (12: 102). Further, we discover that there is a particular affinity between Proctor and the grass, "the whispering grass [. . .] this green harp"; he finds concealment in it, makes a network of paths (18: 147, and see 16: 128). When Proctor eventually dies in an accident, Maitland, casting about, senses "the stronger vibrations of the tall grass growing from the churchyard" (24: 175; there is an old graveyard on the island) and he buries Proctor there.

How does this mysterious emergent richness affect Maitland? The island is at first related to his past (the cinema, the air raid shelter), and to his body. His attitude to his injured leg is intensely alienated. He feels himself to be dragging it after him "like a dying companion on a mountain wall" (6: 48). In general, his body is imaged as something separate from himself: his wet clothes cling to him like a dead animal (6: 46); his legs stretch in front of him like "ragged poles" (8: 61); he wishes he could disconnect his leg and throw it away (16: 127).[13] In this respect, he is alienated from his body, as was Pincher Martin. As the story proceeds, however, Maitland's feelings about his self and the island undergo a change—not transformative, but marked, in view of the text's overall bleakness. In these ways *Concrete Island* is more like *The Tempest* than *Robinson Crusoe*; those on the island come to let its influences work on them.

Maitland sees himself as discarding his body, giving it over to the island, and in turn becoming the island. We are told, "Parts of his mind seemed to be detaching themselves from the centre of his consciousness" (8: 63). He finds himself knowing the place more intimately, and in these invocations not of his wounded body, which he has disowned and tried to shed, but of the island's secret places, there is something more intimate and healing: "The island seemed larger and more contoured, a labyrinth of dips and hollows" (12: 102). The island expands (5: 40, 6: 49), and comes to contain more: relics of the older city, corridors of grass, chambers, such as the room in the old cinema where Jane has taken up residence, and Proctor's quilt-lined hutch.[14]

This strand in the text goes beyond the island being a metaphor for Maitland's mind or his past. There are suggestions that he is rediscovering not some inner self, which is probably better left unvisited, but possibilities of worldness that are denied by the "over-bright" (9: 68) concrete city outside. This is why his growing reluctance to leave the island, his assertions that, though he is losing weight and becoming scrawny, he is also gaining strength and purpose, seem genuinely suggestive (for example, 21: 156). The island replicates and intensifies the exploitation that prevails in the rest of the city, but also offers an alternative to it.

It's true that this is only intermittently apparent. Whatever his relations with the island, Maitland's relations with its other inhabitants are often antagonistic. Jane and Proctor rescue and tend him for a while, though for a variety of reasons they won't help him to leave the island. In return, he sets himself to dominate them, and brings this about in a scene in which he urinates on Proctor, whom he has made drunk, and browbeats Jane. After that, he has Proctor carrying him about the island, a kind of slave. It's only on Proctor's accidental death and Jane's departure that he attains a kind of calm, though we are left uncertain whether this means he is now ready to leave the island himself, or means that he is now ready to stay.

There are ambiguities even here, however. We could take the brutal campaign to dominate Jane and Proctor as an instance of the degeneration into violence and power struggle that kicks in when one is pitched out of ordered society, as in *Lord of the Flies*, but the novel does not in fact depict some substratum of violence and egotism as underlying the veneer of civilization, as is clearly the case with, for instance, Ballard's *Super-Cannes* (2001). Civilization seems *already* violent and egotistic; but in addition, the three characters all in various ways fragment into inconsistent aspects of behavior, aggressive one moment, tender the next. Like Wolfe in his variations on *Moreau*, and Banks in *The Wasp Factory* (as will be suggested next), Ballard seems wary of any depth psychology. Grim circumstances will not necessarily reveal any deep core of personality, because there may not be one. *Concrete Island* does offer psychological analysis at times, as when Jane analyzes Maitland (for instance, 11: 84–85), but this has a desultory air, as if Ballard is not prepared to pursue it very far.

Concrete Island fits the line of inversion and parody that stems from *Moreau*, but ambivalently. It simultaneously demystifies the castaway narrative and remystifies the castaway's relation to the island. It critiques and rejects *Robinson Crusoe* but evokes lyrical aspects of *The Tempest*. It's as if the desert island as a place where the subject might expand and gain power is simultaneously rejected and reintroduced. Maitland's power over the "natives" is in some ways cruder than in fictions actually set on remote islands, yet this island, mere grass and urban wreckage surrounded by concrete, also nourishes something gentler in him. By repatriating the island and its natives, Ballard has ensured that whatever this something gentler is, it is not to be associated with exotic places or natives in orientalist fashion.

Iain Banks's *The Wasp Factory* is not at all ambivalent, and it takes certain features of the post-Moreau island novel to almost absurd extremes; significantly, this entails a refusal of inwardness, a brilliant schematic pattern making.

The Wasp Factory

My greatest enemies are women and the sea.

IAIN BANKS, *The Wasp Factory*

The Wasp Factory is a story about a young man, Frank, who lives with his father on a muddy island very near the coast of Scotland. Frank is the narrator, and he confides in us fully and eagerly. We may well wish he hadn't, because he tells us how he got away with murdering three harmless children of his own family, in alarmingly ingenious ways. In addition, he lets us in on the many obsessive-compulsive rituals and observances, most of them involving violence or petty destruction, by which he structures his life and quarters his island, and he makes us share in his growing alarm at the steady approach to the island of his older brother Eric, of whom by this point it is enough to say that he is possibly even madder than Frank. There are murders and abuses in contemporary fiction or in the newspapers that arouse horror or repulsion, but Frank's behavior does not have this effect, although he is a psychopath. His actions are absurd, though blackly absurd.

Frank is an extension to extremes of the phenomenon of the subject as all-important not only to himself but to the text he dominates. He expresses himself in ways that are, again, an extreme version of the acculturation of the island, and its naming and mapping, that is the work of castaways like Crusoe. Eric's arrival, however, brings about a final series of shocking revelations.

Frank expended huge effort in organizing and controlling his life on the island, but is at last, by these revelations, shown to have lived in fundamental ignorance of who and what he is. This revelation will be discussed later, because it throws a strong light on the castaway novel's concern with masculinity, male work, and male violence. Meanwhile, we can note that *The Wasp Factory* is a rich resume and subversion of many of the tropes of the island novel.

It fits Banks's disruptive style of attack that the island in question is barely an island at all (1990, 15), connected to the mainland by a bridge and by the telephone, by which Eric gives the occasional manic warning of his approach. Frank, however, underlines how he and his father can't bear to be away from it: even when he is on the mainland, he likes to keep his island in view (138). And he emphasizes how thoroughly it is his: it has been mapped with sites that are his own creations, which he meticulously maintains. These sites commemorate violent incidents in his own past, and yet are seemingly archaic (the Sacrifice Poles, the Skull Grounds, the Bomb Circle—as in stone circle).

The island is a little world with its own completeness, attained partly by isolation and partly by Frank's hard work. The effect is to primitivize the island, however, rather than domesticate it as happens in *Robinson Crusoe*. More precisely, if paradoxically, it's the primitive civilization of the security state that Frank evokes.[15] He has an Early Warning system, a bunker, booby traps, a cache system (56–57). He describes his own movements in military terms, or terms derived from war movies—"silent running," or "emergency speed." All this links the modern, the world of the nuclear stand-off, with the archaic, as happens also in Ballard's "The Terminal Beach." The island is repatriated, and put into an unstable temporal zone. Frank says of the Sacrifice Poles, "They were my early warning system and deterrent rolled into one; infected, potent things which looked out from the island, warding off. These totems were my warning shot; anybody who set foot on the island after seeing them should know what to expect" (10).

The Sacrifice Poles are capped with the rotting heads of small animals (frequently replenished by the diligent Frank), and he regularly urinates on them. The poles evoke ideas of fearsome "natives" as well as associating maleness and the territorial, and evoke also the dark side of English history (the rotting heads of traitors on poles), together with the central image in *Lord of the Flies* and Kurtz's heads on poles in *Heart of Darkness*. As for himself, "the unchallenged lord of the island and the lands about it," as he says (139), echoing various British and Scottish titles as well as *Robinson Crusoe*, "I've often thought of myself as a state" (62). It's the military and political aspects of the macrocosm, not as in Defoe the social ones, that are emphasized in *The Wasp Factory*. Banks is equally interested in the politics of gender here, however; all this obsession with defense and control, the war games and games with explosives, is an aspect of Frank's megalomania, but also of his masculinism.

When Frank was a child, his father insisted on his knowing the measurements of everything in the house, which was labeled accordingly. Frank, now seventeen, calibrates and controls obsessively, but mainly he gives names. Much of what we read is his account of how places on his island came to have the names they now have—the Bomb Circle, the Snake Park, and so on. It's a parody both of the way explorers and settlers take it upon themselves to name everything, as in *The Mysterious Island*, for instance, and of the way kids do the same, in their games and fantasies. It is a parody also of Sword and Sorcery epics—Frank's bike is Gravel, his trowel is Stoutstroke, and his slingshot is the Black Destroyer, and after it is broken and he burns it, the place where this happened is named the Hill of the Black Destroyer.

All this is unbalanced and obsessive, though it has a touch of the attractive if it echoes our own fantasies and childhood fetishes.[16] It is closely related to Frank's obsession with power and control. Naming is power with him. Things he has done become the places he has done them in; the name mythologizes, and then he invents some ritual, obsessively repeated, to go with the place. A castaway novel is a novel about a person in a place, and has a particular power because of that. The story is about the person's dealings with the place: we saw just now how description of and response to the place takes over the text in "The Terminal Beach," and how Maitland is changed by the place in *Concrete Island*. In *The Wasp Factory* this quality is pressed to an extreme, for after all, in actuality this particular place is just a muddy islet off the coast. For Frank, events become places; by this, the flippancy and apparent randomness with which he has acted is transformed into something solid, reliable, and old, as if it has been this way for ages. He has rituals he performs at the Sacrifice Poles, or in the Bunker (a World War II construction where he consults the skull of a dog that was very important in his own history), or in the loft of the house in which he and his father live. In the loft he sets in motion the wasp factory, a kind of elaborate machine with many tunnels and booby traps, based on a large clock face scavenged from a rubbish dump, into which he inserts captured wasps: the fate of the wasp, which will be killed in some fashion in one of the tunnels and compartments of the factory, which is therefore a factory for killing not making, will constitute an oracular message for Frank. It was suggested earlier that a significant change comes over the castaway story when its narrative is made to hinge on some final revelation, as in *Pincher Martin*; in addition, we can see a kind of petrifaction overcoming the story in texts such as "The Terminal Beach" and *The Wasp Factory*, where events give way to repetition or routine—though *The Wasp Factory* is also a text that hinges on a final revelation. In the texts under discussion in this chapter, the castaway's work tends to lack a successful onward drive. Frank is active enough, but he seems to be running on the spot.

Further, as is common in castaway stories, there are places within the island, usually manmade ones, where one can't go, or can't go at first. Here, in keeping with this novel's tendency to exacerbation, there are several. Frank's father can't get into the loft (he has a lame leg and can't make the stairs) so he doesn't know about the wasp factory, by which Frank feels he has power over the future. Frank can't get into his father's study, which invariably is locked, and it clearly contains a secret. It is roughly speaking his father's laboratory, site of his experiment on Frank. Frank can't get into the cellar either, though he does know that it contains a load of cordite stolen from the Royal Navy; frustrated, he has to labor over his homemade bombs when there is a wonderful supply of explosive just nearby.

So Frank's control is limited and unstable. There are all sorts of things about his past and his father (a habitual tease and liar) that he doesn't know, places in his obsessively mapped and named and patrolled island that he can't penetrate. His power to name and thence control is disrupted by Eric's sudden crazy phone calls. Eric alternatively reduces language to absurdity (manic childish play on words, for instance, *here*: "Where are you?" "Here." "No, *I'm* here," and so on and on) or to screaming and babble. Frank is the loser in these conversations with his brother—they are absolutely on his brother's terms and he knows it (see, for instance, 100, 131).

The more the limits of his power are emphasized, the more obsessively Frank asserts it, patrolling, arranging, tidying, keeping up the rituals. One of his favorite phrases is "as usual" (for instance, 25–26). He builds elaborate dams, complicated systems to control and channel water, with miniature villages below them; the dams are then blown open and the villages destroyed. Like the wasp factory itself, these constructions are microcosms within the microcosm that is the island, and places over which he can exercise even tighter control, though the matter is not as simple as that, as the wasp factory is an enigmatic oracle, a destiny machine that always kills the wasp but seldom gives Frank a clear message about the future.

Frank's preoccupation with security and control sets the context for the novel's depiction of work. Frank is always busy; he wears a tool belt. We see him making explosives ("I suppose it's a craft in some ways" [53]). We see him making kites—obsessive, and therefore an exaggeration of the concern with physical operations and improvised tools that we get in Defoe or Verne (Banks 1990, 88–89).

Clearly, this novel's relation to the tropes and conventions of castaway narratives is a shifting one: some features are exacerbated, others are refused, though arguably they are refused rather than simply absent. Matters are equally complex with the dramatis personae. We can certainly compare Frank's father Angus to Moreau and to Prospero. He has a laboratory and has operated on Frank in some way, but he has also nurtured Frank. He educated him at home (14); he concealed him from the authorities; there are no public records of Frank. The resemblance of Frank to Miranda can be filled in later; as for Caliban, there is competition for this role. Should we see Frank as Caliban, so profoundly native to his island? Or Eric as Caliban, in his abuse of language and his crazy mocking passage toward the island from the asylum from which he has escaped, burning or eating dogs as he comes?

As in *Moreau's Other Island*, the sea assumes a tantalizing suggestiveness. It's one of Frank's twin enemies, the other being women, as he tells us (43)—wayward, impalpable, flowing, unable to be mapped. Frank's earlier activities with dams and watercourses ("shrouded sexual symbolism," as Thom Nairn comments)[17] can be seen as his attempts to control what he comes to see as uncontrollable:

> I watched the small waves fall on the beach for a while. On the sea, on that lens of water, twice-bulged and wobbling and rolling round the earth, I am looking at a rippled desert, and I have seen it as flat as a salt lake. Elsewhere the geography is different; the sea undulates, sways and swells, folds into rolling downs under freshening breezes, piles into foothills beneath the stiffening trades, and finally rears white-topped and blizzard-streaked in circling mountain ranges rammed by the storm-forced wind. (Banks 1990, 182)

This makes a stark contrast to his attempts to fix and control the land, which have now, as he meditates, just come spectacularly undone.

Angus's experiment on Frank is an allusion, surely, to the plastic surgery by which Moreau is trying to mold the beasts, though the "surgery" was actually done by the dog Old Saul that little Frank had been teasing, which attacked him.[18] He was scarred about the groin but not, as Angus made him think, castrated. After this, and especially as he entered puberty, Angus treated Frank in various ways that were almost as fundamentally intrusive as what Moreau did, though they were concealed from Frank. The line Angus blurred, however, was that between males and females, not that between humans and animals. Angus, whose attitudes to women were perhaps too complex for the word *misogynist* to do much more than gesture at, was trying to delay the onset of womanhood in Frank. The child was never castrated, but only made to believe that he had been castrated, and his plumpness and "downy brown growth" (44) were the result of Angus's hormone treatment. This is what bursts on Frank when he finally gets into his father's study near the end of the story.

Appropriately, given the novel's drive to excess, Frank first thinks that Angus is the one who is the female. And characteristically, he reasons by way of names —Angus is close in sound to Agnes, his mother's name. Agnes rode a motorbike, used it to break Angus's leg when he tried to stop her leaving (hence his limp), and she left the kids to his care: all stereotypical masculine behavior. If Agnes is like a man, maybe Angus is really a woman, is really Agnes. It's not so, and there's a comic, grotesque, and oedipal moment when Frank pulls down his father's pants and sees the latter's equipment (174). It is *Frank* who is Frances: "Now I find I was the fool all along" (183).

After the revelation, Frances says that her boyish murders as Frank must have been the revenge of the unmanned: "Talk about penis envy." That's what men can do, they can bring death, as the wasp factory did also. Now she says,

> Well, it is always easier to succeed at death.
>
> Inside this greater machine [that is, greater than Frank's wasp factory], things are not quite so cut and dried (or cut and pickled). (183)

The allusion is to what he/she had thought were his genitals in a jar; the flippancy here will need a comment, but is this psychology satisfactory? Does the novel *have* a psychology, exactly, as distinct from an intricate schematic sense and a powerful feeling that no earlier island narrative has gone far enough in depicting the savage and "beastly" in the civilized? Can we reread the novel, in the light of this final revelation, as an exploration of how gender is entirely conditioned, entirely a cultural product? Not very easily. Frank, believing he was male, acted in a very masculine fashion, building, patrolling, killing, destroying: a caricature of a version of the male. But then he didn't believe he was male; he believed he was castrated, which is a different thing in his eyes. It is difficult to assess the degree to which a certain castrate's activity is expressive of that of castrates in general, and the novel would appear to mock any attempt to do so. Frank is a social isolate. Once or twice we see him as part of the male drinking culture of Scotland, though it is notable that his best friend on the mainland is Jamie, a dwarf who is almost alone among the personages of the novel in *not* being grotesque. Then there is Eric, whose movement toward the island structures the plot, and whose mad phone calls rip shreds in its isolation and disrupt Frank's efforts at control. Eric and Frank seem to set out some schema of human possibility (id and ego?) that is not to be mapped onto gender. What is important, surely, is the power of the depiction of Frank's megalomaniac egoism in the context the castaway novel sets up—obsession with defense and security; the civilized as primitive, the civilized as archaic; civilizational energies—naming, knowing, building—become ingrown and reduced to the service of ego, or, to put it another way, the ego expanding to include the outside world in an indifferentiation that has a lot to do with Frank's flippant murderousness.

There is a complex both of forces and of deficiencies here that has to run its violent and extreme course, and, having done so, it implodes. The revelation that Frank is not a male or a castrate but a female constitutes that implosion. What is canceled or overwritten in the implosion is both the masculinity of many castaway stories and the revision of the masculinity of these stories in novels about female castaways such as Giraudoux's *Suzanne and the Pacific*, to be discussed in Chapter 5.[19] The castaway story here reaches a kind of null point, in which categories such as male and female, insane and sane, cancel each other out.

The Wasp Factory marks the arrival of the postmodern, and we can measure its distance from, for instance, *Pincher Martin*. Thom Nairn suggests that Banks is postmodern in his awareness of and irreverence about what the postmodern stands for: "Several commentators have recently remarked that we may be in the midst of a post-postmodernist age, where the postmodern itself becomes the butt of elaborate jokes" (Nairn, 131). This is right, though the postmodern hollowness of Frank's (and Eric's) psychology, the novel's flourishing of gestures toward a psychological interpretation which, however, doesn't really take, amounts to a darker response to the situation that the postmodern has put us into. Banks is not being frank about Frank—the name makes that kind of joke, in the light of the final revelation, but the treatment of the self is postmodern here also in being ungrounded. There is no norm against which we can measure the abnormality of Frank's or Eric's psyche.

The Beach

Everything here will fall apart.

ALEX GARLAND, *The Beach*

The Beach concerns the experiences and misdeeds of Richard, who joins a secret commune of young Westerners on an island off the coast of Thailand. The commune seems idyllic, with its easygoing young people fishing, lazing in the sun, keeping things going without much effort or ambition, but it is headed for dispute, mistrust, and eventually violence. Richard learned of the Beach, and obtained a map to guide him to it, when the stranger in the room next door suicided, so the place is marked with blood. In addition, most of the island that shelters the beach and its secluded lagoon is used by armed Thais to cultivate marijuana.

With his careless throwaway style, Richard seems typical of those who take a few years away from the urban West to drift from one more or less cheap and unspoiled Eastern beach or village to another, but he soon sinks into petty deception and intrigue, and from there into hallucination and feckless violence. He resembles the stereotypical sinister, unscrupulous intruder who undermines and destroys innocence, but the matter is not so simple. Richard's path toward violence passes through Vietnam War fantasy and hallucination, and in this he gains a ghostly companion and advisor, Mister Duck (the man who suicided). His drifting casualness and flippancy, indulgence in pop culture trivia and game playing, has this weird shadow extension. At the same time, Richard is the narrator, and his control of the text frustrates the reader's attempts to imagine what the others who are becoming his victims feel about him. It's as if *Victory* were narrated by Mr. Jones. The result is that at its best, *The Beach* retains the frisson of a novel about a psychopath, such as *The Wasp Factory*, without foreclosing the possibility that the castaways as a group have degenerated, as in *Lord of the Flies*. Garland assumes the mask of Richard's narration and doesn't let it slip. Further, Richard never seems *extraordinary* as the clever and witty Frank Cauldhame does in *The Wasp Factory*; he grows in weirdness and destructiveness without ceasing to be shallow.

Clearly, *The Beach* has behind it the novel of imperial adventure as Martin Green has defined it in *Seven Types of Adventure Tale* (1991), but also *Heart of Darkness*, and *Lord of the Flies*. Mister Duck, the character who haunts the narrator, is among other things an ironic allusion to Conrad's Mister Kurtz[20]—ironic because the nickname is also a reference to Daffy Duck. The three pioneers who first "discovered" the Beach that is at the story's heart each took facetious cartoon-character names (Mister Duck; Bugs for Bugs Bunny; Sal for Sylvester the Cat). As for *Lord of the Flies*, *The Beach* is in many ways a revision and updating. The isolated group on the island, which makes first an "Eden" and then starts to divide into factions and succumb to shark attack, illness, paranoia, confusion, and violence, thus repeating the trajectory of *Lord of the Flies*, consists not of schoolboys but of men and women, young people in their twenties or thereabouts, but the difference mainly brings out their dangerous childishness. (The episode in which they enjoy the phosphorescence is a good example

[Garland 1997, 250–51].) Richard is less the sinister intruder than the irritant, the one who stirs up trouble without particularly planning to do so.

The Beach is a tissue of allusions, coming largely from Richard's mediatized imagination, his habit of seeing things in terms of games (Streetfighter II and so on), television shows (*The A-Team*, *The Waltons*), and also a Vietnam imaginary based largely on films. This last is the most significant, as the novel's epigraph and its opening sentence hint to us.[21] The novel thus has some of the qualities of a pastiche as Fredric Jameson has discussed them: blank parody without evident critical purposes (Jameson 1991, 16–19). The allusions, in the chapter and section titles for instance, throw a sort of clever screen across the narration. They are mostly part of the stock of contemporary stereotypes; for instance, there's a chapter called "Ich bin ein Beacher," which includes "Ask not what your beach can do for you" (217–18), so we have the two most familiar Kennedy quotes easily alluded to. Other allusions draw upon another area of popular culture, the realm of buff-fan-trivia. There's a section called "Prisoners of the Sun": the literary reader might wonder if there is an allusion to Ballard's *Empire of the Sun*, but no, as the text makes clear, we have the title of the Tintin book that Mister Duck liked best when he was a child (Garland 1997, 226).

In general, the allusions and pop culture references work to preempt the reader's awareness that the novel is belated, a redoing of a crowd of earlier stories. After all, Richard's journey to the beach begins with a chance encounter and a map that comes into his possession, like dozens of adventure tales: "Naturally, a map," we might say, borrowing from Umberto Eco's gesture at the beginning of *The Name of the Rose* (1980). The allusions are a hint to the reader to allow for this kind of repetition or cliché. And the allusions—especially those to the Vietnam War, which are largely confined to Richard and Mister Duck—also express the *characters'* sense of belatedness, though it's odd to feel regret that you are too late for the Vietnam War.

Richard is the prime pasticheur in the novel. Moreover, Richard's fascination with Vietnam is more than a matter of allusions. In the later part of the novel, he is sent to guard the border of the community, keeping watch on the Thai guards with another of the community, Jed; he lives all this in terms of Vietnam descriptors (for instance, the DMZ) and fantasies, most notably when he gets them out of a tense moment with a Thai guard by means of a clever trick he once saw on *Tour of Duty*. It's Vietnam that structures the increasingly substantial apparitions of Mister Duck, as if the living person and the dead person can make a shared reality because they both love these Vietnam War fantasies and media memories.

It is mainly *Lord of the Flies* that is being revised, and in a sense evacuated, in that *The Beach* eschews Golding's horror and intensity. The novel also brushes against *Robinson Crusoe* a couple of times. Richard discovers a tree on which the three originals carved their initials and the date of their arrival; not 1989, however, but 0000 (136–38), the year zero, another Vietnam War allusion: "Cambodia, Year Zero." We can be reminded of Robinson's carved calendar. Richard himself, however, emphasizes that he has never kept a travel diary or taken photos; these things don't help your memory but confine and constrict it, he says. His opinion is a cliché among travelers, as distinct from the despised tourists.

As for the footprint, the most frequently revised moment in *Robinson Crusoe*, it is provided, and in significant form, because it expresses Richard's growing craziness. Here Richard is walking on the beach, "playing one of my games":

> The aim was to leave the perfect footprint, and it was a lot harder and more preoccupying than it might sound. If the sand was the dry side of damp, the footprint crumbled; the moist side and it melted as the squeezed-out water seeped back in. Then there was the application of pressure. The toes sank too deeply with a normal step and flawed the imprint. The alternative, taking an artificial step with even pressure, created a good imprint at the cost of ethics. This was the compromise I wrestled with. (308)

And so on, until he reaches his friends: "Are you going insane, Rich?" (309).

The differences from *Robinson Crusoe* mark the distance between European settlement and possession in the early days of imperialism (early for Britain, anyway) and their contemporary conditions. Richard reaches the island that hides the beach with two other travelers he has encountered, Étienne and Françoise. They have to swim the last stage, discarding most of the little they have brought with them. Their plan to float their stuff in inflated garbage bags was based on something they had seen in an episode of *The A-Team*, so its failure is unsurprising. Once they join the settlement, they find it already set up, organized, and camouflaged, efficiently enough—Richard feels the toilets are a lot better than most he has encountered on his travels, for instance (99)—but none of this rouses any excitement. There is certainly no desire to replicate "civilization," nor any sense of the effort and ingenuity of survival. The castaways are not free of Western civilization, but its traces are abstracted—nicknames, games, stories of travel. They forget their parents and can't be bothered to contact them.[22] They are a mixture of nationalities. They don't appear to have friends they miss. The material remnants that they desire seem random. Keaty has his Gameboy, which periodically needs batteries. The gifts Richard gets for some of the others when he helps with "the rice run" back to Thailand arouse little interest (193). There doesn't seem to be any longer a material civilization that one might hanker to reestablish as a whole—just a few bits and pieces that individuals might randomly still want.

But haven't they decided to escape from all this, the material baggage that weighs us down in the West? Yes, but not very definitely, and not to anything that figures as an alternative. They don't have an ideology, or even an ethos, really. This could be refreshing, given the high potential for pretension; their leader Sal is said early on to resemble a female Buddha (93), but nothing really comes of this, and there is an emptiness about their sojourn. Sal says the place is a "beach resort" (96); she is joking, but in fact they simply laze about.

Their status as travelers is very important in this connection. They reminisce about their favorite places to travel—all in the non-Western world—but not about their lives before they traveled. They constitute a social and cultural type: backpackers. Their current separation from the rest of the world—though, as will be seen shortly, it is incomplete—just follows the logic of their separation from home, and also from the despised ordinary travelers who flock to any tropical paradise once the word gets around and it is thereby ruined for themselves (139). They have a lot in common:

> "You fish, swim, eat, laze around, and everyone's so friendly. It's such simple stuff, but . . . If I could stop the world and restart life, put the clock back, I think I'd restart it like this. For everyone." I shook my head to stop myself rambling. "You know what I mean."
>
> "All these thoughts are the same as mine."
>
> "They are?"
>
> "Of course. The same as everybody's." (133–34; Richard talking with Étienne)

What they share, and what keeps them from conflict, at least until Richard arrives, is this sense of themselves as freewheeling travelers. Clearly, there are lots of other ways for Westerners to be in the East nowadays—aid workers, business people, soldiers, not to mention the more standard tourists seeking relief from their ordinary life in the sights or the cheap beer—but there is something chilling in these Westerners. They figure an end point, something null. It's an exotic place and the living is communal, but they fish and garden and lounge around just like your uncle and aunt who have retired and moved to the coast.[23] It's true that hippy tourism, like mass tourism in general, could be seen in a postcolonial context, but the situation of the young people in *The Beach* just seems to partake of aftermath, of a tag end, not of anything as definite as the postcolonial.

When Françoise, Étienne, and Richard first arrive on the island, they are horrified to find themselves up on a sort of plateau in a marijuana plantation: there will be guards and they are not likely to be friendly. The island is secluded because it is off limits as part of a national park, but the seclusion that makes the island perfect for the beach resort also makes it perfect for growing the drug. Étienne panics and demands that Richard save them; given no choice by Étienne, Richard can act decisively. Shortly after this, they arrive at the top of a high waterfall, and it is Richard who jumps, impulsively and without actually deciding to. They now find themselves in the commune, which is divided from the drug growers by the waterfall and hidden from the view of the sea by a lagoon and a series of underwater tunnels that connect with the sea. (This answers to a common pattern in castaway narratives—the island within the island; quite often, for instance in *The Coral Island* and *Lord of the Flies*, it takes the form of a hidden, safe swimming place.)

From now on, Richard will act by this random impulsiveness, as if trusting to the shifts of a game. He is not a planner and an ingenious psychopath like Frank in *The Wasp Factory*. Regarding social life, he is most subject to boredom and to irritation or envy. He allows these to structure his feelings about others. He feels some desire for Françoise, but it seems right that he has ended up the third in a trio with Françoise and Étienne. (Danny Boyle's film [2000] gives him a bit more drive and definition: he has sex with Françoise and with Sal, though the woman takes the initiative in each case; and his fantasies are more intensely and even daringly centered around Vietnam War films than in the novel.) His more intense emotional life is elsewhere, in his encounters with the shade of Mister Duck and in his Vietnam fantasies, which give more and more substance to those encounters.

Richard has given a copy of the map to two seemingly harmless American travelers, Zeph and Sammy. There wasn't much thought behind his action. They make it to a neighboring island and wait there. Richard is assigned to watch for them as sidekick to Jed; Jed and Richard do this stealthily from the marijuana plantation, the DMZ in Richard's fantasy. What will they do if Zeph and Sammy manage to get over to the island? It would be convenient if the guards got them first, says Richard. Though the guards tolerate the commune, we know they are rough and armed. Richard describes one of them and, typically, sees his roughness as "perfect"—it fits the image (281). It's as if the "savages" are already on the castaway's island and the harmless Westerners, Zeph and Sammy, are the feared and watched-for intruders. We are never told why the arrival of Zeph and Sammy is to be feared; as this is a commune, the leaders, Sal and Bugs, tend to keep their reasons to themselves, because there are not supposed to *be* leaders.

Zeph and Sammy do make it to the island, with some others, including women; they are caught by the guards, beaten, and probably all shot (the matter is left uncertain). Richard does nothing—even Mister Duck is dismayed by this. Meanwhile, the commune has started to collapse: a bout of food poisoning; a shark attack involving Sten, Christo, and Karl; and increasing tension between Richard and Bugs leading to quarrels and fights. Karl, a survivor of the shark attack, is traumatized, almost insane, and crouches in a hole in the sand, where the impatient Richard comes close to killing him. Garland is careful about all this. Richard had killed a shark—the first time anyone in the group had done this—and he saves Christo, who has been injured by the shark, before turning homicidal against the other survivor, Karl. Richard is a person who *accompanies* violence and deception rather than always causing or exploiting them. He drifts through these episodes: the attempts to revive the injured Sten, the third of those attacked by the shark (289); his search for Christo, missing in the aftermath of the attack, potentially a heroic action but presented in drifting, dreamy fashion ("It was very exciting underwater [. . .] I wasn't hurried; Christo and the shark seemed rather distant concerns" [293]); and his response to the injuries that will eventually kill the man he has rescued ("I'd felt slightly let down by the undramatic nature of his injuries" [304]). Richard's rescue of Christo, one victim of the shark attack, and his subsequent attack on Karl, another victim, cancel each other out because they have the same flippancy. Karl escapes him, and then later, caught up in the urgency of his scheme to leave the beach in reaction to the situation of disintegration and violence he has helped to bring about, he casually suffocates the dying Christo (412). His plan for flight is in turn thwarted by the arrival of the armed Thais, stirred into violence by the intrusion of Zeph and Sammy's party. The Thais kill two of the community, and the survivors mutilate their corpses in a pointless frenzy ("within seconds the corpses were swarmed" [428]).

The will to power and the descent into violence are not seen as rising from the deep natures of the castaways, as in *Lord of the Flies*. These castaways have no depth of nature, or none that is apparent to us from Richard's narration. There is no religious or ritual element, no pig-pilot deity—the feast that goes badly wrong, because Richard drugs it and because the Thai drug traffickers arrive, is just a feast, its purpose of reconciliation after recent communal tension an obvious one. Richard mainly stirs the ill feeling in a random fashion with acts of petty spite or small lies. The coming of Zeph and Sammy was caused by him but hardly his fault, and by the time it brings the Thais down to the commune, he is deep in a scheme to escape with some of his friends, a scheme which in typical Richard fashion also involves a kind of attack on the community—drugging their drink at the feast. In the end he does escape, and so do a few of the others, including Étienne and Françoise, and then they part. In their trips back to the mainland and then away from Thailand, they talk together incessantly, but we are never told what they say (437).

Not that the beachcombers as a group are exempt from blame. There is a general degeneration. This is not a kind of tribe in which one faction succumbs to primitive violence and another clings impotently to civilized ways; most of them deny as best they can that things are sliding downward. "A huge exercise in denial was underway," says Richard, before underlining his main response, that this advantages him: "No problem for me. It meant that no one asked me to elaborate on Karl or brought up the topic of the gunshots. The only downside was having to labour through a few contrived conversations, which seemed a fair trade-off" (371). The conventions of the adventure story (danger, violence, justified deceit in a threatening situation) abet the depiction of Richard's feckless emptiness. (He is referring to his attack on Karl and the probable killing of Zeph and Sammy by the Thai guards.)

Richard himself learns nothing. There is no equivalent to the revelation at the end of *The Wasp Factory*. "I told her that I was very sorry for whatever I'd done, but I didn't know what it was any more. I only knew that I'd never wanted to do anything bad" (Garland 1997, 432). Has the skeptical, violent, or insane castaway story gone as far as it can go, past excess to emptiness? *The Wasp Factory* invites this conclusion, but tempers it with the depiction of Frank's energetic purposefulness; *The Beach* elaborates it through the remorseless presentation of Richard's blank fecklessness. Both novels historicize their stories in contexts of warfare and decline: Frank regresses to the primitive in a context of World War II bunkers, but this is a primitive with a certain materiality to it, while in *The Beach* the primitive is as ungrounded as are Richard's fantasies of the Vietnam War. Frank has a series of projects, which are psychopathic but which he pursues coherently; Richard plays games and responds to impulses.

It may be time to turn to a less extreme tendency in contemporary castaway narratives, in Yann Martel's *Life of Pi* (2001). *Life of Pi* will serve both to conclude this chapter and to prelude the later chapters that examine recent more buoyant revisions of the castaway narrative. As the previous chapter ended with a discussion of *Lord of the Flies*, whose treatment of the degeneration of humans into "beasts" is the most radical and unsparing since *The Island of Dr. Moreau*, this chapter ends with a discussion of *Life of Pi*, a novel centered on the relations between humans and animals—not beasts. In light of this, we can see *Life of Pi* as part of a turn toward reconsideration of humans' place in nature—here, the shared but divergent animality of a boy and his "other" and companion, in this case a tiger. It also stages a sophisticated rethinking of two of the standing anxieties—terrors—of the castaway novel, degeneration and cannibalism. In the last analysis—an analysis that has to center on Pi's relationship with the tiger Richard Parker—what this novel does with these anxieties marks a dissent from the line whose key texts are *The Island of Dr. Moreau* and *Lord of the Flies*.

Life of Pi: the I and the Tiger

I ate like an animal.

YANN MARTEL, *Life of Pi*

My commentary on *Life of Pi* has found a place here because of the book's imagination of violence, startling in such a good-humored and witty novel, but the schematic history into which this book has grouped modern castaway fictions begins to show its ragged edges at this juncture. *Life of Pi* could have been placed in the following chapter, because the tiger Richard Parker occupies the position of Friday in the narrative, as "native" companion to the human castaway, so the novel as a revision of Friday could be put with *Foe*, *The Year of Grace*, and Tournier's *Friday*. *Life of Pi* is the story of a young Indian boy who drifts in a lifeboat for 227 days with a Bengal tiger. It is told by Pi himself, though there is an "author" who figures in occasional interpolations recounting how he met Pi in his later life, after Pi's ordeal. So the intense impression of learning and feeling that the first-person narration conveys needs to be qualified by the sense that this "author" must have shaped the text in some way.

We learn first of Pi's growing up in Pondicherry, where his father runs a zoo—of how he named himself; how he became an adherent in turn of Islam, Hinduism, and Christianity; how the family decided to migrate, with zoo, to America; and of the fierce storm that sank the ship, the rest of Pi's family, and most of the animals. Pi found himself the sole human on a lifeboat, and the story of his time as a castaway began.

The lifeboat has a topography, and Pi reasons and works to survive: this is definitely a castaway narrative, though the "island" perpetually drifts and is threatened by seas and storms.[24] At its heart—and this is a novel with heart on sleeve—this is the story of Pi's relations with Richard Parker, whom he fears, tames, comes to love, and comes to resemble. Combine the relationship with Richard Parker and the overall intense up-closeness to nature and the body (sea, storms, fish, blood, vomit) that results from the fact that Pi's island is a small boat and from his struggle to survive, and we have a reassessment of the castaway's life in nature. Nature here is not something the castaway can use or enjoy or destroy at will, yet Pi is working with it, not, as in many narratives of shipwreck and survival, simply drifting and starving. Further, there are values and realities beyond the scope of reason, as Pi says: "I applied my reason at every moment. Reason is excellent for getting food, clothing and shelter. Reason is the very best toolkit. Nothing beats reason for keeping tigers away. But be excessively reasonable and you risk throwing out the universe with the bathwater" (Martel 2002, 298).

Beyond reason, and defining its limits, there are the spiritual and the imaginative, both of them often invoked by Pi.[25] "The world isn't just the way it is. It is how we understand it, no? And in understanding something, we bring something to it, no? Doesn't that make life a story?" (303). Conversely, the struggle for survival, shaped at every step by reason, brings Pi to the brink of the degeneration and cannibalism that have haunted the castaway narrative in its modern revisions.

Pi has always been a gentle boy, and one attuned to what he happily acknowledges as greater than himself, as we see in the early account of his embrace simultaneously of the Hindu, Christian, and Moslem religions, though this also illustrates his readiness to go his own way. He loves his family, admires his religious mentors, is grateful to his teachers.

He doesn't leave his family behind; he loses it in the shipwreck that begins his lonely voyage. Individualism is certainly not his creed, but on the lifeboat he has to see to his own survival. The task leads to some tough choices and some fierce actions. The novel's deepest testing and rethinking of the castaway as isolated subject comes in the connections and contrasts between his dependence on the tiger (and the tiger's dependence on him) on the one hand, and on the other hand the violence that intensifies as the story unfolds. In my judgment, the connections and contrasts are left unresolved at the end of the novel.

It is an amazing story: 227 days in an open boat with a ferocious tiger. Perhaps more amazing than true, perhaps more true than plausible. (Yet we have recently had the yearlong drift of José Salvador Alvarenga from Mexico—where Pi and Richard Parker will drift—to the Marshall Islands.) There are plenty of postmodern signals and winks. Martel has written that the novel's theme is that "reality is a story and we can choose our story and so why not pick 'the better story' (the novel's key words)."[26] While demonstrating in detail the inescapable demands of material needs and realities, *Life of Pi* continually reminds us that the world is malleable and indeterminate. It's not just that these contending elements interplay in the novel; each is pressed to its limits.

Pi has renamed himself, and his given name referred to a swimming pool ("Piscine"). Richard Parker received his unexpectedly dull and Anglo name by bureaucratic mistake.[27] Pi's self-given name is that of the number that "runs on forever" (Martel 2002, 285), indeterminate like his story, and one doesn't know whether to laugh or cry at the irony of his original name, given his fate as a castaway on the wide ocean. The story is grim and testing; the text is embroidered with verbal and conceptual play. Early on, Pi several times teases us by mentioning Richard Parker but withholding the fact that this is a tiger not a man (and he works the same tease with the orangutan Orange Juice).[28]

The shipwreck that initiates the central episode plunges us into the full-on drama of the adventure novel: "I was alone and orphaned, in the middle of the Pacific, hanging on to an oar, an adult tiger in front of me, sharks beneath me, a storm raging about me" (107). At a later crisis he tells us, "I felt like a prisoner being pushed off a plank by pirates" (154). This is a story, and stories plumb the heights and depths. It's a postmodern story, and postmodern stories know that they are stories and recognize that the world is as we imagine it—or is partly as we imagine it, a significant qualification. Awareness of story embraces awareness of castaway stories: we can note that Pi keeps no calendar (194), but does keep a journal (208); that of course he has read *Robinson Crusoe* (73), and that there is a variation on the trope of the footprint.[29] "Ultimately, a foot is the only good judge of land" advises the survival manual that Pi finds on the lifeboat, so he tests the seeming island that he and Richard Parker reach late in the story by gingerly stepping on to it. The place seems to pass this practical test, but even at the time, Pi is dubious (258).

The story is also controlled and serious, as (arguably) stories should be. The element of knowing tricksiness is persistent but never dominant. Pi realizes that he cannot hope to kill Richard Parker; he will have to tame him and keep him alive, and we learn in great detail how he does both these things. The narrative of Pi's early life with his zookeeping family in Pondicherry carefully prepares us for what he does on the lifeboat.[30] In this preliminary section of the text, we learn a lot about zoos and about animals: Animals can be perfectly content in zoos, provided they are kept comfortable and have a clear territory and a clear routine (they like monotony: we must not see their situation in human terms). Animals are ferocious (Pi's father teaches his family this by means of a shocking demonstration involving a tiger and a goat), but they are capable of accepting incongruous relationships with members of other species (we learn of rhinos and goats happily cohabiting). And this is the clue to how a fierce beast can be tamed: the lions come to accept their trainer as the alpha male in the pride.[31] All this is reasoned and plausible and helps us to accept what Pi achieves with Richard Parker as they drift alone across the Pacific. It also clears the ground for the complexity of what happens between Pi and Richard

Parker, by refuting various assumptions and sentimentalities about animals and zoos.

It follows from this reasonableness that, once Pi is cast away, the novel gives a lot of scope to the attitudes of the classic castaway narrative. Pi reasons and plans; he devotes himself to his own survival; he works with what he is given. We learn the exact topography of the lifeboat (137–39). We have an inventory of everything in the supply locker, and this is the equivalent of the episode of salvage that is commonly part of a castaway narrative (145–46). Fortunately the boat—intended for thirty-two survivors—is well supplied and all the equipment works well, including the rain catchers and the solar stills. There's a kind of luxury about this that updates the abundance of eighteenth-century material goods that Robinson Crusoe's salvage details. Nonetheless, Pi has a lot of work to do, and he has to think hard about details. He makes himself a raft out of oars, lifejackets, and rope; towed behind the lifeboat, the raft is safe from Richard Parker and gives Pi time to consider how to tame the tiger. (The image of the bulky lifeboat with Richard Parker on board, and Pi on the small, fragile raft attached to it, is a memorable feature of Ang Lee's film of the novel.) He plans, and defines his tasks:

> I had to devise a training program for Richard Parker. [. . .] I had to start fishing very soon. [. . .] I had to find a means of sheltering myself. [. . .] I had to improve the raft. At present it was seaworthy, but hardly habitable. I would have to make it fit for living in until I could move to my permanent quarters on the lifeboat. [. . .]
>
> [. . .] Survival starts by paying attention to what is close at hand and immediate. (168–69)

He realizes that the raft acts as a sea anchor for the lifeboat, and then sees that by rocking the raft, he can rock the lifeboat and make Richard Parker seasick, and this helps him to tame the tiger. All this is like an epitome of the practical, detail-oriented aspects of the castaway narrative.

But this account of reasoning and working is only one of the text's modes, or rather moods. The narrative has a characteristic rhythm, whereby crisp clarity collapses into anticlimax or shifts into lyricism. The passage just quoted continues:

> There was so much I had to do.
>
> I looked out at the empty horizon. There was so much water. And I was all alone. All alone.
>
> I burst into hot tears. I buried my face in my crossed arms and sobbed. My situation was patently hopeless. (169)

Even this is not so very different from the abrupt alternations of practical work and religious musings in *Robinson Crusoe*. It's simply compressed by this restless rhythm, with a quick allusion to "The Rime of the Ancient Mariner" thrown in.

Other revisions of common preoccupations of the castaway narrative are more compelling, and more disturbing. Martel expresses and revises the fear of degeneration and the anxiety about cannibalism that haunts the genre. The two are welded together, made to stem from the obsession with eating that belongs to any story about drifting in an open boat, and brought into a revealing connection to Pi's relations with Richard Parker.

Even the sinking ship has gross bodily processes. It goes down with a "burp" (97, 303). "All around me was the vomit of a dyspeptic ship" (101). Pi at first finds himself in the lifeboat with an injured zebra, a hyena, an orangutan, and Richard Parker. Hyenas, we are told, eat anything—practically everything. They sometimes eat their own kind (117). This hyena eats the zebra while it is still alive, and from the inside. The text goes into detail (not so the film):

> There was no order to what it was doing. It bit here, swallowed there, seemingly overwhelmed by the riches before it. After devouring half the liver, it started tugging on the whitish, balloon-like stomach bag. But it was heavy, and the zebra's haunches being higher than its belly—and blood being slippery—the hyena started to slide into its victim. It plunged head and shoulders into the zebra's guts, up to the knees of its front legs. It pushed itself out, only to slide back down. It finally settled into this position, half in, half out. (125)

It's enough to make the reader into a vegetarian—but necessity is forcing Pi in the other direction. Next the hyena kills and eats Orange Juice, the motherly and loveable orangutan, but—"it would get its own just desserts soon enough" (136)—Richard Parker, who had been suffering from seasickness (more vomit), revives, and eats the hyena. In a way, Pi doesn't *experience* the loss of his mother, father, and brother; they are simply gone. Instead, soon after the ship sinks, he experiences this ghastly, but natural, animal ferocity. Perhaps the second trauma masks the first. At the very end of the novel, in response to the skepticism of the first hearers of his story, Pi will retell his story, substituting humans, including his mother, for the animals in this episode, and a shocking scene of murder and cannibalism will follow (304–11).

As time passes, Pi learns to kill enough for himself and a hungry tiger, and he learns to eat raw and rapidly. There is a graphic early description of his agonized efforts to kill a flying fish, wrapping it in a blanket and breaking its neck. Later, he bashes a big threshing dorado with a hatchet, and witnesses its "iridescent" death, stabs young sharks through the eyes, hauls turtles on board, butchers them, and drinks their blood.[32] He marks his portion of the lifeboat, his territory, with his urine just as Richard Parker marks his territory; he takes possession of the tiger's feces because he is the dominant male on the boat (211). He eats in a rush because Richard Parker is hungrily waiting:

> Sometimes I just didn't have the time to consider what was before me. It either went into my mouth that instant or was lost to Richard Parker, who was pawing and stamping the ground and huffing impatiently on the edge of his territory. It came as an unmistakable indication to me of how low I had sunk the day I noticed, with a pinching of the heart, that I ate like an animal, that this noisy, frantic, unchewing wolfing-down of mine was exactly the way Richard Parker ate. (225)

This is the trope of degeneration, so important to *The Island of Dr. Moreau* and *Lord of the Flies*. But the significance is different. Neither Richard Parker nor Pi is a "beast," in the language of the earlier depictions of degeneration. Richard Parker is an animal and Pi has become one, but the novel gives a detailed, sympathetic picture of what it is to be an animal, especially in the way it sees Richard Parker—awe-inspiring, submissive, grumpy, content, bored, living magnificently in the instant. Pi doesn't cease to fear Richard Parker—he tells us that he fears him when it is necessary to do so (222)—but he comes to love him, and simply to live with him. (The hyena comes close to standing outside of the circle that encloses humans and other animals and thus, in effect, to being a "beast"; and hyenas are capable of cannibalism [117], but the hyena is also depicted as a kind of parody or caricature of an animal [116].)

This blend of love, respect, fear, control, and fascination in Pi's relationship with Richard Parker is surely what most readers remember from *Life of Pi*. In finding things in himself, as castaways do, Pi has found things in himself and Richard Parker. The novel defines their utter separateness (human being and tiger), yet intense togetherness and interdependence. Humans are bodily creatures who are part of nature as tigers and sharks are, but they are something else as well: rational, spiritual, imaginative. Martel makes a compelling narrative intervention in a range of scientific, ecological, and posthumanist thinking about animals, humans, and nature.[33] The arguments and studies are made flesh in the dealings of Pi and Richard Parker.

The final effect of the novel is, however, more equivocal. As the story of Pi and Richard Parker's long adventure nears its end, we have two episodes of increasing weirdness, stretching the credibility of the novel's realism. They are followed by a grisly coda that is challenging in the same way. The first involves the encounter of Pi (temporarily blind and starving by this stage) with another drifting castaway, also blind and starving. It begins with an exchange of food fantasies, Indian and French, segues into talk of eating cigarettes and boots, and culminates in death and cannibalism (240–56). The stranger, who may be the cook from Pi's ship, confesses that he has already committed murder, tries to strangle Pi and get at his heart and liver, and is eaten by Richard Parker, after which Pi fishes with some of his remains, and eats some of his remains. Extraordinary coincidence is combined with black comedy and ghastly violence. The second episode involves a sojourn on a green, lush island that turns out not to be an island, because it floats, and is also sinister and carnivorous (256–83). The episode combines comedy (the multitude of tame meerkats, the only animals on the island) with the grotesque that out-Poes Edgar Allan Poe (the discovery of thirty-two human teeth embedded in what Pi has taken to be fruit: evidently the last remains of some unfortunate earlier castaway). Then, when Pi has arrived in Mexico and been rescued, he tells his story to a pair of Japanese marine investigators. When they are skeptical, he offers them by way of alternative story a grim narrative of murder and cannibalism. This narrative is based on, but easily exceeds, his first horrific hours on the lifeboat with the killing and eating of the zebra, orangutan, and hyena in the story we have been reading. According to Pi's alternative story, the cook, Pi, his mother, and a sailor with a broken leg made it into the lifeboat. The others forcibly amputated the sailor's broken leg; Pi and the cook secretly ate the lifeboat's supply of biscuits; the sailor died, and the cook was caught eating part of his corpse; the cook killed Pi's mother, and Pi killed the cook and ate him. It's not hard to see this as parody, but not easy to be sure what lies behind it in Pi's feelings about his mother's death.

By inserting these extreme episodes, Martel qualifies the warm and complex impression left by the relationship between Pi and Richard Parker. Each episode comes to rest on cannibalism: the encounter with the hallucinated other castaway and the sojourn on the floating island more or less obliquely, and the alternative story of Pi's time on the lifeboat explicitly in a welter of blood. These passages parody the trope of cannibalism in the castaway tradition, pushing it to an almost ludicrous extreme. It's as if the novel gets rid of this material by exaggerating it, vomiting it forth, to borrow one of *Life of Pi*'s habitual images. This can happen because at the heart of the novel is the relationship between Pi and Richard Parker, and this clarifies what a human is and what an animal is, so that Pi's degeneration, if it is that, in the main story is degeneration to animality not "bestiality."

This discussion of *Life of Pi* has emphasized the complex way in which Martel draws a line under two of the anxieties that haunted the castaway narrative in its many grim and violent twentieth-century revisions: degeneration and cannibalism. *Life of Pi* also finds space in the skeptical maneuvers of the postmodern novel for a more positive depiction of the subject's place in nature, and with nature.

3

Reconciliation

5

Always Another Island

Females and Fridays

Il y a toujours une autre île.
JEAN GUÉHENNO

But my poor island's still
un-rediscovered, un-renamable.
None of the books has ever got it right.
ELIZABETH BISHOP, "Crusoe in England"

This chapter[1] discusses a variety of novels that in very different ways rethink or revise or laugh at the Crusoe tradition, and this without the violence and insanity that entered the castaway novel with H. G. Wells's *The Island of Dr. Moreau* and was explored in a series of later fictions, many of them in direct intertextual relations with *Moreau*. Wells's novel intervenes so forcefully in the tradition of the castaway novel as to divert its course in radical ways, but the texts considered here ignore it and make *Robinson Crusoe* their target text. This chapter begins with Jean Giraudoux's *Suzanne and the Pacific (Suzanne et le Pacifique*, 1921), and then discusses Michel Tournier's *Friday or The Other Island* (1967, revised 1972: *Vendredi ou Les Limbes du Pacifique*), Cristina Fernández Cubas's *The Year of Grace* (*El Año de Gracia*, 1985), and J. M. Coetzee's *Foe* (1986). This diverse set of texts shares critical or ironic attitudes to Defoe's *Robinson Crusoe*. It is not argued here that these novels make a tradition or are influenced by each other, but that their revisions of Defoe share significant similarities. As the title of this chapter suggests, female castaways are introduced, and the figure of Friday is revised. Female castaways challenge the tradition's emphasis on practical work and on making use of the resources of the island (and other people, such as Friday). Regarding the relations of Friday and Crusoe, and regarding what they show us of language and textuality, these various castaway tales end up in similar places. Friday is no longer to be taken for granted as simple and subordinate. He is elusive and challenging or demanding. The business of naming the island, and of making a narrative of the castaway's sojourn on the island, for instance in a journal, is made problematic. In this chapter, these threads of revision are traced.

These novels don't belong with the phase of violence that has been discussed in the previous two chapters. They do question *Robinson Crusoe*'s (and its nineteenth-century successors') confidence in work and improvisation, and in the sovereignty of the Western male, but this questioning doesn't lead to the headlong degeneration into violence and irrationality that we observed in castaway tales from *Moreau* to *The Beach*. Nor do they quite initiate the phase of reconciliation that will be discussed in the next two chapters, although in a general way their confidence in human imagination and in the unpredictability of nature anticipates themes to be traced in this phase. This refusal to fit into a clear pattern is inconvenient, considering the argument of this book and its reliance on the contention that there are three phases in the history of the castaway tale; but history is not always neat, and this group of texts includes some of the most intelligent and most enjoyable to be discussed in *Castaway Tales*.

Suzanne and the Pacific concerns a lone female castaway on a comfortable island, and the castaway's femaleness, indeed her femininity, is central. As we will see, Suzanne has plenty to occupy her time, but is never involved in work or struggle, and never seems lonely. She is scornful of castaways of the Crusoe type. She plays with language. Tournier's *Friday* is set in the eighteenth century and gives us a Crusoe and a Friday but, as we will see, reverses their relationship. In this version of the castaway tale, Crusoe's work is hardly practical; it is a matter of almost ludicrous organization of a replica of civilization. It is brought to an end by the actions and free spirit of Friday, even though Crusoe had rescued and attempted to educate him, as in Defoe. In *The Year of Grace*, Daniel is on a year's holiday (a year of grace) when he is shipwrecked on an island off the coast of Scotland, already inhabited by Grock but otherwise wild and deserted. This time, Daniel, civilized and educated, becomes the servant, and eventually the companion, of the illiterate but strong-willed Grock; his main work is to read to him. The relationship between the equivalents of Crusoe and Friday, Daniel and Grock, is again reversed.

Foe, like *Friday*, replays *Robinson Crusoe* in that we have a Cruso (so spelled) and a Friday. This Cruso is taciturn and unenterprising, and this Friday, a figure of mystery, has been mutilated and cannot talk. The story begins with the arrival of another castaway, Susan Barton, who already has a complicated past, including a sojourn in Bahia. Not long afterward all three leave the island, Cruso dies, and the story continues back in England where (to simplify) Foe is trying to get Susan to acknowledge a person who might be her long-lost daughter. Susan is trying to get Foe (that is, Defoe, the author) to write her story, and eventually trying to teach Friday to write. Susan's story as we have it in the novel is thus superimposed on Defoe's novel, which is not yet written at the time of Susan's involvement with Foe and with Friday. *Foe* thus centers around contests over language and narrative, but, as will be argued here, these contests are enlivened by Susan's vitality.

In the discussion of *Robinson Crusoe* in Chapter 1, it was suggested that the novel's plain style tends to exclude or at least firmly control whatever might threaten or disrupt practical reason and concentration on the here and now of material things. In Chapters 3 and 4, the irrational and even insane surfaced and took control, but the creative powers of the unconscious were hardly in evidence. Now, with these revisions of Friday, the impulsive and imaginative, and that which resists or eludes language, makes a return, in varying forms, touched with Tournier's didacticism in his Friday, darkly elusive in Coetzee's Friday, rough and uncompromising in Fernández Cubas's Grock.

Suzanne and the Pacific

Un parc, un salon.

JEAN GIRAUDOUX, *Suzanne et le Pacifique*

Suzanne and the Pacific was published in 1921, well before the grim and disabused revisions of the castaway narrative that after Golding broaden to a flood. It makes a remarkable contrast to all these works, because its take on the castaway's subjectivity is so different, and it displays no interest in the idea that either the necessities of survival or the nature of the human animal will bring out a toughness or a violence in the individual. Even its most strikingly serious passage, in which sailors killed in a naval battle in World War I are washed up on Suzanne's remote island, is tender and almost domestic in style. Yet its refusal of the tradition of Protestant shipwreck narratives is emphatic (Giraudoux 1961, 6: 100), even before the passage in which Suzanne reads and mocks a copy of *Robinson Crusoe* that has also usefully come ashore. In spirit it's Watteau not Defoe. The postwar context is also important: a refusal of seriousness and a delight in play might well take on a new salience in 1921. The parallel would be with figures such as Colette, Cocteau, and Dufy.

Suzanne and the Pacific could possibly be read as a novel about the passage from adolescence to womanhood in Suzanne, the island as a liminal place marking her passage, just as the narrative moves from the belle époque through World

War I to the 1920s, a crucial passage for France. Yet if this structure is put in place, it is not filled out: Giraudoux emphasizes ease of transition rather than breaks and changes; and Suzanne is sophisticated from the beginning and not overly mature at the end (for instance, she falls in love with each of her three rescuers in turn, and rapidly).

Suzanne is an alert, sunny, well-brought-up French girl, eighteen at the beginning of the story. It's characteristic of her to involve herself with a group of friends or companions, evoke them lightly, with appreciation rather than intimacy, and then leave them behind.

The story begins with a stroke of luck. She wins a prize from a newspaper, the "Sydney Daily," for the best saying about ennui: "Si un homme s'ennuie, excitez-le; si une femme s'ennuie, retenez-le," and the prize is a trip: "En échange d'un conseil aussi utile pour elle l'Australie m'appelait" (1: 25).[2] Derrida begins his seminar on Crusoe in Volume II of *The Beast and the Sovereign* by musing, "Was Robinson Crusoe bored? Was he even alone, this man, because this man is a man, a human and a male human (not a woman), let's never forget it; nothing equivalent or similar, analogous, was ever, to my knowledge (but I may be wrong) written about a woman alone: like an island in an island" (Derrida 2011, 2).

It would have been fascinating to have Derrida's thoughts on Suzanne, who is solitary but not sovereign; but he is right here, in that the topic of boredom is what wins Suzanne her cruise, but she is never bored on her island. Again, if her stay on the island is to be an idyll, so, largely, were her earlier sojourns in Bellac and Paris and on the ship. Each time, people reveal and then reassuringly repeat themselves, and seem little different from the natural things that accompany them (a pet monkey, a pet owl: "La chouette, qui tous les soirs sortait de la cale saluée par le mot 'chouette' en toutes les langues du monde, et voltigeait autour du navire" [Giraudoux 1961, 3: 54]).[3]

Then we have the shipwreck. This is seen so thoroughly through Suzanne's eyes (bewildered, though not frightened) that it's not altogether clear what sank the ship, or how all the others drowned. What is clear is that she is shepherded and helped by her friends and companions, Naki and Nenetza, who make sure she has her life jacket on, that she has a raft, with a few useful things on it (an umbrella, a fur), and in effect sacrifice themselves. Giraudoux is here organizing the requisite shipwreck and the usual deaths of everyone but the future castaway.[4] There is usually a contrast between the luck that is necessary to get the castaway onto the island when others perish and the hard work that will be the basis of survival once there, and in many castaway fictions this introduces an alternation of powerlessness and power that extends through the narrative as a whole. Here, her friends serve and cherish Suzanne just as will the island.

She is cast away in a very comfortable place. Everything she could want is provided—fruit, cosmetics, hot and cold baths, flocks of birds, feathers for her bed. She settles in quickly. She doesn't marvel at the isle and its provisions, because its scents remind her of ones she knows already ("Rose D'Orsay, Ambre Antique, le Mouchoir de Monsieur" [4: 66]), and even the vivid green of the neighboring island shines "comme les arrêts facultatifs des tramways, á Paris" (67).[5]

Suzanne and the Pacific uses the island sojourn as opportunity for exploration and expansion of subjectivity. There are no dangers, no challenges to exertion. We have in fact a long list of the things that did *not* happen to her on her island ("Ce n'est pas vrai . . .": a passing ship that tragically could not hear her cries or notice the tunic that she waved, not to mention her body left naked while she waved the tunic; all the deaths she might have met or desired; and so on). She imagines all the winds that buffet the island during a storm as desiring to win her favor and become gods of this or that (the god of caresses, for instance), and feels privileged, with her European education and the power it gives her to bestow names, so that the winds have chosen her for their appeals over some Polynesian queen on a neighboring island (5: 93). She subjectifies the island—humanizing a twisted tree trunk that seems like a hip, holes in bark that seem like eyes. It's not that she needs the isle and what can be made out of it, as in most castaway stories; the isle needs her—to kill a boa that comes ashore on some driftwood for instance; she knocks it on the head as it sleeps (5: 88). This might lightly recall the power that castaways or other sojourners on islands enjoy, from Prospero to Moreau and through to the insanity of Frank in *The Wasp Factory*. But the inscription that will eventually be carved on a rock on what is called, for the first time in the novel, "L'Ile de Suzanne" is surely right in saying that egoism is one of the things she conquered. Earlier she talks of "Cette île qui est devenue de mon âme un miroir que je confond avec elle," which is rather different from identifying the island with oneself (9: 167).[6]

Once we accept the Cockaigne-like plenitude and hospitality of this island, we see how thoroughly masculinized is the island that Crusoe works and shapes, and how abstract the island in many later stories. We enjoy the flourishing of Suzanne's sensibility and imagination, the recovery of a sense of the mild and beneficent in untouched nature—the nature that doesn't need to be worked on or that you wouldn't bother to work on. It's all carefully limited, however, just as was the possibility of loneliness and depression for Crusoe. The island is not so much strange for Suzanne as new: even the sparrows are colorful, but they are still sparrows; she wakes up "près des cacaos embaumes," as formerly next to "mon chocolat"; everything on the island had its equivalents in Paris. (No doubt the luxurious or comfortable things she enjoyed in Paris had a colonial origin in the first place: chocolate came from cacao.) When she is imagining the winds appealing to her to make them gods, what recalls her to herself is the thought of "mes vrais maîtres" who turn out to be the mundane authority figures of home, the tram conductor and so on (93). She deheroicizes Crusoe's experience. She mentions some small hurts and cuts, and says that these scratches were the nicks ("des coches" [97]) that marked the passing of time, in allusion to the way Crusoe recorded the passing of his heroic twenty-eight years on his island with notches on a pole.

"Everything that only poets see in France, here one sees with the naked eye," Suzanne proclaims (9: 166), but it's also true that she makes the island into an equivalent of France. When she eventually shows her island to her three handsome rescuers, she says that she has spent five years preparing it, and has made the island into "un parc, un salon" (10: 201).

There is too much of this blitheness and whimsy in the novel, but still it's notable that as other contemporary authors revise Defoe, or revise Wells's revision of Defoe and Swift, they only tighten the grip of necessity, or the power of uncontrollable or insane ego or instinct. Suzanne is merely annoyed by the drifting ashore of a map that discloses the "stupid" name of her island, which she won't even mention (8: 176). She uses language in an arbitrary and fanciful way. She devises names for unique island sights and phenomena: 200 invented words that will never leave the island where they were born, nouns with switched gender or that change gender—her moon is sometimes male and sometimes female. (Derrida [2011, 4], in meditating on Robinson Crusoe, plays with language and gender, making a concordance between "une île" and "une 'il,'" the words for island and he, but the play is his, and Robinson Crusoe has no such option.) Even Frank in *The Wasp Factory*, who has his own whimsy and wit, is the prisoner of obsessions and compulsions. He gives everything a name but he feels under pressure to get the names right; they are portentous not freewheeling, though in the end when his control and his sense of himself has unraveled, he will have to change his own name. Suzanne alone among the castaways discussed in this chapter feels no impulse to set down her experiences in a journal, as Fernández Cubas's Daniel and Tournier's Robinson do, or to make a text of them as Susan wants Foe to do in Coetzee's novel. Suzanne has lots of desires but few needs; she is an Eve without an Adam, and she knocks the snake on the head before it can do any harm.

Giraudoux includes two passages that strikingly widen the scope of his story. One concerns World War I, the other, *Robinson Crusoe.* Suzanne is awoken at night by the sound of a cannon.[7] She imagines the advent of rescue and almost decides to swim out to the ship, like someone catching the all-stations train because they can't be bothered to wait for the express, as she characteristically puts it. But there is more gunfire, and more: not a rescue, but a battle at sea. Then a corpse is washed up, and the text lingers over this—the tattoos that announce him to be Johnny Smith from Leeds, tell us his various girls in various ports, and so on. Then more bodies: eventually seven German and ten British. Here Giraudoux offers serious parody of the lucky retrievals of Crusoe, most obviously from his shipwreck. Suzanne, for her part, ends up with rum and ink, and a collection of things found in the dead sailors' pockets, such as tram tickets that evoke various homely trips around Heidelberg or Coblentz (8: 159–60). It's lightly done, and there is no description of wounds or the effects of drowning, but Suzanne realizes she is at the extreme edge of a vast conflict, and a newspaper gives her the casualties so far: 8 million. This is how men enter her agreeable and feminized island, as tenderly cared-for victims, with behind them the almost unimaginable carnage of the war.[8] And there is an allusion to Crusoe's discovery of the footprint: as she drags the dead English sailor ashore, Suzanne looks back, "j'eus la même angoisse, à voir mes empreintes profondes, en me retournant, qu'à voir celles d'un inconnu" ["I felt the same anguish at seeing my deep prints, when I turned round, as in seeing those of an unknown man"] (157). We guess that her footprints are "profondes," and she is making a mark on her island for the first time, because she is dragging a corpse. This is the moment that suggests she has passed out of her phase of self-sufficiency, not the later passages in which she falls in love with her rescuers or comes to terms with the inexplicably evil man she meets in New York. Again, there is a contrast with Tournier's Robinson, who also encounters his own footprint, but in a way that sums up how the island is all about him—his values, his psyche, his sexuality (*Friday*, 53/56).

The second passage actually arouses more heat in Giraudoux and Suzanne than the one about the war. Various scraps of the classics drift ashore—a page or so for all but one—*Robinson Crusoe.* (There is no particular attempt to make any of this plausible; the narrative is a series of tableaux and games.) Suzanne reads the novel with growing anger and contempt. She sees Crusoe as a Puritan overwhelmed by reason, certain that he is the plaything of Providence but not trusting it for a moment, working obsessively. "'Cet homme hardi' ['this bold man'] shivered ceaselessly with fear and only dared to explore his whole island after 13 years"; him with his ten kinds of basket and his three kinds of sickle; fussy and superstitious; with never a thought of a woman. She rounds on him: don't labor three months making a table, squat on the ground; don't waste six months making a prieu-dieu, just kneel down (171–72). There's some knockabout chauvinist scorn: "Encombrant déjà sa pauvre île, comme sa nation plus tard allait faire le monde, de pacotille et de fer-blanc" ["Already burdening his poor island, as his nation was going to do later to the world, with cheap tat and tin"] (9: 171). She says she would have liked to put a handprint on his island, and then disappear: "Que diable aurais-tu dis de cette main de femme" ["You would have said 'what the devil' at this woman's hand"] (172). So much for Crusoe's prudence and ingenuity, his delight in material things and his stubborn work, his complex fear at the sign of a footprint on his island: "Because above all he never imagines for a moment that the footprint might be a feminine footprint. Il, the Il, an il, him, an island [*île*] and not them [*elles*], no woman" (Derrida 2011, 55).

Eventually Suzanne is rescued, by a party of handsome rich English milords, and returned to civilization. Giraudoux has some astute points to make about her transition from idealization, to disillusionment, to a kind of balance. We end with the dawn of her arrival back in France, the rural sights and sounds, mist and birdsong, and also her encounter on the road with, as it were, the spirit of the Third Republic, the Controller of Weights and Measures, with his grand moustaches and his grey stamp collector's eyes ("avec l'amour des collections de timbres" [10: 219]).

Friday, or The Limbo of the Pacific

I grope in search of myself in this forest of allegory.

MICHEL TOURNIER, *Friday or The Other Island*

TOURNIER AND DEFOE

Michel Tournier's *Friday* is explicitly a version of *Robinson Crusoe*—Robinson and Friday have the same names, many incidents are repeated, Robinson spends the same span of time on his island ("twenty-eight years, two months and an unspecified number of days" [Tournier 1969, 206/1972, 235]).[9] There are lots of variations, however, in the circumstances and details, even before we get to the major and drastic changes in significance, style, and psychology. Tournier's Robinson is married and a Quaker, not a reckless restless sailor and slave trader. His memories of his youth in York are mostly peaceful ones centering on his mother. Friday is neither Robinson's slave nor his servant for long; he is the means of his transcendence, a feckless child of nature who helps precipitate a metamorphosis that Robinson has himself begun to await by this stage of the novel.

Tournier's Friday doesn't have much relation to actual Native Americans or Africans, though he is said to be a combination of both. He is an idealized figure, the male equivalent of a nymph, though with touches of wildness and roughness. When a British ship eventually arrives off the island, it is Friday who embarks, however, and Robinson who stays, to resume his sun-bronzed idyll with another boy, the oppressed cabin boy who has sneaked ashore from the ship, and whom Robinson rechristens Sunday after the day of "the youth of all things and the day of our master, the Sun" (224/254).[10]

So *Friday* orients itself in relation to *Robinson Crusoe*, and then takes the story in a very different direction. Regarding Friday himself, Tournier takes Defoe's framework and then revisits the long French (and British) debate on the innocence and free sexuality, or the licentiousness and cruelty, of the natives of the South Seas. This is a debate that is launched in Bougainville and Diderot and in a more general way in Rousseau in response to the first European sojourns on Tahiti, which took place during the years in which the novel is set.[11] Tournier exaggerates, embroiders, and makes comic the elements of the picture that emerged in the eighteenth century and that continued to fascinate Westerners to the times of Robert Louis Stevenson and Gauguin. In Friday he intertwines free sensuality and unconscious cruelty, but refuses anthropological specificity of a kind that often tripped up the earlier voyagers and commentators because Tahitian customs were much harder to read than they supposed. In his reflections on *Friday* in his autobiography, Tournier says that the novel was inspired by his time at the Musée de l'Homme and the "tutelage" of Claude Lévi-Strauss, but nonetheless indicates that this is not an anthropological novel, because he makes no attempt to give the details of Friday's indigenous culture.[12] Instead, Friday more or less floats free, exotic, unsocialized, and tethered, if to anything, to hints of classic pastoral, for instance in the making of his Aeolian harp—but as soon as one notes that, one has to note Tournier's selective and even parodic relation to pastoral. The way Friday feeds the lame vulture, for instance, goes beyond the pastoral, as of shepherds and goatherds, into the gross. He chews the maggots himself before giving them to the bird.

The tropes and the constitutive conditions of *Robinson Crusoe* figure in *Friday*: the futile construction of a boat that can't be gotten to the water, and later the more successful making of a smaller canoe;[13] the recording of the passing of time (Tournier's Robinson goes further and devises also a water clock); the interest in growing wheat and making bread; the discovery of the footprint; the visits of frightening natives; the rescue of Friday; the looming of madness in solitude; and the urge to order and name. The novel is in effect inserting Tournier's own investigation of the solitary life in nature into the framework that Defoe provided, and combining Defoe's eighteenth century with a very different one, that of the South Seas voyagers and their commentators. At times Tournier breaks this double framework, at times he leaves it in place, but when there is parody in the novel, it is at least as often parody of his own inventions as of Defoe's.

Friday is taking Robinson on a journey of radical self-transformation that will bring him to bronzed solar nakedness and brotherhood with Friday, and in the course of this journey, behaviors that might seem reminiscent of Defoe's Robinson and behaviors that are excluded from Defoe's novel are both taken to extremity and then abandoned, or surpassed. Like Defoe's Robinson, Tournier's cultivates wheat, and refrains from eating any of his first crop so that he may have plenty of seed corn; but the novel's pull is toward sensuous metaphor: the warm bread dough that Robinson remembers from his childhood, and that is associated with his mother and with the moist warmth of the inside of his island (73/81). We pass from administration and cultivation, which is already schematized and engaged in for symbolic rather than practical reasons, to indulgence of the flesh, in contact with the body of the island, and then to a kind of idyll with Friday in which sexuality is diffused, a matter of "a soft jubilation that exalts and pervades me from head to foot" (201/229) and the sun is worshipped.[14] We go deep into the darkness and milky moistness of the telluric and then high into the airy and solar. The result is that Defoe's novel provides us with lots of fascinating points of view on Tournier's, both when the latter touches on the earlier text and when it deliberately (and to extremity) opens matters that Defoe excludes—the possibility of madness and the irrational; sexuality; self-abandonment.

Friday begins with a prologue in which the ship's captain turns over Tarot cards that image what is going to happen to Robinson on the island, so that the schematic, symbolic, and fated are underlined from the beginning. Tournier's Robinson is not going to *make* his life on the island; he is going to experience it, to pass through it in experiencing a series of phases of transformation. He faces the possibility of a kind of fugue and regression to mindlessness almost from his first arrival on the island. Once the fear of madness has entered his mind, we are told, "It was never to leave it" (20/23). He doesn't bother to salvage from the wreck at first, though it is clearly visible; nor does he take measures to mark the passing of time at first, so that when eventually he does, he has no idea how long he has already been on the island (which explains the puzzling phrase "an unspecified number of days" for the notation of the duration of his stay on the island).

He does construct an ambitiously large boat, as did Defoe's Robinson. This is virtually the only time one of his projects of work and ordering is described in detail, though he has plenty of these projects in the early phase of his time on the island, as will be seen in a moment. Even though his boat (the "*Escape*" or "*Evasion*") is clearly something of a technical feat for one man, we are told that as he labors, he exists "in a kind of somnambulistic torpor, beyond weariness or haste" (28/29). He is scarred and bruised by his work: "There was no builder's time-sheet, but his own body was record enough" (32/35). The emphasis on the body is characteristic of the novel; so is that on an absorption in some state, or place, or time, in which the mind is suspended or blank. It is not that Tournier's Robinson does not think—as will be seen, he thinks a lot, but by way of philosophizing, not by way of practical reasoning such as we find in Defoe.

Sometimes the text briskly cuts Defoe off, as it were, or turns aside indifferently. This is very notable in the vital matter of the visits of the natives. These visits are violent, as in Defoe. The Araucanians come ashore to choose a sacrificial victim, and then kill, dismember, and burn him. Robinson witnesses this a first time without particular horror, and instead quotes the Gospel, "if thy hand or foot offend thee, cast them off and cast them from thee": the Araucanians are evidently primitive Christians in his view. Robinson nonetheless leaves the scene "with a mind beset by doubts" (70/78) and shortly after this, as if by magic, has constructed elaborate fortifications.

The crucial incident in which Robinson saves Friday is even brisker. This time the Araucanians kill one man and begin to turn on another, perhaps, we are told, because he is different, being darker. He runs, Robinson hesitates whether to shoot pursuer or pursued, decides on the latter (better calculated to avoid suspicion), but finds himself shooting the former instead because his dog has bumped him (128/143). There is roughly the same result as in Defoe, because the escapee is grateful and is renamed Friday, but the incident itself is a matter of accident, and there has been none of the worrying about whether one is justified in killing cannibals that is to be found in Defoe.

It will turn out that Friday's gratitude is relatively superficial, because, being young and also a creature of entire, blithe naturalness, everything he does is superficial, and superficiality is what he has to teach. This Friday laughs at Robinson's heavy-handed attempt at Christian instruction, one of the moments in *Robinson Crusoe* where Friday displayed some autonomy, when he asked Robinson some theological questions that he couldn't answer (Defoe 1987, 279–82). This Friday can't work as Robinson demands; even when Robinson beats him he cannot but go his own way, and anyway, at that point Robinson is beating him for imitating Robinson himself in sexual relations with a tree. He is not to be molded by Robinson, as Friday was in Defoe; his function is to mold Robinson, but to do it by his fine ideal superficiality and carelessness.

This takes us closer to the nub of *Friday*. It's a book that is in its way as centered on its hero and his fate and development as was Defoe's. The more the self, the ego, the man of order and administration, timekeeping and routine, is peeled away, the further Robinson penetrates, sinks, and climbs into new realms of the natural, the more thoroughly, ambitiously, and at times ludicrously the text centers on him. The novel is named after Friday because of the importance of his effect on Robinson.[15] Development of the island, as of a colony, a possession, and therefore an expression of one man's power and command, gives way in Tournier to development of the self, in relation to a Nature that for a long time adapts itself very biddably to the self's desires. An illustration of this shift that is not altogether a shift comes with Tournier's rendition of the trope of the footprint: here it is Robinson's own footprint, "his personal signature, the unique token of Robinson, impressed in the living rock," the "seal" of the island's "lord and master" (53/56). This is different from that paradoxical horror at the thought of another human presence that Defoe's Robinson feels: that he might have made the footprint himself, as he suspects for a moment, merely redoubles his vertigo. It is true that at this point, Tournier's Robinson is well into a project of order and administration that can be read as a parody and critique of this enterprise in Defoe's Robinson, because it is taken to such lengths and scarcely has utility as even a pretext. It would follow that he sees the footprint as sign of his rule of the island, though it is significant that the print really is "impressed in the living rock."

Everything becomes a symbol or moral exemplum. Tournier's Robinson builds a house but only sleeps in it on Saturday nights, and dresses in his best to visit it: "By degrees the hut became for him a sort of shrine of human living" ("une sorte de musée de l'humain" [59/66]). He builds a temple dedicated to measurement. He wants a label on each plant, a ring on each bird, a brand on each animal; he wants to change the place into "une construction abstraite, transparente, intelligible jusqua l'os" (67; "a calculated design, visible and intelligible to its very depths" [61]). Not only does he tame the goats, as in Defoe, but he gives each a letter and a number: B13, L24, and so on (83/91). He wants not only to control the island ("Construire, organiser, ordonner" [44/50]) but time itself, which he feels he has "regularisé, maitrisé" (61/67).[16]

This extremism is characteristic of the lengths to which this Robinson goes in all of his phases and changes, whether literally wallowing in the mire with the pigs or erecting a temple to measurement. Is it Defoe's Robinson that is being parodied in the passages about order and administration, or is it self-parody that accompanies the enterprise at each step? It's as if Tournier has seized on the very things that Defoe refuses: on the one hand, that years in total solitude might threaten madness or, at least, strangely unhinged behavior; on the other, that, outside society, almost anything is possible if one wants to indulge in it. Whatever one does, there is no one to watch or talk to. Years pass without Robinson looking in a mirror; when he does, he is disconcerted, feels "disfigured," because he has not smiled for years. Then, in a ludicrous but charming passage, he smiles at his only companion, his dog Tenn, and the dog smiles back (81–82/89–91). Meanwhile he can indulge in his filial or marital relations with his island (to be detailed shortly) with no one to tell him no, or to laugh at him, at least until Friday arrives, and Friday's laughter is not social: he laughs out of enjoyment, not satire. For Tournier's Robinson, solitude, at least on an island like this one, brings both a self-alienation and a sensual freedom, while Defoe's Robinson was almost immune to the first and never experienced the second.

A condition for this new freedom of the castaway is that nature is responsive to all Robinson's plans and fantasies. It's not only that, as in Giraudoux, the island is comfortable and fertile and there seems no particular need to work. It's also that the island is not anthropomorphized, but feminized. Its outline resembles that of a headless woman, "in an attitude wherein submission, fear and simple abandonment were inextricably mingled" (43/46). The name Robinson gives it is female, Speranza. The crucial question will be whether the arrival of Friday, which is what moves Robinson into a new phase of personal development, corrects or simply subtilizes this fantasy of a perfectly biddable nature whereby, it is suggested here, the self-concern always potential in the island narrative is taking a new direction in Tournier.

Here it is useful to backtrack a little. *Friday* brings home forcibly how the island novel allows for the schematic and symbolic. The story of the lone castaway who achieves his survival and makes a version of civilization, thereby showing what he or the author thinks civilization is, cannot be read any way but symbolically or generally. We may no longer see the castaway as Man, but we do commonly see him as Western Man. Tournier is very conscious of this aspect of the island novel; he plays with it, sends it up perhaps, but he also takes it seriously. Robinson lives a good deal of the time inside his own head, and when he acts, his actions are symbolic. He knows this: at first he sees "Friday" as the name neither of a person nor of a thing, and this interpretation reflects his philosophical problem with subjectivity and objectivity, with which he is grappling in his "Log-Book"; later he sees the name as referring to Venus ("la vénusté de Vendredi" [200/228]).

There is perhaps a split, and certainly an unease. The novel oscillates between preoccupation with representation, with signs and symbols, and biological reductionism (masturbating; vomiting; a leech attached to the corner of his mouth when Robinson comes back to himself after wallowing in the mud; rats disgorged from the corpse of the captain of the *Virginia* when Robinson revisits the wreck).[17] Like Defoe's Robinson, Tournier's castaway keeps a journal, called a "Log-Book" (using the English word), not, however, a record of daily events but a series of meditations on subjectivity and objectivity, solitude and society, knowing and being. "Do I possess in myself the massive dose of rationality I wish to administer to Speranza?" says Robinson early on (63/70). The answer in many ways is in the affirmative. The intellectual is embraced; then it is abandoned, but Tournier knows that he is caught in the same trap as other writers who try to imagine total abandonment of ego and mind, such as D. H. Lawrence or J. G. Ballard. The further down this path you go, the more you need symbols, and (so it seems) symbols that you have to label, and labor, so that the path curves back toward the mind after all. The logic of your position tells you to stop writing this book and go outside and sunbathe, but your urge is to use words and symbols to capture the transcendence of mind by body. Robinson at the top of the araucaria, having completed his ascent from the dark inside of the island, imagines his lungs growing outside himself: "He would flaunt that delicate efflorescence, that bouquet of fleshly flowers, in the wide air while a tide of purple ecstasy flowed into his body on the stream of crimson blood" (185/204)—which sounds like the lyrics of a 1960s album featuring very long guitar solos.[18]

ROBINSON: MIND AND BODY

In his "Log-Book," Robinson reasons on the fundamentals of his situation. He emphasizes the implications of solitude. Language depends on society; without others to hear and respond, language goes dead for us. Similarly, personality depends on society; without the need and practice of communicative expressions, one's face becomes expressionless, "disfigured." Because others in the rest of the world who have known him must think him dead, he is effectively dead (117/130).

He analyzes existence and subjectivity in similarly skeptical terms. We can't be sure that when others experience, they experience as we do; we can't ascribe our experiencing to them by way of analogy. And knowing—sensing—does not give us access to the world but obliterates it by centering the world on our sense data. "My eye is the corpse of light and colour" (90/99). Things in themselves have existence, they shine out their beings, but the subject is only intermittently a self, in moments of reflection (88/98).

Tournier is exploring the consequences of solitude, which in this part of *Friday* are bleaker than in *Robinson Crusoe*—Defoe's Robinson is for Tournier in his comments on *Friday* in *The Wind Spirit* "a hero of solitude," "so marvelously adept at coping with the solitude that afflicts us all" (Tournier 1998, 184, 188). He is suggesting the trouble we get into when we detach ourselves from the rest of existence. In *Friday*, however, the problem is largely an intellectual one. Robinson has reasoned his way to this position, and in fact he has come to find himself envying the world apart from himself for a richness of being—of existence—which he finds only intermittently in his knowing and sensing self. And his recourse is already present, both in the rich fertility and femaleness of his island, and in the division in himself that he in effect comes to accept. One part of himself will continue his project of organization and control, while the other prepares for the emergence of a new self, and an other island, by a series of sensual engagements. We have the island as wife, then the island as mother (162/180), and at last his idyll of brotherhood with Friday, through which he comes to a solar self and a diffused, nongenital sexuality.

This different phase of Robinson's experience is written in a different mode, not intellectualizing as in his journal, but by way of actions and places that have a kind of literalness to their symbolism. He enters into a dark cavity inside the island, one that is perfectly shaped to his body. To slide down into this place, he rubs himself with milk and goes head down as if through a gullet. It's a place of "stony nipples and protuberances," "curled papillae," a big mineral flower (95/106). Suspended in this darkness, in a "happy eternity," he recalls his mother. He draws back; he is not a child, and spilling his semen in his island-mother would be incest (103/114).

The next stage in this process is, however, equally literal in what it expresses and signifies. After some observations of the vegetable loves of insects, in the form of the orchid that lures one of the hymenoptera with its imitation of the female genitals, he wonders whether he himself might find the same opportunity, and he does, in a pink combe (punning on the French word for loins) with an acceptant tree. "His liaison with quillai lasted several happy months" (108/120); what is more, it produces offspring, mandrakes, his daughters as he calls them. Even his beard, "growing in the night, had begun to take root in the earth" (123/137). The episode is ended by the arrival of another person, the end of solitude, the beginning of a kind of social difficulty. But even Friday, who accepts that he should be Robinson's slave, has his own will and waywardness. Robinson suspects the adolescent of visiting the pink combe himself, and comes across him there, "the small black buttocks hard at work" (158/177).

FRIDAY: UPWARD TO THE SUN

Friday's arrival, and his submission to his rescuer, at first exacerbates Robinson's urge to control. He disciplines him, sets him useless tasks, beats him. He recognizes a freedom in Friday, and a different relation to nature, but is enraged by his blitheness and his innocent laughter at Robinson's tasks and projects. Chance has to take a hand. Friday has learned to smoke, though he is not supposed to. He carelessly tosses aside his pipe, and all of Robinson's gunpowder—forty kegs of it salvaged from the wreck—goes up in a big explosion. So does much of what he has constructed. Robinson is now released from labor and control that he knew to be futile: "A new Robinson was sloughing off the skin of the old, preparing to accept the decay of his cultivated island and, at the heels of an unthinking guide to enter upon an unknown road" (171/189).

Friday himself changes, opening up vistas for Robinson by a series of actions that have symbolic bearings, but also come to seem more complex and more testing. His relation to nature poses an alternative to Robinson's, which had become split between the intellectual and the sensual. It is not simply idealized, however: Friday gets along with animals, and in effect seduces them away from Robinson, but he can be cruel and violent. He carves a living turtle out of its shell when he wants to make a shield; he fights the great goat Andoar, and out of its remains makes both a kite and an Aeolian harp.[19] The products of his work are suggestive of the Greece of myth rather than the modern West, but the details are described here, as seldom in *Friday*, and in the way Friday goes about his projects we are closer to practical work than with most of Robinson's projects on Speranza. Friday is *making* symbols, without the use of words—words that, according to Robinson, cut us off from objects and imprison us in subjectivity, though they are exuberantly foregrounded in Tournier's writing. *La Vie Sauvage*, Tournier's later revision for children, adds an episode in which Robinson and Friday are imitated in everything they say by a flock of parrots that have come to the island to breed. Friday shows Robinson how they can resort to sign language to communicate silently, and says that anyway, it is better not to talk much (Tournier 2005, 92–96).

Friday draws Robinson toward the sun, the solar, and that is his function in the narrative, but he does so from the basis of this tougher relation to natural things. Robinson climbs dangerously to help Friday when he and Andoar have fallen off a precipice in their combat; Friday's arrows and his kite draw Robinson skyward, and eventually he climbs the tall araucaria and experiences a new being, "sky-love," "a soft jubilation" that "floods with a renewed vitality" (201/229). There's a contrast between these images of openness (climbing up into the sky; making an Aeolian harp) and the lush images of refuge and confinement from Robinson's earlier life on the island. Friday won't even allow the turtle to be safe and confined in its shell; he cuts the shell away and leaves the creature to wander off unprotected into the surf. There's no sex with Friday, who is now felt to be a brother, indeed a twin, but of an exalted kind, as with Castor and Pollux.

This transformation that Friday is bringing about in Robinson is interrupted by the arrival of a British ship. In his new enlightenment, Robinson feels disdain for the grossness of the sailors and the world of war and slavery they belong to, but Friday is fascinated by the ship, named for a bird, with its towering mast, and the new life it brings. It is Friday who leaves, and Robinson who stays. He is plunged into despair by this return to solitude and seeks oblivion, returning to the cave he visited in his telluric phase. Luckily, he there finds the runaway ship's boy Jaan, another young companion, and renames him as he had Friday.

Tournier and Tournier

Tournier has suggested that writing for young people involves an effort to purify and to achieve clarity, so that it is harder than writing for adults.[20] Certainly his version of *Vendredi* for young readers (*Vendredi ou La Vie Sauvage*, 1977) is simpler than *Les Limbes du Pacifique*, much more concentrated on the moral and cultural contrast between Robinson and Friday, and on the change in their relationship: from Robinson as master to Friday as leader, and from work to play. Robinson's confusion and introspection is largely eliminated. In this version, it is obvious that Robinson should abandon his efforts at work and order, and follow the playful and free-spirited Friday, and he does so promptly after the explosion of the gunpowder has wrecked his work, which he admits has become boring and annoying ("ennuyeuse et tracassière" [Tournier 1977, 74]).

This simplification has useful effects. *La Vie Sauvage* makes very clear contrasts between Robinson's effortful and complicated labor, for instance in the cultivation of rice, and Friday's quick work when he feels like it—and often in order to make playthings, as with turning the carcass of the goat Andoar into a kite and an Aeolian harp.[21] In most castaway novels, the details of practical work are associated with the Western castaway's survival and therefore with the project of settling and civilizing the island. The fact that indigenous people are just as practical and handy is concealed by the fact that the castaway is laboring at what seem distinctly Western tasks, such as baking bread or making a fortress. Tournier refutes this impression and, for good measure, makes the native a much more efficient and ingenious worker.

In addition, *La Vie Sauvage* shifts the textual relations of Robinson and Friday. Robinson's meditations are omitted. His passage toward solar transcendence is omitted, as is the emphasis on how he follows Friday's lead and learns from him. The result is that *La Vie Sauvage* is much less the story of Robinson than was argued to be the case with *Les Limbes du Pacifique*.

Nonetheless it is still Robinson who has interiority, even if the implication is that he would be better off without it. He devotes himself to elaborating schemes of civilization and order not exactly because he sees the mission to civilize as good in itself, but to stave off boredom and, still more threatening, the desire and temptation to wallow in the mire like an animal or to sink into a blissful no-time in the warm maternal hollow in the island. He has the remnants of interiority: neurotic urges and anxieties. The emphasis in the passage on his climbing the araucaria in *La Vie Sauvage*, for instance, is on the fact that when he gets to the top he sees Friday's new kite flying, and he has made the attempt, we are told, because he now takes Friday as his model (106–7). His ascent is a matter of his overcoming his congenital vertigo, that is, more a matter of the neurosis of the civilized. The earlier novel's schema of Robinson's ascent, from the mud of the wallow and the moist close darkness of the womb-like hollow and the fecundity of the cleft in the tree, to the top of the tree and the sun, is largely replaced by images of Friday as delighted by flight—shooting arrows ever further until they don't come back, making Andoar fly or having the winds play him. These images and actions in *La Vie Sauvage* express the power and playfulness of Friday, and Robinson's task is to imitate and learn.

Friday comes into Robinson's life as a Child of Nature, and as such he doesn't have doubts or worries or, as far as we can see, inner life. He has responses and impulses. His life is with and in the rest of nature, his cubby next to the tree with his favorite things, his pet goat Anda (an addition to the story), his relations with the fledgling vulture, which he feeds on chewed maggots, with the tortoise and the goat Andoar. Hence the sublime moment when the storm makes the Aeolian harp sing: the song of the harp seems to come at once from the earth and from the stars; and in contrast, the grisly scene in which Robinson comes across Friday cutting the shell from the still-living turtle. The contrast exhibits Tournier's lyricism at its most effective:

> Serrés tous trois sous un rocher, Robinson, Vendredi et la chevrette Anda regardaient de tous leurs yeux ce spectacle terrible, et ils écoutaient de toutes leurs oreilles ce chant qui semblait à la fois tomber des étoiles et monter des profondeurs de la terre. (113)

And

> Pendant ce temps, Vendredi avec un couteau coupait à l'intérieur les parties qui restaient encore collées à la carapace. Tout à coup, la tortue roula sur le côté en laissant sa carapace par terre. Elle retomba sur les pattes et se mit à galloper vers la mer, suivie par Tenn qui courait derrière en aboyant. Puis elle s'enfonça dans les vagues.
>
> —Elle a tort, dit tranquillement Vendredi, demain les crabes l'auront mangée! (62)[22]

Friday as personage is to be seen as free, without purposes, and ageless, because he does not develop or change, while Friday as literary function has the task of educating Robinson and introducing him to a better way of being. Everything he does is invented by Tournier to that end, though this kind of purpose is largely alien to his nature. "Vendredi lui avait enseigné la vie sauvage, puis il était parti" ["Friday had taught him wildness, then left"] (126): without the presence of a teacher such as Friday has been for Robinson, it's not clear what Robinson will do now, except perhaps educate his new companion in his turn. But no doubt this is why the book ends when it does.

The Year of Grace

> *aquella isola de vapores y sombras*
>
> CRISTINA FERNÁNDEZ CUBAS, *The Year of Grace*

Cristina Fernández Cubas's *The Year of Grace* (*El Año de Gracia*, 1985) is narrated by Daniel. The novel is named for the narrator's sister, who financed the year of adventure that led to his being marooned on Grock's island. At one point he remembers the immensities that he and Gracia made of the small territories of their children's games (150). It's a remark with resonances for the whole tradition of the castaway novel, because that small territory of childhood which becomes big in play and imagination is always present, or potential, in castaway novels, where the castaway is given an island to make into his or her territory. But this innocent fascination is certainly buried deep in *The Year of Grace*. When he has this thought, Daniel is realizing how Grock deceived him as to the size of his island, leading him roundabout in the mists, and the island itself may be the most harsh and uninviting of any discussed in this book, except perhaps for Pincher Martin's lonely rock. Grock's island is misty, rocky, and poisoned by anthrax experiments dating from World War II. It is inhabited only by sheep given to outbreaks of unpredictable savagery, and by Grock himself, Daniel's "variable Viernes" (Friday), capricious, demanding, old and weather-beaten, yet like a child, and almost languageless.

The narrator of this castaway adventure is particularly "thin-boundaried."[23] The world is certainly rough, strange, and hostile, and so are the people he encounters—or at least he comes to believe so. Yet he is open to the world; he does try to impose a pattern and an explanation on it and to use it, as every castaway does and perhaps must, but he never succeeds in making that distance between self and other, subject and objects, that then allows the castaway to plan and work and even exploit and dominate. If grace in the theological sense is something bestowed on the subject undeserved, then Daniel's life is shaped by grace as well as Grace.[24] He veers between increasingly disillusioned invocations of literary precedents—he is very aware that he is willy-nilly living out a modern version of an old adventure tale—and retreat into reverie, alcohol, hallucination, or fever. In this flickering of moods, impulses, suspicions, and surprises, he grasps at a series of momentary companionships—with his sister Gracia; with his Parisian lover Yasmine; with the old seafarer Jean with whom he embarks; with the rum he resorts to when he suspects that Jean has evil plans for him ("el amigo ron" [58]); with the imaginary reader of the journal he resumes after he is cast away, an ideally sensitive reader, as he fantasizes; and at last with Grock, his rescuer and enslaver, rough and capricious. Daniel's relationship with Grock, on Grock Island, is at the heart of the story, and the heart of *The Year of Grace*'s rewriting of *Robinson Crusoe*. Grock is the most challenging and capricious of all those he encounters, and he does learn to accept and even love Grock before he loses him.

Daniel is a scholar of Latin and Greek who has left his seminary and embarked on his year of travel, financed by Gracia. He's a reader, fully aware of the ironic parallels with *Robinson Crusoe*,[25] and of the deceptiveness of adventure novels when brought into contact with his disillusioning experiences (see, for instance, 67). He is quick with intertextual analogies, whereby, for instance, his rescuer Grock becomes the old man of the sea in Sinbad's tale of nightmarish oppression (125); and he himself, once he discovers Grock likes to be read to each night, goes from slave to Scheherazade (137). When he washes his filthy hair in a spring, "of strange taste and worse appearance," Daniel compares himself to a Spartan warrior getting ready for battle (74). He becomes a writer, composing, of course, the narrative we are reading; we see him fix on the title of the text we are reading and write the sentence we read at its beginning (85). He flees into this writing, first from his troubles on the *Providencia* (the boat on which he embarked with Jean), then from Grock's demands. He fantasizes an ideal reader, one who is attentive, who makes allowances for the concision of his text, who is a kind of alternative to Grock, his actual companion and yet master (139–40).

Grock has a strong quality of autonomy; as with the boy Friday in Tournier's novel, there are things he has to teach the literate and supposedly civilized Daniel, or rather things the latter comes to learn and accept. But one does not feel that Grock's *function* in the text is to educate Daniel in the way that Friday's function in the text is to lead Robinson to solar transcendence. That is, for all his vitality and beauty, Tournier's Friday is present in order to do something for the castaway. In this respect, Tournier's is a Eurocentric novel even though it idealizes the Araucanian Friday, or because of the way it idealizes him. Grock is Grock: he goes his own way, and his effect on Daniel is for Daniel to come to terms with. In this important aspect, *The Year of Grace* is a postcolonial novel; nonetheless, although Grock is illiterate and from the wild Hebridean fringes of the continent, he is as European as Daniel or Gracia or Jean, all of whom present as changeable and unstable, at least in Daniel's narrative. The sole representatives of Western rationalism and structured order that the novel offers are the policemen and scientists who arrive by helicopter near the end and murder Grock, assuming that in doing so they are killing the other inhabitant of the island, Daniel, whom they have just recently come across.

Grock is illiterate and has virtually no words, though we learn he does speak a mixture of Gaelic and English. Grock is his name for himself and for his island, and for the pile of stones outside his hut, crowned with a cross where, as Daniel learns, Grock buried the sheepdog that had been his faithful companion, and perhaps a more satisfactory and capable one than Daniel ("Nunca existió en el mundo un ser tan inteligente como su compañero" [121]).[26] Grock doesn't converse; he gestures, shoves, repeats. Yet Daniel, literate, imaginative, daydreamy, hardly names himself until he discovers the Bible from which he will read to Grock. Grock names it "madre" and Daniel realizes it belonged to Grock's mother and perhaps stands for her as the island stands for Grock, or is Grock. For the reader, Daniel is simply the "I" of his first-person narrative, and we don't learn his name until this very late stage; it is Grock, in fact, who precipitates this self-naming by Daniel by his obsession with the Book of Daniel. "'Tal vez,' dije en el mismo tono en el que leía las Sagradas Escrituras, 'de lo primero que se olvida un ser humano es de su propio nombre'" ["'Maybe,' I said in the same tone as I was reading the Scriptures, 'the first thing a human being forgets is his own name'"] (134). As he names himself, he remarks that loss of your name is the first sign of loss of your humanity. Yet this apparent spiraling down of the narrator to Grock's level is powerfully both a degeneration and a progression, and it's out of the novel's revision of the relationship between indigene and castaway, Friday and Robinson, that this complexity comes.

The mistakes and revelations that will structure the narrator's relationship with Grock are foreshadowed in his dealings with Jean ("tío Jean") and Naguib. He befriends Jean by the dockside in St. Malo and, seduced by his old-fashioned sailor's tales and his old-fashioned boat, the *Providencia*, embarks for Glasgow with Jean and the other member of the crew, the Egyptian Naguib, who seems resentful of his friendship with Jean. It's not until they are well at sea, however, that the increasingly uneasy Daniel comes to believe that Jean and Naguib mean him no good: he guesses that they are planning to hold him captive and blackmail Gracia into paying them for him. His recourse is to lie low and get drunk; meanwhile, there is a violent storm and Naguib is lost overboard. Daniel blacks out, and when he next awakes, he is cast ashore and the *Providencia* is wreckage on the dismal island. There is no sign of Jean.

Plainly, Daniel has been something of an innocent, entrusting himself to Jean and the apparently sinister Naguib. In what follows, he will be stripped of any remaining powers and pretensions and reduced to the level of the primitive and illiterate Grock, and indeed to below that level as the latter's slave and prisoner-companion. There will be no evidence that he has any of the abilities of a classic castaway, though the wreck is available for salvage in the usual way, and Daniel takes advantage of this. (There is a cursory list of what he got from the wreck; the operation is largely described in general terms.) The process of degeneration to the level of primitive beasts and to slavery will involve a kind of rebirth, a discovery of love, a discovery, perhaps, of the true meaning of his name, Daniel.

The central episode of the novel begins when Grock tends Daniel through a fever. Daniel does not encounter Grock, and he certainly doesn't rescue him as Friday was rescued by Crusoe. He comes to himself and finds Grock tending him, just as he did not experience the wreck of the *Providencia* but came to afterward on the shore.

The fever is precipitated by Daniel's savage and uncanny encounter with a flock of sheep, a kind of parody of the Biblical Daniel in the lions' den. First he comes across a trapped sheep with its lamb bleating by its side. This arouses no pity, only salivation and lip-licking in a hungry man. Neither does the fact that the sheep is of a strange kind, very shaggy, and moreover stinking and diseased ("cubiertas de pústulas y eccemas") deter him. He changes to savagery in a few instants ("había pasado de pobre náufrago a cruel y voraz hambriento" [90]).[27] He kills, skins, butchers, and roasts a leg of the lamb in front of its bleating mother. What follows is just as savage and almost stranger still. He finds himself confronted by a whole flock; the flock falls silent, two rams fight, the loser is savagely torn to pieces by the rest, and its gizzards and organs seized on. Roused to a frenzy by the struggles to escape of the sheep he had captured, Daniel turns on it and kills it. Before he passes out, he hallucinates the hooves of the sheep as cruel knives; when he comes to, he finds Grock caring for him. The savagery, including savage eating, that castaway narratives usually dramatize by way of the incursions of natives and pirates, is here incorporated in this incident of Daniel's violence with the sheep and their violence with each other. It seems to happen in a delirious gap, after which he has met Friday (Grock) and his life on the island is set on a new path. As in *The Island of Dr. Moreau*, the difference between human and animal is put violently into question: the sheep are savage, but so is Daniel; the savagery of the sheep is structured, as by a ritual, whereas that of Daniel is insensate and delirious. Stripped of civilized restraint, he is perhaps ready to encounter Grock.

Daniel's life becomes centered around his relationship with Grock. He makes discoveries, he reasons about his experiences, but this concerns Grock. He does not ask himself why the island is poisoned and then set himself to solve that problem. Attempting to run away from Grock, who has made a slave of him, he finds himself in the midst of a wood of dead trees whose sudden fallings tell him his hiding place is no refuge. He thinks about Grock's refusal to enter this place, Grock who so possesses the rest of the island that he identifies it with his self, and speculates that Grock has made the dead wood into his god: "Su movilidad en la isla es absoluta, con la excepción de un lúgubre bosque sin vida al que no accedería por nada del mundo. El bosque es su dios" (141).[28] Daniel's theory is that Grock believes that his rule over the rest of the island and its creatures (the sheep) depends on his never entering the wood. It's an uncanny place and a fascinating speculation, with its analogy to the conditions on which Adam enjoyed his rule in Eden, but Daniel does not think to put the deadness of the wood into any other frame.

Similarly, Daniel sees their discovery of the Bible and their coming to an arrangement that he read from the Book of Daniel every third evening very much as an event in their life together—with more reason this time, because none of this bears on the mystery of the island itself. Daniel goes from slave to Scheherazade,[29] and the custom of reading regularizes their life together and moderates Grock's capriciousness. (The English-speaking reader may notice a contrast with the final pages of Evelyn Waugh's *A Handful of Dust* [1934], where the unfortunate Tony is trapped in the jungle and compelled to read Dickens to Mr. Todd.) The emphasis is less on how Daniel is literate and Grock so ignorant that he doesn't even know the name of the book he is being read, and more on how they have come together in fascination with the Book of Daniel—Daniel because of the name, Grock because his favorite passage deals with the confrontation of a ram and a horned goat, and he identifies the second with himself, having had a good deal of experience with fierce rams. Now it's true that Daniel turns to his journal with renewed confidence, and, for instance, writes his speculation that the lifeless wood is Grock's god; but the episode of the Bible reading overturns any stereotype of the settler bringing the word to the ignorant native. It's a shared experience: Grock needs Daniel for the reading, and Daniel needs the reading for his relationship with Grock to attain stability. Daniel compares himself to a lady-in-waiting and to Scheherazade, but he finds this amusing rather than humiliating, and the reader is anyway free to reflect that Scheherazade was more creative in these nightly sessions than Daniel is. By this stage, Daniel has started to repudiate the old tales of adventure such as *Robinson Crusoe*, though he is clear enough about Grock's resemblance to Friday. He finds himself going back to yet older tales—Sinbad, Scheherazade, the passing image of the Spartan dressing his hair—and this is better seen as acceptance that one cannot escape stories than as persistence of an immature habit of seeing the world through books. The island with its forbidden wood is a place of myth, not of practical reason.

There now follows an episode that very closely reprises one in *Robinson Crusoe*. It is significant that one of Robinson's most conspicuous failures is reprised—the construction of a boat that cannot be gotten to the sea. Daniel does make a raft—he draws plans, hunts for suitable timber. Even in this, his most sustained practical action, he becomes obsessed (144). To no avail: the raft won't float, and he is brought to face "los insondables misterios de las leyes de flotación" (145).[30] He finds himself cast back on shore more or less as when he first came to the island. But nonetheless this is a breakthrough, though by accident. The last plank washed up is a sign warning of contamination and forbidding entry to what he now learns is the island of Gruinard. He begins to realize what kind of island this is, though it is not until later that he learns that Gruinard and its sheep were poisoned with anthrax in 1942,[31] and all the human inhabitants but Grock were evacuated. (So the dead wood that Grock saw as taboo must have been poisoned.)

The last incident in Daniel's life with Grock corresponds to the moment in a castaway narrative when the island, long unvisited, begins to be invaded although, as we have seen, important aspects of this phase have already happened, in a form that is internal to the island and to Daniel (violence; savage eating). But, in accordance with the island as a place of myth, the violence will take the form of sacrifice. When Grock hears the noise of a launch, he ties Daniel up, but Daniel escapes and witnesses what follows. Some of the six intruders are uniformed and armed, some dressed official style. Grock is by this time wearing the red sheepskin jacket that Daniel once got from Jean; when he approaches the intruders, they shoot and kill him. Then they roughly bury him. Daniel witnesses this as if in a dream—the state he falls into in each moment of crisis in his story. The intruders discover him, he recovers enough to yell out "Don't shoot" ["¡Alto!"], and then they dismiss him: "—Es Grock . . . Simple e inofensivo como un niño" (163).[32]

Daniel realizes that Grock has been mistaken for the stranger in the sheepskin coat and died for him, and he has been taken for Grock: if he is Grock, the man just buried is Daniel (164). And it's even possible that Grock was once himself a marooned sailor and Daniel has now succeeded him in a chain of castaways molded into becoming Grocks by the island: Fernández Cubas discusses this possibility in her interview with Katarzyna Olga Beilin (2004, 136). Grock has remained utterly distinct from Daniel, who scarcely understood him: even at the last, "El viejo me miraba con una expresión indefinible" (157)[33]—this just before Grock ties him up for his own protection and advances toward the intruders with intentions Daniel can only guess at. Yet they have become one. Between this Friday and this Robinson there is a gulf, yet they are friends and companions, and one has died in place of the other, and one has become the other. It's a tragic fable of the coming together of Robinson and Friday. The primitive aspects of the island and the story—the savage sheep, the forbidden wood—play a role in this. Robinson and Friday act out different parts in a transformed version of the castaway tale; yet, insofar as it still is a castaway tale, the effect is comic as well as tragic: Daniel has repeatedly misinterpreted clues and failed tasks, and we can't be sure that the sacrifice of Grock was not another misidentification.

The rest is anticlimax for Daniel: the island is soon visited again, after the frequent pattern in castaway narratives, and he is taken off by a group of ecologists who patronize him as long as he is useful to their cause, and then drop him. He travels again, to the scene in St. Malo where he discovers that Naguib has survived and prospered; and he even marries, but his heart is left with Grock on the island. The last page of the novel finds him in bed with his wife, but going back in his imagination to "la apacible y tranquila Isla de Grock" (184).

Foe

The story I desire to be known by is the story of the island.

J. M. COETZEE, *Foe*

Foe is the culmination of a trend to be seen in fictions responding to *Robinson Crusoe*, and also to *The Island of Dr. Moreau*. Intertextuality prompts awareness of a narrative as a made thing, something contingent. The story we read in *Foe* is the story of Susan Barton's attempt to get Foe to write the story of her time on Cruso's island.[34] Susan has taken on Friday as servant, companion, and substitute for her lost daughter, and she gradually comes to accept that he too needs to tell his story. The texts proliferate: what Susan wrote to guide Foe in his writing; her letters to Foe, some not posted, most not delivered; his other works by which he is bringing other stories and lives into existence; even, at the very end, what Friday is starting to write. Foe and Susan propose contrasting versions of the narrative structure that her story might assume, and these are also contrasting versions of what makes up her story. Foe: "We therefore have five parts in all" (a quest story [117]). Susan: "The story I desire to be known by is the story of the island," which would nonetheless involve several other, inset stories (121). Foe wants the story to include Susan's quest for her daughter, which took her to Bahia and eventually the voyage on which she was wrecked; Susan insists that she have control over her story and that it center on the island. The story of Cruso, Friday, and the island rewrites, or preempts, *Robinson Crusoe*; the story of Susan and her daughter rewrites, or preempts, Defoe's *Roxana*. What we get in *Foe* is somehow more authentic than what was—or would be—written in these other novels by Defoe, but it defines itself by opposition to them, and it revolves around the difficulties of writing any narrative.

At first glance, it seems that what Coetzee does is to set *Robinson Crusoe* firmly before us, because this is a story with a Cruso and a Friday and even a Defoe —and then deny or refuse much of what we get in Defoe's novel. This is indeed so, and often in very striking ways; but it is equally true that he opens out the latter, introducing the tantalizing, the mysterious, the poignantly unfulfilled. In doing all this, he critiques colonialism and especially slavery, a kind of heart of darkness at the center of the story. But he also draws on various more positive aspects of eighteenth-century culture, especially in the person of Susan Barton, the first-person narrator of this text. In what follows here, the discussion begins from what in *Robinson Crusoe* is denied or refused in *Foe*, sometimes bluntly, sometimes more subtly, and then characterizes what Susan brings to the narrative. Coetzee is writing his novel over the top of *Robinson Crusoe*, around it, and, so to speak, before it. The process is so intricate that *Robinson Crusoe* (not yet written by the time *Foe* comes to an end) might as well be a response to or a parody of *Foe* as the reverse.

Robinson Crusoe, which depicts Robinson as so productive and enterprising, and Friday as so simple and biddable, is not history as *Foe* specifies it with its counter narrative, and in fact it is refused, but it perhaps expresses a desire that narrative answer to our desire that is not yet satisfied at the end of *Foe*. It's true that not all desires are legitimate. For instance, the desire to possess others by appropriating their story is illegitimate, and this is something of which both Coetzee's novel and all published criticism on it are aware; indeed, a good deal of the latter is concerned to police the novel's dealings with power and narrative. Nonetheless, desire in general is given a good deal of scope in *Foe*, especially in the person of Susan, and the desire for narrative is not something a novel can easily repress. Not many novels would be written were the novelist to accept that the only person permitted to tell the story is that person himself or herself; yet Coetzee's dealings with the problem are indeed rich and indirect.[35] It's a huge and inescapable fact that slavers have exercised cruel power over Friday, because he has lost his tongue and probably been castrated, and this is reemphasized near the end of the novel when a figure who is in effect Coetzee discovers a scar around Friday's neck. This is so, and as the mutilation has happened, it is inexpugnable; yet in our narrative, if Cruso and Susan and Foe exert some power over Friday, in the aftermath of what the slavers did to him, Friday for his part exerts some power over Susan and Foe, Foe over Susan, and Susan over Foe. Power, curiosity, desire, and simple interest in another all tend to operate at once in the triangular relationship of Foe, Susan, and Friday that is at the center of the novel. This relationship is shaped by slavery, gender, and colonialism, but also by power, curiosity, desire, and simple interest as they shape most relationships. If there is a thesis, an end in view in the windings of the fiction, as there is in *Friday*, for instance, it is not easy to define here. There is room for testing and exploration.

Regarding the experience of being cast away, Coetzee/Susan provides a much barer account. Susan denies the most famous moment of all: "I saw no cannibals; and if they came after nightfall and fled before the dawn, they left no footprint behind" (54). (But she tantalizingly remembers the bed she slept in, "which perhaps still bears the imprint, fainter every day, of my body" [54], and she is by no means rid of thoughts of cannibals.)[36] This island is windswept and rocky, the trees stunted. There is no salvage from the wreck, though the wreck itself is going to have a rich symbolic life in the text, and there is no active program of manufacture and homemaking. Cruso and Friday do have a rough dwelling and enough food (Friday goes spearfishing), but there is no providentially sprouting and then extensively cultivated grain. Susan finds it unsatisfactory:

> How long before I am driven to invent new and stranger circumstances: the salvage of tools and muskets from Cruso's ship; the building of a boat, or at least a skiff, and a venture to sail to the mainland; a landing by cannibals on the island, followed by a skirmish and many bloody deaths; and at last, the coming of a golden-haired stranger with a sack of corn, and the planting of the terraces. (67)

There is intense labor, however, though to Susan it seems so empty that she calls the island a place of sloth not labor (88). In the oddest detail of Cruso's bleak arrangements, we find that he and Friday have labored making stone-embanked terraces for grain that might arrive, but never has. Perhaps this is an image of the sheer negativity and blankness of the colonial project, or of its South African version. In that case it would join the image of the silencing of Friday, whose tongue has been ripped out. But perhaps we are simply to read the image of Cruso struggling with stones as a sign of the hardening and narrowing that is a likely result of years of isolation in a tough place. If you can't have children or interact with others, you will end with this husk of production. Cruso is driven in on himself. He doesn't want to leave the island, and he dies when he is rescued, but neither does he want to do very much when he is on the island, and is, like Robinson, its ruler: no attempt to make a boat, no lookout or signal fire, no journal or marking of the passage of time, no memories. Susan keeps prompting him, and he keeps rejecting or denying.

The effect is that Cruso fades into the background, and we are left with the silent but always haunting Friday, and Susan. Susan is not so quickly characterized as Cruso. Certainly, she is alert, eloquent, and sexually alive: "How dismal a fate it would be to go through life unkissed!" she exclaims at one point (80).[37] It's her fate to spend her time with Cruso, who is morose and negative, with Friday, who is tongueless and keeps his feelings about her unexpressed, if he has any, and with Foe, who is mostly absent and elusive. In a sense her buoyancy is as remarkable as was Robinson Crusoe's in the original story. She finds herself submitting to Cruso, and accommodating herself as best she can to this, but having raped her once he seems to lose interest (30, 35–36). She does have sex with Foe, as we shall see, and significantly enough it is as the Muse, the goddess who comes to the writer and impregnates him that she does it.

To allegorize her or in some way see her as representative (of white liberals, for instance) is not the best way to approach her. It may result in a misleading selectivity, because, for instance, her remark about being unkissed and her dangerous trek with Friday to Bristol do not seem very obviously to say something about white liberals. It is better to see Coetzee as revising, rather than refuting, the valuation of individuality that is so important to *Robinson Crusoe*. Here it is better to speak of individuality than of individualism. Individuality, the individual's need for autonomy and for his or her own story, is put into an intricate dancing with interdependence. Susan is assertive, she demands and rebuffs and denies, then she feels remorse, and apologizes. Even at the end of the story, after she has committed herself to Friday in so many ways, she is still giving him orders and expecting him to eat only after she has eaten, yet she realizes that her story and Friday's (and Foe's) are interdependent. She accepts Friday as her shadow (115), and burden (like the Old Man of the River, she says).[38]

Further, she appeals to a view of civilization as sociability: what Cruso lost, Friday cannot have, and even Foe is a bit unreliable on, though in his elusive way he does like to exchange ideas. She speaks out for "the fullness of human speech," "the pleasures of conversation," "the world of speech" (8, 22, 79). She sees how music might be a form of conversation, call and response (96). She sees how the tongue as well as the genitals expresses desire, so it's not surprising that Friday dismays her, because he lacks the first and may well lack the second. In addition, in her speculations, mostly about Friday, she develops (or Coetzee does, through her) a kind of anthropology of human needs, a sense of human variety. It's another side to eighteenth-century culture than the slave trading. Here she thinks over Friday's failure, or refusal, to respond to some pictures she has drawn for him:

> And how did he understand my gesture of putting out my tongue at him? What if, among the cannibals of Africa, putting out the tongue has the same meaning as offering the lips has amongst us? Might you then not flush with shame when a woman puts out her tongue and you have no tongue with which to respond? [. . .]
>
> Who was to say there do not exist entire tribes in Africa among whom the men are mute and speech is reserved to women? Why should it not be so? (69)

Finally, Susan is a woman, both in her sense of herself (her desire, for instance, or her image of herself as like a tall goddess come from the sea to Cruso's island [86]) and in her social circumstances, such as her encounters with predatory men; yet she wants to "father" her story on Foe, and she tells her would-be daughter, having led her into the dark heart of the forest as the father did his children in "Hansel and Gretel," that she had a father but no mother, she was "father-born" (91). And this desire, to "beget" like a male, but while acting as a goddess, a Muse, yet not to mother the daughter that she thinks Foe is pretending to provide her with, this desire is itself complex and split. At first she says that to "father her story" she needs to withhold, but this is not what she does when she has sex with Foe to impregnate him with story.

The first result of Foe's intercourse with Susan as the Muse comes almost at once, like the working of a very quick-acting drug. He produces a wonderfully rich image of the scene of the shipwreck, a place that Susan had noticed Friday visiting and scattering with flower petals. (Cruso had denied that this place that Friday visited was in fact the site of the wreck [32].) Perhaps there was a sea monster down there. The heart of the story, anyway, like a dead eye down there, or, says Susan, collaborating with Foe in imagining, a great mouth (141), reminding us of the darkness of Friday's mouth with the stump of a tongue in it, at which she had been afraid to look. There they leave their imaginings, for the moment, though this is where they get the idea to try to teach Friday to write. But on the last pages of the novel, another I, Coetzee,[39] rewrites the first time Susan climbed the stairs to see Foe, and then dives down to the wreck. As Dominic Head says (1997, 125), this conflates the ship from which Robinson Crusoe salvaged so much, the ship from which Susan was cast away, and the slave ship that carried Friday. Here, in these images of intimate enclosure (Foe's staircase, the depth of the wreck), the novel finds the intimacy, the insideness, of the house, the dwelling, which it could not find on Cruso's island, though the castaway's island can often offer seclusion and enclosure. This too is the heart of the story, the same spot that Foe and Susan saw as eyes and mouth, the history out of which Coetzee has narrated Susan and Friday and Foe into life, to struggle with and achieve their own stories. Here, the I who dives experiences an unending stream that comes from Friday's mouth, a stream that still cannot be translated but cannot be stopped either: "an extraordinary literary gesture," Head calls it (126), and a literary gesture that might be taken as expressing a novel's power to say, rather than signify.

In *Friday* Robinson is set a series of rites of passage, so that he learns not to obsess about organizing and ordering, works through a series of sexual relations with his island as mother and lover, and at length finds a model of release and ascent into solar sensuality. His trajectory is clear, and richly detailed, but it is set out for him, and in the course of it inwardness is first literalized, in the passages in which Robinson penetrates inside his island, in all its uterine sensuousness, and then dissipated, because Friday is without inwardness and, it would seem, all the better for it. In *Foe* the characters' narratives, in the plural, are in process and uncertain, and neither the mercurial Susan nor the mysterious Friday nor the elusive Foe can be pinned to a meaning. Behind these differences between the two novels there are differing assumptions about signification. It may be that *Friday*'s enthusiasm for freeing oneself from mind and will, and its literalism about symbolism, both stem from a Cartesian assumption of the gulf between mind and the material. *Foe* refrains from categorizing; aspects of the world or experience that we might label as mind, will, body, signs, things—all dance and shift and merge.

Foe teases us with its denials or revisions of *Robinson Crusoe*, showing how one story can feed a very different one—and must, because we can no longer accept the earlier novel's ideologies. It laments all the stories untold or untellable, especially Friday's, but it also breaks open the closure of the island novel, the closure that follows on its choice of the limited, controllable microcosm, a man on an island with a parrot and a dog and some goats and a lot of stuff. Of course *Robinson Crusoe* already has a before and an after to the twenty-eight years on the island, but their interest is limited, and this is partly because there is really only one person in the novel, Crusoe himself. (Friday troubles this, especially for the modern reader, but Defoe has shut him into his demeaning pidgin English.) Susan has a point when she invokes various, multiracial Bahia, with its free women/whores adorned with gold: "How can you ever close Bahia between the covers of a book? It is only small and thinly peopled places that can be subjugated and held down in words, such as desert islands and lonely places" (122). (Defoe's Robinson Crusoe also lived in Brazil for a while, though we learn only about his career as a planter.)

There are several images in the novel of closed systems, self-stultifications, which might remind us of the other aspect of the island as little world—not so much complete as impoverished: "Growing old on his island kingdom with no one to say him nay had so narrowed his horizon—when the horizon all around us was so vast and so majestic!—that he had come to be persuaded he knew all there was to know about the world" (13). "Nothing I have forgotten is worth the remembering," Cruso proclaims to Susan (17).

In a sense it is this "silence," "emptiness," which Cruso imposed on his island, which dogs Susan after her return and which she sets herself to fight. The paradox is that its representative for Susan becomes Friday—himself, as she often sees him, a closed system, "made cold, incurious, like an animal wrapt entirely in itself" (70): "To tell my story and be silent on Friday's tongue is no better than offering a book for sale with pages in it quietly left empty. Yet the only tongue that can tell Friday's secret is the tongue he has lost!" (67).

Yet the story we read, though troubled, is very open and fluid, not at all closed. *Foe* releases us into the before and the after, puts Cruso into the background as a morose, negative, in-turned but rather sad figure, and expands with Susan, Foe, the substitutes for Susan's daughter, even the daughter herself because she is a presence in the story in her painful absence from Susan, and most of all Friday (a tour de force because of his lack of speech: the representation of what cannot be represented, as Head says [1997, 121–22]). And the story reaches no ending but an opening to a new beginning, Friday's writing; not to mention an affair between Susan and Foe, which itself is the seed of writerly inspiration for Foe. There is no rescue, as with the arrival of the naval officer at the climax of *Lord of the Flies*, nor settled prosperity as with *Robinson Crusoe*, nor even startling revelation as with *Pincher Martin* and *The Wasp Factory*. Or perhaps it is better to see the novel as poised between a beginning that cannot be told and an ending not yet told and maybe—if we think of the passage in which "Coetzee" dives into the wreck—not yet tellable. Foe wants to tell how Susan lost her daughter, which Susan refuses. Susan wants to know how Friday lost his tongue, and how he became a slave; at the end this is still untold, and there are plenty of hints that Friday may be no more willing to tell of his past than she of hers. Whether the ending not yet told will come from Friday, who is learning to write as the text ends, or Defoe, of whose version this version is so preemptively aware, we can't say. And it is a story that is repeatedly retold, or restarted. The moment when Susan launched herself into the sea to swim for the island is repeated, and so is the moment when she climbed the dark stairs to Foe's room in London to get him to turn her story into a book. But this repetition is not best described as a faltering or a looking backward; it's more like the return of a theme in a piece of music. It measures the same action in a new situation.

Further, this novel, which asserts people's right to strong individuality and right to own and withhold their stories, also expresses a complex sense of their interdependences and overlaps. Here we have a group of persons who are strangers to each other, isolates or isolated, like the whales and spiders of one of Susan's images (59), and, with the exception of Susan, rather in-turned and, as she says of Cruso and of Foe, secretive. Yet they overlap, converge, swap positions. There is an openness in this history that is missed if we see these overlaps and convergences only in terms of, for instance, complicity and collusion.[40] Susan at one point sees Friday as a burden, like the Old Man of the River in Sinbad's tale (147); but when they first met, just after she had been washed exhausted ashore, it was Friday who carried her (6). She also sees Foe's writing and his family (if he has one—she doesn't know) as a burden to him (52), feels willing to "bear you and your troubles on my back" (63), and realizes that Friday may well find life with her as "burdensome" as she finds life with him (104). Everywhere back in England she sees analogies with the situation of the castaway, isolated and "confined": imprisoned debtors ("castaways in the very heart of the city" [62]), Foe laboring in his attic, herself and Friday when they sojourn in Foe's house at Stoke Newington (71). She sees a darkness at the center of the silenced Friday, but this darkness is everywhere in the novel. "The heart of man is a dark forest—that is one of the sayings they have in Brazil" (11).

It's the cruelty of the mutineers who kill Susan's lover/captain and cast her adrift with his corpse that prompts this thought, though we may well think of Conrad and perhaps of Golding's allusion to *Heart of Darkness* in *Lord of the Flies*. Then later, when Susan leads her would-be daughter into the woods, we think of the dark forests in the Grimms' fairy tales. But inner darkness is widespread in *Foe*, and the image gathers density even as Susan both commits herself to Friday and struggles with her thoughts about his darkness; and she experiences some more of the darkness at the heart of man that prompted this remark, for instance, the soldiers who try to rape her on the road to Bristol, and the dead newborn she finds in a ditch (101, 105). When Friday dances and spins, so that Foe's robe that he has taken to wearing is lifted in his spinning, she sees "the dark pillar at its centre" (119), and the phrase suggests the column of smoke and pillar of fire guiding the Israelites in their wanderings. Later we have Foe's tale of the condemned woman who kept confessing to more crimes so that the priest would have more to absolve and the execution be longer delayed, a version of Scheherazade the archetypal female storyteller: "and is it [my repentance] truly felt?—I look into my heart and cannot say, so dark is it there" (124).[41] Then later, Foe and Susan speculate about "our darker selves" into which we descend in sleep (138). It is Foe who wonders if some of us, such as Friday, are "written by another and darker author" (143), but Foe also who shifts the bearing of the phrase, speaking of Friday, in his visits to the sunken wreck, as being at "the heart of the story" (141)—this being the place to which the I of the last pages of *Foe* will descend.

All these shifting dark places can be seen as equivalent to the secret or locked place within the island that is part of the spatiality of so many island stories, but with a difference because they so recur and vary, paradoxically freed. The process of the text is this turning about of a phrase or an idea so that it shifts position and location, appears in different lights and associated with different characters. And this can be so dynamic because the phrases, and the concepts behind them, are themselves in play. They are not static; we can't attach the one connotation to them as they thread and vary. Toward the end, Foe gloomily sees his role as a writer as being like a whore's: "An old whore who should ply her trade only in the dark" (151). But Susan has just made a wry joke about Foe giving her sixpence for breakfast after their night together ("no great payment for a visit from the muse" [145]), and anyway she has her own ideas about whores, as we see from her brisk decision to see the whores of Bahia as free women, able to go about and wear their gold (115).

Many of these images are images of interdependence—whore (or writer) and customer, man and woman, burden and one who assumes the burden, "substantial body" and shadow. Admittedly, this only constitutes an element in the whole; there are just as many images of closure and isolation and of collusion and complicity in the novel. The novel does not commit itself or finally resolve itself, or at least its very rich resolution is itself unresolved. What I want to underline here is the strength of this element of openness and interdependence in *Foe*. Susan and Foe and Friday share a troubled but poignant togetherness. Defoe's Robinson Crusoe is solitary, and his companionship with Friday, when it arrives, hardly modifies this because it is so easy, so untroubled; it is striking that Coetzee's revision of Defoe produces this haunting trio. Susan, Foe, and Friday are not originary, not like Adam and Eve, not like Crusoe whose being cast away means he can begin again. On the contrary, they are marked —scarred—by the histories of their lives, their secrets and unfulfilled desires, and in a broader way by the histories of genders and races that the novel reminds us of, and it is the awareness of all this that is behind the haunting quality that I am pointing to here. As coda to the way in which the island is almost displaced in Foe's revision of the story, and Friday is set at its center, yet almost unreachable, a glance at Elizabeth Bishop's "Crusoe in England" (1976), and Derek Walcott's "Crusoe's Island" (1965) is helpful.[42] Both poems are about solitude, and both come to a point of rest on Friday, as companion in Bishop's poem, and as productive ancestor in Walcott's.

In "Crusoe in England," Crusoe almost loses confidence in his human distinctness:

> The island smelt of goat and guano.
> The goats were white, so were the gulls,
> and both too tame, or else they thought
> I was a goat too, or a gull. (lines 100–103)

But then Friday comes, all is well, and that is all Crusoe wants to say about the matter—no slave or servant or master or convert, just a companion:

> Just when I thought I couldn't stand it
> another minute longer, Friday came.

(Accounts of that have everything all wrong.)
Friday was nice.
Friday was nice, and we were friends. (lines 142–46)

Better for Robinson had he been a woman so they could propagate, the poem goes on to say, but in any case this interlude is soon over:

And then they came and took us off. (line 153)

Back in England ("another island, but who decides?" [line 155]) Crusoe is unhappy, nostalgic for the island or at least for the life on the island that, when he lived it, he could not feel was home. The poem ends with a different kind of loss:

—And Friday, my dear Friday, died of measles
seventeen years ago come March. (lines 181–82)

On the island, Robinson was only alone until Friday came; now that Friday is dead, he is alone forever, as any bereaved person is, and as Daniel is without Grock. He has rejoined a larger, human condition. His time on the island can now be seen as the time that came before this time.

"Crusoe's Island" is a poem of turmoil and restless unhappiness. It begins with the sound of the chapel's cowbell, "like God's anvil," (line 2) intensifying the fierce island heat and underlining for Walcott how "My father, God, is dead," (line 19) he has chosen art, and, in his isolation, he fears the love of self:

Some lesion of the brain
From art or alcohol
Flashes this fear by day:
As startling as his shadow
Grows to the castaway. (lines 24–28)

This introduces Crusoe, whose island seems to offer a homely Eden ("Goats, corn crop, fort, parasol, garden"), but instead intensifies the heat and unease Walcott was suffering on his own island:

Exiled by a flaming sun
The rotting nut, bowled in the surf,
Became his own brain rotting from the guilt
Of heaven without his kind. (lines 35–38)

The image of the brain as a rotting nut has appeared in another poem in the sequence, "The Castaway." Walcott returns now to his own plight, and the image recurs, this time somehow bred of the "Compassion, supposedly inherited with the gift / Of poetry":

> Its brain a white, nocturnal bloom
> That in a drunken, moonlit room
> Saw my son's head
> Swaddled in sheets
> Like a lopped nut, lolling in foam. (lines 57–61)

With this image of his son's head both "swaddled" (like a newborn) and "lolling in foam," the poet's anguished sense of stalemate and of aloneness ("O love, we die alone!" [line 62]) reaches a climax. Now we have the saving appearance in the poem of Friday, or rather his children:

> Now Friday's progeny
> The brood of Crusoe's slave,
> Black little girls in pink
> Organdy, crinolines,
> Walk in their air of glory
> Beside a breaking wave;
> Below their feet the surf
> Hisses like tambourines. (lines 92–99)

When Walcott sought a kind of relief from thinking of Crusoe in his Eden, his own fears and nightmares were doubled, then redoubled in the vision of his son's severed head. Now it is Friday, his ancestor as a slave, who sponsors the beautiful and sane image of the "black little girls in pink organdy":

> At dusk, when they return
> For vespers, every dress touched by the sun will burn
> A seraph's, an angel's. (lines 100–102)

Even the heat, so fierce earlier in the poem, has become beneficent.

The sequence of texts that groups *The Year of Grace*, *Foe*, "Crusoe in England," and "Crusoe's Island" has set Crusoe and Friday in a series of new relations, with an effect of refreshment and even liberation. This points toward the recognition of indigeneity to be examined in the castaway novels for children in the next chapter.

6

Recent Children's Novels

Recognizing Indigeneity, Facing Death

This chapter discusses a selection of recent castaway novels for children:[1] *Island of the Blue Dolphins* (Scott O'Dell, 1960), *To the Wild Sky* (Ivan Southall, 1967), *Nation* (Terry Pratchett, 2008), and *Kensuke's Kingdom* (Michael Morpurgo, 1999). Each of these novels finds a way to revive the buoyancy and confidence of nineteenth-century castaway novels for children, such as *The Swiss Family Robinson*, *Masterman Ready*, and *The Coral Island*, and in this respect they resemble the science fictions to be discussed in the next chapter. What is most striking about them is the decisions they each make about their main characters: girls and non-European people are given new importance, and the altered angle that this provides is perhaps the clue to their achievements. It certainly lends each a thoughtful quality; the constituents of the story cannot be taken for granted. Each has to rethink the elementary matter of getting the castaways onto the island, which in O'Dell's and Pratchett's novels has been their home.

The nineteenth-century novels mentioned earlier often concerned a castaway family in which adults were the reliable leaders and instructors. In the more recent novels under discussion here, arrival on the island marks a break, a rupture, from the castaways' previous lives as children, or teenagers, that is, as part of a society of which they are not yet full members; indeed, the narrative of this rupture occupies most of *To the Wild Sky*. Each of the more recent novels features an indigenous castaway who can no longer live as her society requires (Karana in O'Dell), or has only just recognized that she is indigenous (Carol in Southall), or is caught between man and boy, like a hermit crab that has abandoned one shell and not yet found another, and besides is in revolt against the religion of his people (Mau in Pratchett).[2] Experimenting with an indigenous castaway, and yet subjecting this character to the rupture with the grownup world that is frequent in novels about growing up, and making this world an indigenous one—all this makes for a rich revision of the castaway novel. In addition, girl castaways figure in three of these novels—Karana is Native American; the castaway teenagers in *To the Wild Sky* are a mixture of males and females; Daphne, who is English, is paired with Mau in *Nation*. Finally, each novel confronts death, in this facing something that is often taken for granted in earlier castaway narratives, the deaths of all but the survivor or survivors on whom the novel will concentrate.

Island of the Blue Dolphins

It was a good day to begin my new home.

SCOTT O'DELL, *Island of the Blue Dolphins*

Island of the Blue Dolphins tells the story of Karana, a Native American girl left behind by mischance when the remnants of her tribe left their island. She is forced to fend for herself for the years of her growing up. The story is based on that of Juana Maria, as her eventual white rescuers called her, marooned on San Nicolas Island off California from 1835 to 1853, though the novel's confinement to Karana's point of view means that the scandal of Juana Maria's being left on her island for almost twenty years is unexamined. Karana is female, Native American, and she is not a settler on her island: her people have always lived there. O'Dell thus departs from the template of the castaway narrative in important ways.

The island is Karana's ancestral home, and her task as castaway is defined in relation to that fact. At one point she finds a cave with the skeleton of one ancestor and effigies of others: this cave, flooded by the tide and very dark, is a variation on a common feature of castaway narratives; it is the island within the island, the place apart from the place apart. "We will call it Black Cave and never in all our days go there again" (20: 129). The island has been the home of her people, but now it is hers alone, and she is discovering its hidden places as castaways often do. But this place, cave of her ancestors, containing death, is off limits. She can't bear to stay in the now ghostly village; she burns it to ashes (3: 49–50). Perhaps these incidents in Karana's life on the island should be seen as the shadows of something hard to face, the cultural death of her people. In the sequel, *Zia* (1976) we find them in effect imprisoned in a Californian mission, and struggling for their autonomy.

Island of the Blue Dolphins is a coming-of-age story; the combined freedom and necessity of Karana's solitude as a castaway means that she can take on different, male and female, roles as she grows and changes. Again, the point of reference is the way of life and culture of her own people. She grows into a young woman; for instance, she makes herself a beautiful skirt out of the skins and iridescent feathers of cormorants (21: 135). But she also eagerly takes on the roles of a young male hunter and the tasks otherwise reserved for the males of the tribe. She hunts the wild dogs that killed her younger brother in her first days as a castaway, wounds their leader, and then cares for him so that he becomes her companion (a kind of Friday, in fact); she hunts the sea elephant for its tusks, useful for spearheads, and the "devilfish" (an octopus) mainly for the challenge of doing so. To do all this, Karana has to make a bow and arrows and various kinds of spear, though this is man's work, taboo for women, and she does it with trepidation, as well as having to work out the technique for herself in castaway fashion. Each of these hunts leads to something other than a simple victory, because the story has another goal than domination or domestication of the island: the leader of the dogs is not killed but becomes her companion; the sea elephant is eventually killed by a rival male and she scavenges the tusks later; the devilfish is successfully killed, but the hunt is exhausting and never repeated. O'Dell combines what Karana's people would do and believe with the ways in which her situation and her own boldness and activity make her into a different person—a loner, a girl who takes on male enterprises.

Then there is repetition (a second pair of parrots; a successor to her dog Rontu after he dies) and a kind of diminuendo. Karana's interest in making companions and pets of animals and birds rather than hunting them means she has moved on and become a kind of mother (she sees this herself); in another way, she seems to move away from any defined roles.

The novel also recapitulates or varies a series of the familiar castaway tropes. As noted, Karana follows a common pattern in making a "new home," a hut, protected by a fence of whale bones, equivalent to Crusoe's stockade, and later setting up a cave as bolt-hole. She doesn't make her own boat, but succeeds in dragging down to the sea one of the big canoes that the tribe left behind: a variation of an episode that marks a limit and anticlimax for Robinson Crusoe and several other European castaways. She sets out for the east, only to have to turn back and return to her island when her canoe leaks (it had been left too long in the sun). Then later, she rebuilds the canoe to make it more wieldy, but this time, like Robinson in his second, less ambitious vessel, uses it only to circumnavigate her island. As in *Robinson Crusoe* and in some other castaway narratives (for instance, *The Island of Dr. Moreau*, *Friday*), the message is that the castaway's ingenuity as a builder has limits, and that he or she must remain on the island until rescue comes from across the sea. In this case it is softened a little by the way Karana seems to be guided back toward her island by friendly blue dolphins, a foretaste also of her later relations with wild creatures.[3]

In other ways the story diverges from Defoe and many of his successors: there can be no journal; there is no salvage—she in fact digs up a buried chest only to reject its contents and rebury it (there are no weapons such as spearheads in it, so it is useless). There is a calendar, about which we are told quite late in the story, and it is like Robinson Crusoe's (notches on a pole), but toward the end of her stay, Karana gives up recording even the years (25: 158). Mainly she measures the passing of time from the seasons, the flowering of plants and arrival of migratory birds—from the changing natural scene that is already familiar to her.

The ending is a little sad. Her white rescuers make her a dress and insist that she wear it and put aside the finery she had made for herself. She looked better in the skirt she made herself in her people's style than in the white men's dress; she got further communicating with the Aleut girl who befriended her during the episode of the Aleuts' visit than she does with the white people who will take her away from the island. The notion of rescue is undermined. Yet the overall effect of *Island of the Blue Dolphins* is buoyant and reassuring. Karana is quietly strong, and she succeeds in her undertakings without feeling the need to dominate or proceed to interminable tasks and feats as tends to happen in *The Swiss Family Robinson*, *Masterman Ready*, and *The Mysterious Island*. It is arguably because O'Dell's castaway is female and indigenous that *Island of the Blue Dolphins* finds this alternative, calmer texture.

To the Wild Sky

Ivan Southall's *To the Wild Sky*[4] carries similar implications to *Island of the Blue Dolphins*, in that the work of a female castaway of, as it turns out, indigenous origins is again highlighted, but this novel is more troubled, and it finds so many tensions to explore among the castaways that it gets only as far as their first days on the island. The reassuring confidence about the child castaway's making do and prospering on the island, which *Island of the Blue Dolphins* carries over from earlier castaway stories about children, is replaced by a questioning that takes no difficulty for granted, but the castaways do cope, and they are ready for further struggles by the end of the novel.

These children are neither heroic nor violent, but changeable, touchy, and quarrelsome. By the end, after much labor and many diversions and disputes, they have achieved the kind of material success that most castaways achieve without fuss, often by using what they salvage from the wreck. They've gotten a fire going and gathered some edible shellfish and seeds. It's not what they salvage or happen to bring with them that launches them on their career on the island, however. (The light plane in which they were traveling has crash-landed just off the island.) Their luggage is drowned, their radio won't function, rafts and messages in a bottle are pointless though they naïvely contemplate them; what works for them is a couple of sticks, and these have indigenous resonances that Southall carefully structures into the story and that take *To the Wild Sky* beyond its sensible realism about children.

The novel begins by cutting the group off from adults and their life as supervised by adults, and then plunges them into a crisis that they have to solve by themselves. The early chapters, which get them away from home and into the air, give us adults who are either fussy or grumpy with children, and children who find the adult world annoying and negative—this in spite of the privilege they are enjoying (they are being flown to a huge cattle station owned by a rich family, the Hennessys, to celebrate the birthday of one of their number, Gerald).

The children have their tensions and disagreements. They are differentiated according to individual character and the roles and reputations the others allot them, as in almost all children's novels involving a group, including *The Swiss Family Robinson* and *Masterman Ready*. The result here is a down-to-earth toughness. There are class tensions, because Gerald is rich, confident, and expects to lead them, but not all the others are happy with that. There are gender tensions, stemming from puberty, and illustrated by Carol, who seems sophisticated and mature and is keen on Gerald, and by Jan, who feels bad about herself and had almost pulled out of the trip. So from the beginning and for the duration, they are uneasy with each other.

Not long after they have taken off, the pilot has a heart attack and dies. The children have to cope with death at very close quarters, and also fly the plane. Gerald takes over; he gathers some command of the plane, and they fly on and on. This has been an achievement, but there is a dust storm, a wind that carries the plane a long way off whatever course the pilot had been following, and cloud hiding the land below. They fly on as if frozen in their positions, Gerald locked in concentration, the dead pilot on the floor, the others in their separate seats, unable to talk to Gerald because of the engine noise. It's a wonderful image of being severed from ordinary society, that of adults *and* of kids, and pitched into an ordeal: "They seemed to be flying away from everything they had ever known; school, home, mums and dads, friends, relations, and everything else that had added up to their lives" (72).

They will find themselves in a different place, a very long way from Coonnabibba, because they have gotten as far as the Gulf of Carpentaria. Gerald, absorbed in keeping the plane in the air, has not been able to set a course or measure how far they have flown. He doesn't dare to land through the cloud. When the cloud comes to an end, a kind of void opens in the evening that has come on: "Suddenly the cloud was gone and there was a void, a pit; two vertical miles of nothing" (73). They descend and eventually crash-land near a beach.

The unexpected sequel deepens the divide from their previous lives. Gerald had assumed leadership and bravely flown the plane; now he has a breakdown. The others have to take over ("It would have been better if Gerald had been dead" [89])—and their first task is to bury the pilot, who really is dead. There's a continual shifting back and forth of capacity and initiative, and those involved feel the humiliation and uncertainty of this, though what is emerging is that the group as a whole is capable, and can do without a leader.

Meanwhile, the text underpins this realism with a clear and wide-ranging contrast. The first—the only previous—white settlement on the island had failed; and the one who finds food for them is Carol, who is able to do this because she listens to the voices of her aboriginal ancestry. Southall handles this in the terms of the culture of Australia in the 1960s. When Carol first thinks of her ancestry, she despairs: "She had a white girl's body, a white girl's skin, a white girl's mind and a white girl's instinct. Nothing of the Aboriginal was left; it had been bred out; it had been lost in white generations. What a shame" (125). In Australia of the 1960s and earlier, it was expected that the "Aboriginal" would be "bred out," extinguished in the white population. Carol is recalling this in ironic circumstances.[5]

She comes across the grim, even sinister remains of the failed settlement, when they are all still hoping to discover a cheerful resort or town around the next headland. Jan responds to the place:

> It wasn't a settlement at all. It was as though men had come here just for the sake of a stupid fight against the bush, just to show how clever they were, just to show how brave they were, but had never looked like winning; had been whipped and beaten and broken and stamped on. They should not have come here—any more than she should have come here.
>
> [. . .] These were strangled ruins, where people had been lonely and desperate and cut off. (151)[6]

Carol wanders off into the bush, and there she is able to open to the voices of her ancestors, and the land, and find seeds and berries that, no doubt, the earlier settlers never noticed and would have rejected. She goes into a kind of trance, and awakes to find two emus regarding her. She throws her stick at them and misses: "She remained there, breathless, trembling, peering out through golden hair into a golden bushland ruled over by two giant birds" (166). She tries again, and this time Gerald finds her, "digging industriously with a stick." She has uncovered food. They have a quarrel in which, disoriented and perhaps ashamed, she accuses him of thinking blacks are dirty: "He let her walk on, away from him, and made no effort to overtake her again. She was walking into the setting sun, a black silhouette crowned with gold" (178).

This contrast between the failed white settlement and Carol's recovery of her aboriginal heritage reconfigures the castaway story. Southall only takes the castaways up to the initial moment of basic settlement (food and fire), but, on the other hand, he underpins the climax of the narrative with a glimpse of the hidden history of human settlement in Australia. This contrasts in turn with the modernity of taxis and planes, and the hints of the power and wealth of Coonabibba, their original destination, whose location was always rather vague and which is now thousands of miles away.

Nation

It Takes a Lifetime to Learn How to Die

TERRY PRATCHETT, *Nation*

Should we generalize on the basis of *Island of the Blue Dolphins* and *To the Wild Sky*, and say that shifting the focus from males and/or a family to indigenous females enables the castaway story for children to recover its earlier capacity to reassure and teach? The evidence of two novels isn't enough for such a generalization, but it is suggestive. Terry Pratchett's *Nation* (first published in 2008) strengthens the possibility.

Nation is breezy and funny. There are comic incidents and much enjoyment of the messy and gross—clumsy, constantly vomiting vultures; an early incident in which Mau has to get milk for a starving infant and does so by making a sow drunk and stealing her milk, getting very mucky in the process (5: 122–24); an old woman who has to have her food chewed for her before she can swallow it (8: 207). The novel is enlightened on matters of race and gender: the original castaways, soon joined by many other refugees from a giant tsunami, are an English girl, Daphne, and the sole survivor of the island's people, Mau, a teenaged boy. (The novel is set in an alternative history, but in a Victorian age in which the English still rule much of the world, contribute much to Science, and confine women in narrow morals and voluminous clothes.) Mau and Daphne get on well, and both find liberation from the restrictions of their cultures. In keeping with this relaxedness, the novel is adept in its variations on common tropes of the castaway narrative, such as the discovery of the footprint and the salvage from the wreck.

As was mentioned earlier in Chapter 1, Mau encounters mysterious footprints in traumatic circumstances. He has been sent apart from the rest of his people for the initiation test that will change him from boy to man; the tsunami strikes, and when he struggles back to his island, he finds it has killed all his people, who were gathered on the beach to welcome him. His first grim task is to dispose of their corpses. During his subsequent exhausted sleep, someone leaves a mango for him, on a metal disc that we recognize as a plate:

> He looked down at the sand. There were footprints there, not large, but they had no toes.
>
> He stood up very carefully, and looked around. The creature with no toes was watching him, he was sure. (2: 35)

"The creature with no toes" is Daphne, the sole survivor of her sailing ship, which was washed right up onto the island by the tsunami. (In fact, she was christened Ermintrude, but she has renamed herself, and this makes a parallel with Pratchett's placing Mau on the cusp of initiation as a man.) Pratchett develops this variation on Crusoe's experience into a comic reversal of the European anxiety about being properly clothed, seen sometimes from the point of view of the islanders, who call Europeans "trousermen," and sometimes from Daphne's point of view, because she is a free spirit in many ways but feels she absolutely must not show her legs. The culmination of this is the scene in which Mau has tentatively put on pants salvaged from Daphne's ship the *Sweet Judy* (the pants seem to him pointless, but he appreciates the idea of pockets) while Daphne has allowed the other, indigenous women who have by this stage reached the island to put a grass skirt on her, but will not yet shed her longjohns. Still, her feet are bare, and, as a voice says in her head, "Everyone has toes!" (6: 178).

Regarding salvage, the islanders take as much as they can from the *Sweet Judy*, and much that is very useful: crowbars, for instance. Mau's thoughts on this are complex. A boat has a spirit of its own, and this is violated here ("They were still stripping her like termites" [9: 250]); and their reliance on the European vessel is a bit demeaning ("How did the trousermen get to have all this stuff?" [6: 158]), given that there is clearly nothing special about the ship as far as the trousermen are concerned. Pratchett does not underplay this; new thoughts have to come before new things, but the castaways need new things, and the pliers and crowbars point the way (6: 168). In addition, he cleverly postcolonializes the impact of the salvage from the western vessel in two ways.

The first happens when Mau and Daphne explore the hitherto completely taboo Cave of the Grandfathers, which has a stone door barring it, which, significantly enough, they can open because they have a crowbar (Chap. 10). The cave is stuffed with the withered or skeletal corpses of male ancestors, so their venturing into it takes courage and defies the dead, but at the farthest end is a series of statues—statues of the gods, but evidence, as Daphne realizes, that the islanders in former times had circumnavigated the globe, mapped the stars with the aid of telescopes, and also (this being a Pratchett novel) devised false teeth made of gold. So the crowbar leads to a complete revaluation of the civilization of the island. Daphne appreciates this because, unconventionally for a girl in her society, she is interested in science.

The second happens when the motley community of refugees, now led by Mau, confronts the formidable and scary "Raiders," led by the villainous Cox. The Raiders are the traditional cannibals or headhunters of castaway and other adventure stories, and Cox is the traditional murderous pirate. The islanders have cannons salvaged from the *Sweet Judy*, but as Daphne knows—and so does Cox, who was the leader of mutineers on the *Sweet Judy*—the cannons are full of holes and not to be fired; so why are Mau and the others pretending they will work? Yet a cannon is fired, knocking over a couple of the Raiders' canoes. Apparently, they do work! This persuades the Raiders to agree to the single combat that Mau eventually wins. But the cannon that fired was not one of the old iron ones from the wreck; it was, as it were, an indigenous one, made of wood and papervine by one of the islanders, already known as the papervine woman. It could be fired only once, but once was enough for the trick to work.

This is all skillfully done, and by making Cox the leader of the Raiders, Pratchett organizes things so that Mau's climactic combat is with a bad white man not a "savage." But the novel also works at a deeper and more challenging level. This concerns confrontation with death. The sole survivor who figures in so many castaway narratives is a sole survivor only because his or her companions or crewmates have all died. This is something that most castaway narratives pass over, or merely allude to, as with the "three of their hats, one cap, and two shoes that were not fellows" that wash up on Crusoe's island (Defoe 1987, 58). Mau's first task after he got back to his island, however, was to dispose properly of the corpses of his people, and he had to split himself into two selves to do it—a "grey body made of mud" that did the work, somehow curled inside the body of Locaha, the god of death (2: 55), while the rest of Mau remained apart. The shock of all this makes him cry out against the gods in protest and rejection so that later, when people from different islands arrive and try to settle, and he becomes their leader, he is still separate, questioning and dismissing tradition, a "demon boy," venturing into the taboo cave of the Grandfathers. (There is a parallel here with *Island of the Blue Dolphins*, where Karana has to take on male tasks formerly taboo to women.)

Daphne also has to dispose of a corpse, that of the captain of the *Sweet Judy*, but the deaths that haunt her are those of her mother and newborn baby in her past back in England, grief unresolved: "The little coffin, so small on top of the big one. She'd never forget it. She'd wanted to look inside, but they wouldn't let her, and they wouldn't listen, wouldn't let her explain" (6: 145). So far, Pratchett exploits the concern of the castaway narrative with practical arrangements; in similar fashion, the children in *To the Wild Sky* had to bury the corpse of the pilot. He will follow this up with variations on the adventure plot. Daphne kills one of the pirates (but she insists that she be put on trial for this, though the islanders have no concept of a formal trial; fortunately, they acquit her). Mau kills Cox in single combat. More interestingly, the confrontation with death is played out in a form borrowed from myth.

Mau begins to succumb to the strain of leading the island community, a strain intensified by the fact that the disaster that overcame his nation has disillusioned him with their gods, and he has said so, loudly. Now he is seen as running, ceaselessly, under the sea, toward a death of exhaustion, and it is Daphne who is deputed by a wise old woman to descend into or near to death and bring him back, out of the grip of Locaha. She succeeds; quotation here will give an indication of Pratchett's range and of how he combines cultures:

> Silence fell like a hammer made of feathers. It left holes in the shape of the sound of the sea.
>
> They stopped running, not because they intended to, but because they had to. Mau's feet hung uselessly above the ground. The air turned grey.
>
> "We are in the steps of Locaha," he said. "He has spread his wings over us."

Daphne has to act. She calls on her memory and finds the right words:

> Words seized Daphne's tongue. It was only a few weeks since she'd heard them before, at the funeral of cabin-boy Scatterling, who had been killed in the mutiny. [. . .] Captain Roberts was a member of the Conducive Brethren, who accepted a version of the Gospel of St Mary Magdalene as, well, gospel. [. . .] now it came out, screamed like a battle-cry:
>
> *"And those that perish in the sea, the sea shall not hold them!*
> *Tho' they be broken and scattered, they will be made whole!*
> *They will rise again on that morning, clad in new raiment!*
> *In ships of the firmament they will climb among stars!"* (8: 226)

This pastiche of bits from "the cauldron of story,"[7] classical, European, non-European, illustrates in miniature the freedom available to fiction for children, as on a grander scale does the whole novel's reorganization of adventure story and castaway tropes, its comic inventiveness (as in the culture of clothes —but even the clumsy vultures are called "pantaloon birds"), its easy didactiveness, its reorganization of our imperial age into that of an alternative history. It can even be a freedom to misconstrue, as when Daphne interprets a patriotic picture of the Empire as showing "the Nobbly Savage," or Mau fails to realize at their first meeting that Daphne has just tried to shoot him (5: 139, 2: 53). *Nation* is on the whole a very positive novel, about gender, for instance: Daphne finds a role among the women of the island, even though the sexes are segregated, but also breaks free of Victorian prudery and acts boldly. It is positive about race and friendship between races: the customs of the trousermen are mocked or tolerated in the novel, but their scientific achievements are celebrated—while those of Mau's ancestors are rediscovered and then vindicated by Daphne in rigorous scientific argument with her father when he has arrived on the island, argument that meets the standards of the Royal Society. Meanwhile Daphne finds plenty of overlap between the culture of the island and that of the novel's version of Victorian England. For instance, when one of the islanders gives an electrifying—and heroicized—narrative of Mau's courage in driving off a shark, Daphne remembers Mr. Griffith the Baptist: "He preached as if he had a flaming sword in his hand. Bats fell out of the rafters. The organ started up by itself. The water sloshed in the font" (8: 214).

Nonetheless, accompanying this buoyancy and wit are serious matters. Death haunts the castaways from first to last, and has to be coped with, or confronted face-to-face, or dealt out. The novel is fun, but the way its characters confront death makes a profound point in the context of the castaway novel. Death—the deaths of all but the castaway or castaways—is set aside in many castaway novels and the narrative devotes itself to survival and settlement, until the stage when various invaders arrive and, if necessary, are killed; but, as we have seen, death and the past (with its ruins and memories) are not so readily dismissed. In the different mode of the novel for children, Pratchett confronts this omission and this haunting, as do O'Dell and Southall in more restricted ways.

Kensuke's Kingdom

In this story, Michael the boy narrator is cast away on a desert island in the Pacific and eventually rescued, but the twist is that he is the second castaway on this island, which is Kensuke's Kingdom. In effect, in the common structure of the castaway story, Michael is the invader, the later arrival that disrupts the ordered settlement of the original castaway. The bulk of the story of his time on the island tells of his relationship with Kensuke, a difficult, bewildering, but eventually warm and productive friendship. Behind the story of how Michael (and his dog Stella, short for Stella Artois) got to the island, which is frightening but within the compass of a twelve-year-old's experience, is the story of Kensuke, which gradually emerges, and takes us into the darker history of the twentieth century. The novel poses what we can call ordinary adventures and troubles against troubles and decisions whose painfulness would challenge any story, let alone one about and narrated by a child; so these troubles and decisions are slow to come to light and are narrated barely and plainly by Kensuke in his newly acquired but simple English. *Kensuke's Kingdom* confronts the limits of what can be told in a children's book or, really, anywhere.

Michael's story takes up the first half of the book; then we have the story of Kensuke and Michael, out of which emerges Kensuke's brief telling of his own story. Then Michael is rescued, and Kensuke chooses to stay behind.

Michael and his parents and dog make up an ordinary English family, hit by ordinary troubles (unemployment), but responding adventurously, setting forth in a yacht until their savings run out. Things begin to go wrong, however, and eventually Michael, on deck alone at night, goes overboard trying to rescue Stella. The yacht sails on; boy and dog are left in the vast dark ocean. All this gives us family life with its normal troubles and affections, a possible adventure for a young person, and a frightening outcome.

When Michael and dog find themselves alive and washed up on a beach, a new kind of adventure begins. It's not really a Robinson Crusoe adventure. They don't support themselves. They don't find food—fish can't easily be caught, and all the fruit that they might have been able to reach has been eaten by the island's gibbons and orangutans. They can't even find water. Instead they are saved and fed by an invisible benefactor who leaves food and water for them. This turns out to be an old man, Kensuke, a Japanese sailor living in solitude on the island since World War II, recalling a modern myth, that of the Japanese soldier living on in the jungle, refusing to acknowledge that the war has ended; a myth with affinities to the castaway tale.

Kensuke doesn't reveal himself until Michael does succeed in accomplishing one of those Robinson Crusoe castaway tasks, lighting a fire. At this point an angry wizened man almost indistinguishable from an orangutan appears, extinguishes the fire, and prohibits the lighting of any fires, including the immense pile of wood that Michael later collects in case he sees a ship. Kensuke at first seems all prohibitions, the more bewildering because he must also be the invisible benefactor. He draws a line across the island and forbids Michael to cross it: each is to keep to his own half. He forbids Michael to swim. None of these orders and prohibitions is or can be explained at first, if only because the old man has little English. Yet he is kindly; he cares for Michael when the latter disobeys the seemingly perverse prohibition on swimming and is nearly paralyzed by jellyfish stings. At this point, as Michael has been moved to Kensuke's cave to be cared for, a reconciliation and revelation begins.

First we learn what a successful and enlightened Crusoe Kensuke has been. His cave (unlike Michael's on his side of the island) is well equipped and furnished, with bamboo partitions and woven mats in Japanese style. He has a warm relationship with the island's orangutans. He spends a good deal of time painting, in classical Japanese style, with octopus ink and brush hairs plucked from the orangutan matriarch as he grooms her. He gradually opens up to Michael, patiently teaches him how to paint, and shares his life on the island. Eventually we learn the grim history of Kensuke's arrival on the island and, more, his wish to remain there, hidden, until his death—hence the prohibition on fires. Kensuke is a doctor; he was drafted into the Japanese navy, leaving behind a wife and son in Nagasaki. His ship beached on the island, with himself the sole survivor. From a visiting party of American sailors he overheard news of the total destruction of Nagasaki and the defeat of Japan. He stayed on, not as one who saw himself as fighting on, as in the familiar story, but disillusioned by the war and the loss of his family. His rejection of humanity was sealed when a party of men from a junk came ashore and began shooting the animals of the island.

Kensuke's relationship with Michael brings him out of himself, as it has led him to reveal the secrets of the island and tell his story; but not very far out of himself. He eventually allows Michael to light his pile of wood and alert a passing yacht, but before this the men from the junk had returned and Kensuke and Michael had only just succeeded in hiding the orangutans from them, and this decides Kensuke not to reveal himself or leave the island. The yacht is the *Peggy Sue*—Michael's parents have never given up their search for him. So the novel ends with his reunion with his real parents and parting from his foster parent, the wise but wounded Kensuke.

The adult castaway, Kensuke, repeats Robinson Crusoe's story of successful settlement, with the added touch, appropriate to our eco-sensitive times, of his companionship with the orangutans. The child castaway depends on Kensuke for his survival, and while he learns castaway skills from him, such as how to fish with a spear, the most interesting and intimate thing he learns is the discipline of painting, a skill belonging to civilization but not particularly to the work of survival or settlement. Meanwhile, Michael draws Kensuke out of himself, and he forgets his division of the island into two and his harsh, nervous prohibitions, and eventually tells his story. It's a story of trauma, unhealed, or, at least, not to be healed by returning to the Nagasaki of his past. Morpurgo balances this, however: Kensuke has a positive role on the island as guardian of the orangutans.

Yet it turns out that his wife and son did in fact survive the destruction of Nagasaki. Michael learns this only after he has published the account we have been reading, and he had agreed with Kensuke that he would wait ten years before doing this. By this time Kensuke's wife is long dead, and it is his son who makes contact with Michael. These complications cast a shadow over the ending of the castaway story, Michael's reunion with his parents, which was already rather implausibly lucky. Michael's castaway story is concluded but Kensuke remains on the island, hidden, as he was before Michael was cast away; and because his story can't be told for ten years, we have to assume that Michael's could not be told for ten years either. There is no hint of what he did tell his parents in the meantime, and his now remarkable skill as an artist in ink must have puzzled them. Michael's parents, bravely sailing in their yacht named for a pop song, are themselves marked by their times—discarded by their society but not really emigrating to a new one, just doing a round-the-world trip while their money lasts. We don't know what they did after that, just as we don't know what story Michael told them, concealing the existence of Kensuke, after they rescued him. It's as if these more domestic stories are pushed out of the way by the grim dimensions of Kensuke's story.

Kensuke's Kingdom is a complex handling of the situation of the castaway narrative in the modern world, after the end of colonialism, after the end of World War II. It binds together two castaway stories, one of them coming out of the darkness of twentieth-century history, which leaves its indelible mark on the castaway; this story shadows and has to be (for ten years) hidden by the more reassuring story of the boy castaway.

There are probably other recent castaway stories for children than those discussed here, but it is interesting that all of them rethink the traditional focus on a Western castaway, either by concentrating on a single non-European, or by adding one to the Western child. It seems that the pleasure and buoyancy of the castaway tale can be recovered for children's stories if at least one of the castaways is not European. It is not surprising that there is practically no killing or violence in these stories, but it is probably significant, again, that there is a lot of death. Evidently the survival and thriving of the child castaway can now be celebrated on condition that death is nonetheless a presence—in the past of the story (Daphne; the caves of death in O'Dell and Pratchett; Nagasaki in *Kensuke's Kingdom*), or the present of the story (Southall, Pratchett).

7

Recent Science Fiction Novels

Science Reaffirmed, Nature Rethought

This chapter discusses *Second Nature* (1986) and *Signs of Life* (1996) by Cherry Wilder, *Across the Sea of Suns* (1984) by Gregory Benford, and *Teranesia* (1999) by Greg Egan. Like the novels for children discussed in the previous chapter, these novels find ways to recover some of the confidence in the castaway's ability to reason and improvise that had marked *Robinson Crusoe* and its successors in the castaway tale of settlement. They do this by reimagining nature and the castaway's relation to it. In Wilder's novels, nature is seen as elusive and a source of wisdom, to be approached with caution and humility. In Egan's and Benford's, it is something that the hard work of reasoning can hope to understand, but which is seen as too powerful and dynamic to be exploited or used. In each of these novels, to rethink nature is to rethink science and its capacities.

In Chapters 3 and 4, discussing castaway tales of the phase of violence, we noted a different temporality: no longer, as in *Robinson Crusoe* and its immediate successors, a progression into the future, toward a developed and civilized island, marked step by step by practical improvisations and achievements, but rather degeneration; decline into violence; the narrative often hinging on some revelation about the past. In those novels the castaway's island might be littered with remnants from the past, often from past wars. The repatriation of the castaway's island that features in several of those novels expresses the feeling that imperialism is coming home in the form of a nemesis or grim joke on the descendants of the confident, energetic colonizers and settlers of its heyday. In the fictions discussed in this chapter, the story happens in the future or on another planet, or both. The shift has no intrinsic meaning, but it allows for distance and the exploration of alternatives, and often accompanies a more inward and ramified depiction of the postcolonial. It's not that the stability and confidence of the phase of settlement is simply restored. The present situation of the various worlds treated in these novels is unstable, not necessarily determined by past history, and therefore of uncertain potential.

In Greg Egan's *Teranesia*, the setting is a postcolonial Indonesia—but it is the breakup of the Javanese imperium that is under way—and the main character, Prabir Suresh, is troubled, gay, Indian,[1] and fiercely committed to scientific rationality, as were his parents for whose deaths he is painfully guilty. In this novel the equivalent of the superstition of the "natives" in earlier fictions is a fatuous blend of New Age religiosity and postmodernism: very much a Western product. In Cherry Wilder's *Second Nature* and *Signs of Life*, the culture of the more recent castaways is shown to consist of an unstable combination of advanced science, New Age dance matriarchy, and macho militarism, while the castaways they encounter from centuries ago have lost both the arrogant confidence and the useful knowledge that go with advanced science, and have come to terms with the vastness and often uncanniness of nature on the planet. Greg Benford's *Across the Sea of Suns* is very much concerned with a lone Westerner, reasoning and improvising in classic castaway fashion, but there is no sign that domination, of nature or of the various alien, mysterious, and powerful creatures he encounters, is even worth contemplating, and he is quite mistaken in his assessment of the one "native" he has to deal with.

Second Nature and *Signs of Life*: Versions of Reunion

"What you mean," he said mildly, "is that I'm not Robinson Crusoe."

CHERRY WILDER, *Signs of Life*

The castaways in Wilder's unfolding narrative find themselves among those who had already been cast away, perhaps generations or centuries earlier, so that the story is then about contacts and clashes between the two sets of castaways. *Second Nature* and *Signs of Life* in fact double the effect of repetition by telling two overlapping stories, both stemming from the same event—the crash-landing of a spaceship on a planet on which humans had crash-landed some centuries earlier. We have the stories of two separated groups of recent castaways, each eventually encountering descendants of the original castaways. The descendants of the earlier castaways have developed a simple agricultural and fishing society but are modestly aware of their ignorance of their past, of much of the planet, and of science. The new arrivals are advanced, with sophisticated technology and enlightened notions of how settlement or first contact should unfold, but in *Signs of Life* it's the new arrivals, nonetheless, who make a hash of their task and degenerate into violence. There's a more positive meeting of older and new castaways at the end of *Second Nature*. "Second nature" refers, after all, to an inbuilt skill that comes naturally, and the descendants of the earlier castaways are closer to having this than the new arrivals.

The two novels explore in different lights both the advanced technology of the more recent castaways and the moment of their contact with the earlier castaways. In *Signs of Life*, the technology is mostly mishandled by a faction of the castaways, the Silvos, who are organized on militarist lines and behave like caricatures of US soldiers in Vietnam. They are ready to find any inhabitants a threat, and stumble into pointless conflict with them when they encounter them. In *Second Nature*, the strand of the story that concerns the recent castaways follows two who have been thrown together and have to reason and collaborate, and culminates in a moving scene of contact with the earlier castaways, the Rhomarians who have meanwhile been searching for survivors and interpreting the clues provided by various bits of wreckage, though uncertain who or what has come down. The moment of contact is a moment of rescue and reunion, as in Shakespearean romance, but its practical aspect is that the recent castaways possess advanced medical knowledge and can now bring it to those who lack it, notably the doctors among the Rhomarians.

Further, both novels reimagine the nature of nature on Rhomary. The tendency of some of the recent arrivals, notably the Silvos, to see nature as something to be feared and dominated, is emphatically repudiated, but what is put in its place is elusive and open. The planet is a source of wonder and the uncanny. It is still largely unexplored, so that the Rhomarians are humble in the face of its size and its unknowns. There are delphins (dolphins), intelligent, able to communicate, and benign; and there were once the Vail (a word obviously related to whale), huge, tentacled, many-sensed, wise and aloof sea creatures whose time sense was alien. The Vail communicated with human representatives, the Envoys, only every seventeen years, when the planet's comet reappeared. *Second Nature* opens with a prologue recalling, from the Vail's point of view, the Rhomarians' first encounter with the Vail; the Rhomarians then came to believe that the Vail died out in "The Great Drought," but live in sad hope of their return. At the end of the novel, their wish is granted. The story of the recent castaways and their eventual meeting with the Rhomarians, the castaways of centuries ago, is thus framed by the story of the finding, loss, and refinding of the Vail. The Vail can be seen as standing for a yearned-for, possibly lost, certainly desired connection with nature in our time. The Rhomarians' feeling that they are bereft ("This world is full of lost things" [*Second Nature*, 227]) stems both from the seeming loss of the Vail and from their awareness of having declined since they were cast away: "by the standards of those first castaways and the standards of Old Earth we have lapsed into barbarism," says Los Smitwode, the doctor, as they contemplate the first-aid box they have found drifting from the recent wreck (*Second Nature*, 77).

In addition, something about the planet has brought the possibility of "dreaming true," prophetic dreams, to the Rhomarians, who regularly tell and respect their dreams. (It's the planet, or aspects of it, that communicates the dreams—the recent castaway Dr. Valenti, while still delirious from the wreck, is given such a dream by one of the Vail [*Second Nature*, 84].) Further, though only a few Rhomarians know about this, there is the presence of aliens called shape-changers, powerful and cold, who take human form and have fabricated a religious sect, the Jenz, for their own purposes, or perhaps out of a sort of callous alienated playfulness, as they too turn out to be marooned and isolated on the planet. These various creatures tolerate the Rhomarians more or less benignly, and there is no way the Rhomarians can claim to be superior to them or to understand them. At one point in *Second Nature*, the delphin, very usefully, pass over to the Rhomarians something they have recovered: it turns out to be the oxper, a kind of android, John Miller. There is some communication between the two species, but then the Rhomarian leader reflects that "there was nothing one could offer such a being but acceptance, even love" (129). "Acceptance, even love" is in striking contrast to the use, even exploitation, that is a common response of the castaway to nature, but it is a response to the huge differentness of the delphin, which consigns the Rhomarians to passivity.

Wilder is very clear on the blundering violence of the Silvos in *Signs of Life*, but in *Second Nature* she involves her text in a more complex weighing of the elements of passivity or bereft helplessness, as compared with the elements of practical activity, in the Rhomarians' lives. The Rhomarians respond intelligently and actively to the signs that a spaceship has come down on their planet, and eventually they do encounter both the castaway party whose fate is treated in *Signs of Life* and the pair of castaways whose fate is treated in *Second Nature*. In *Second Nature*, however, the Rhomarians search the Sooree swamp where Rose Chan and Dr. Valenti have come down just as the latter have left it. The castaways will eventually meet the Rhomarians elsewhere in the form of a young boy flying a kite, and instead it is the Vail the Rhomarian search party encounters in the Sooree. The effect is to weave the two novels out of a whole series of losses, discoveries and contacts; the various castaway stories make one strand in this pattern. The elements of the castaway tale are revised to serve a larger theme, the desire that what is lost be recovered. For the Rhomarians, what is lost is both connection with nature (most strikingly, the Vail) and knowledge of modern science, which the recent castaways, for all their faults, bring with them to the planet.

In novels closer to the *Robinson Crusoe* tradition, rescue and reunion, if it occurs, is played down. The castaway has made a substitute for home that is better, more complete, more in his control, and also in certain ways more natural, than what the wreck has cast him or her away from, so that rescue or reconnection with his or her own kind, when it comes, has no great emotional force, or, in later and bleaker versions, can scarcely happen. Suzanne's return to France, with her happy encounter with the long-mustached Controller of Weights and Measures, is the exception that proves the rule, because *Suzanne and the Pacific* is an anti-Crusoe. In Defoe, Robinson's emotional connection is with Friday, and forged on the island; his later marriage is passed over in a few sentences. The effect is repeated in *The Year of Grace*, where Daniel's eventual marriage is given a little more attention—only for us to be told that he lies awake in the marriage bed pining for the now dead Grock, his companion on the island.

The Rhomarians have scrabbled to make a simple way of life and culture on an inhospitable planet full of mysteries, but they are gripped, some more, some less, by a kind of nostalgia for what has been lost and forgotten since their landing—a feeling the reverse of the colonist's or settler's go-ahead confidence—but also an eagerness to recover it. And they do; by the end of *Second Nature* they have learned a good deal from John Miller, and have made contact with two other survivors, Chan and Valenti, a distinguished surgeon whose knowledge will no doubt be valuable. This contact when it comes at last is moving, because it follows from hard work on both sides, and mobilizes the thoughts about the past and the present, modernity and what is lost in modernity, which shape the novel. It takes the form of rescue and reunion, and in giving it this form, Wilder is revising some fundamental aspects of the castaway narrative, which are most visible in the range of its usual denouements as sketched earlier. Valenti mistakes Ben's kite for a hawk, then realizes it is a kite, and then he meets Ben: "The boy, running and shouting, seemed to be reaching for both of them: he was the boy, the boy was himself, the boy was proving their common humanity" (234). Then the bells of the settlement ring in celebration, reminding us, however, of the way the bells fell silent just a little earlier in the story because a portion of the community left it, unwilling to live in the same place as the android John Miller, of whom they had a religious fear.

In *Second Nature* the castaways rejoice when they encounter an already civilized and ordered society of settlers. Partly by necessity, because they have been cut off from the resources and even, over time, the knowledge and memory of the advanced civilization that built their spaceship, and partly by social choice, these settlers have shed a good deal of what makes for modernity, while retaining other aspects. They have shed advanced technology and the will to dominate nature while retaining, for instance, gender equality. As was discussed earlier, their sense that they are bereft and their humility before nature sometimes lead them to a certain passivity—in fact both the Vail and the shape-changers accuse them of self-pity (169). But there is no doubt that they are hungry for practical knowledge, especially for medical knowledge of the kind that Valenti brings.

As for Valenti and Chan, they have survived, in spite of fever and bewilderment, but there was never any chance that they would or could settle in Crusoe-fashion.

> On the second day as [Valenti] walked on the strip of beach he found the pug mark of a large animal. He shouted for Chan and they bent over the footprint, measured it, sketched it, speculated, peered into the swamp, cracked as Crusoes.
>
> "At least *he* knew what to expect!" said Chan. (*Second Nature*, 146)

(It turns out to be a creature like a sea urchin.)

The environment they find themselves in is inhospitable, and dangerous to their health, the natural life of the place not totally alien but hard to live with—regarding what to eat, for instance. They cope, but they begin to stagnate:

> The new world had narrowed to a warm, interminable day on the small strip of sand and brown grass (166) [. . .]
>
> the brown and blue longueurs of the new world rolled over them [. . .]
>
> It was difficult to keep a diary, it was impossible to develop a routine, he did things out of order because they were small, heavy, boring tasks. (230)

Settled castaway routine is not a possibility for Valenti and Chan. They have to keep moving, even though it is only late in their adventure that they realize the planet might already have human inhabitants. So the successful, settled castaways, who have made a simple abundance as Robinson Crusoe did, are the Rhomarians, and it has taken them centuries; and the planet (their island, as it were), though they have settled it in a civilized, ordered way, remains mysterious and unexplored: it is not a possession and there are no Fridays to be dominated.

In *Signs of Life*, the outcome is more equivocal. The more liberal and enlightened among the castaways are ready for free exchange with the Rhomarians, but this can happen only after the militarized and aggressive faction among them has been defeated in an attack on the Rhomarians, and then in effect exiled. They will be left to their own settlement on the island where the recent castaways landed, began to settle, and fell to violent disputes; from now on they will be cut off from contact with the rest of their own companions and with the Rhomarians. The novel turns away from whatever they may do to survive and settle.

The earlier phase of *Signs of Life* concerns the strains and antagonisms among the castaways. Again, it is modernity that is being reassessed. It turns out to be so riven by divergences as to make coherent settlement impossible. From the picture of the future that Wilder gives in *Signs of Life*, it appears that modern society has developed on a set of tracks that were already laid down in our time, but have since diverged more and more. It's not only that technology has advanced, as in many sf stories: we also have a New Age culture of meditation, peace, and art, represented by the konos, a kind of art and dance troupe headed by a wise matriarch (Myrrha Devi);[2] and we have a curdled macho militarism, represented by the clan of Silvos (from Silver Cross), who are supposed to be technicians but behave like a particularly coarse and irrational set of soldiers. There is no suggestion that there are any wars in the novel's future; the context in which the reader naturally sets the Silvos' behavior is really the Vietnam War rather than anything in the world of the future. In the middle are the regular crew and various scientists, also with ranks (Lieutenant, Sergeant, and so on), but ready to implement settlement and first contact in thoughtful fashion. In addition, a degree of gender equality prevails (the primary point-of-view character in the novel is female) though this is clearly an unstable matter, given the matriarchy of the konos and the machismo of the Silvos. To further complicate matters there are the oxpers, who communicate telepathically, tend to act as advisors to humans in authority to ambiguous effect, and are perhaps evolving—starting to dream, for instance—in the uncanny environment of the new planet. And everyone takes mood-altering drugs as a matter of course.

The castaways' arrival on the planet provokes a widening of their differences and divergences. Once the story gathers speed, this is expressed by a bundle of, by my count, five separated plot lines following groups or individuals that have split apart or split off. There are plots, murders, and secessions; settlement is a mess and first contact, when it comes, is jeopardized by the Silvos' violence. The Rhomarians are represented by the crew of a sailing ship that arrives off the island, and they carry the novel's vision of a modest, uncoercive attitude to nature, which in turn is at times unknowable or uncanny. Regarding the recent castaways, the logic of Wilder's depiction is that the splits and contradictions of their modern society, which is a pointed development of our own, render them incapable of the kind of settlement and development that happens in earlier castaway fictions.

Across the Sea of Suns and *Teranesia*: Sophisticated Science, Unstable Scientists

The rest of this chapter concerns narratives belonging to a very different genre, and thus arriving at their reassessment of science and of nature by a very different route. In Greg Benford's *Across the Sea of Suns* (1984) and Greg Egan's *Teranesia* (1999), relations between the castaway and nature are again rethought, while science, as what promotes the castaway's practical engagement with nature, is taken seriously and carefully expounded. The ingredients of castaway fiction are shaken up and rearranged. The inadequacy of trying to know and exploit nature and natives as if one were separate from them is approached through an awareness of shifts and paradoxes in science that stem from the contemporary sense of the paradoxical and shifting nature of nature: paradoxical and shifting, but still accessible to reason. In each case the text pays careful attention to human, scientific work and thoughtfulness, but there is a transference of understanding and creativity from humans to nature itself.

The effect is that we are asked to slow down and take a close, detailed look at the modern form of knowledge of and reasoning about natural things: science. Sf is a form of fiction well equipped, by tradition and array of story types and protagonists, for this closer look. The result is a set of shifts in the castaway tale: the lone castaway in his work on nature is contrasted with the social aspects of science, collaborative or competitive, and the sojourn on an island is made one of a series of episodes.

This development takes place in a different generic space: that of Hard Science Fiction, so called. The term is a tendentious one. Is the implied opposite of "hard," "soft," or "easy," and why should we bother with the polemical intention behind this labeling and dividing? Nonetheless it is the term that prevails and will be followed here.[3] Hard sf sets out to make narratives of the most advanced science of the day, usually that which is "hard" in the sense that it makes clear predictions and depends on mathematics. This kind of sf has regularly presented individuals coping with difficulties and solving problems in such a way that their ingenuity reaffirms their self-sufficiency as heroes, to paraphrase Benford (1984b, 6), and it is this relation between ingenuity and self-sufficiency that island fictions have dealt with since Defoe—but with increasingly corrosive effect as self-sufficiency becomes domination or madness. *Across the Sea of Suns* and *Teranesia* both reaffirm the value of ingenuity while questioning the self-sufficiency.

Hard sf has often seemed indifferent to sciences and disciplines other than physics and astronomy, and has often seemed indifferent to or conservative about matters of domination or patriarchy. This is where the blended sf and fantasy of Ursula Le Guin and Cherry Wilder entered the picture, drawing on anthropology more than physics or astronomy; but both *Across the Sea of Suns* and *Teranesia* allow a sense of the paradoxes of science to lead the fiction to some radical conclusions. The relation between human as knower and as one who works on nature, and nature as that which is known and worked on, is surpassed. The bridge to this surpassing in the case of *Across the Sea of Suns* is the figure of the alien, close to central to sf.[4]

Egan and Benford are both engaged in modernizing the hard sf tradition in the context of the extreme sophistication of recent advances in, for instance, astrophysics, cosmology, and cybernetics, advances which mean that what science comes up with is in many ways weird and (even more than before) contrary to common sense.[5] Each also explores the subjectivity of scientists, their emotional vagaries and uncertainties. The bluff, uncomplicated go-ahead personality, or what Benford calls the tone of the "wiseguy insider" (1984b, 8), is no longer adequate to the human and social complexities of science as scientists actually do it, nor to the challenging strangeness of contact with the alien. To depict what actually happens when scientists do science is to depict subjectivity and intersubjectivity in its complex fallibility and depth. Benford has been working on this for some time, while polemicizing against other varieties of sf that he considers less disciplined, polluted with fantasy, and so on. *Teranesia* marks something of a turn in Egan's longer fiction in this respect, though it is anticipated by many of his short stories. Prabir, the main character in *Teranesia*, is troubled by his past and his sexuality and dogged by his clumsy body; personages in Egan's other novels, such as *Permutation City* (1994) and *Diaspora* (1997), tend to leap confidently into a hyperdeveloped future, discarding their bodies, if they ever had them.

Across the Sea of Suns

Across the Sea of Suns is a novel about doing science: how scientists behave; the social life of scientists. Indeed, as it develops, *Across the Sea of Suns* expresses reservations about the capacities of humans, humans in groups anyway, to do science. This aspect of the novel hinges on a contrast between the loner and the group that can't always bear the weight that is put upon it, but it does mean that in this novel we have fundamental critical scrutiny of science itself, or at least scientists themselves. Benford gives us the talk, the dispute, the speculation, the rivalry and politics, of scientists at work. There are interwoven snatches of scientific dialogue, mixing speculation, reportage, and discussion, showing how scientists might organize vast amounts of data coming to them almost always from their instruments not their immediate senses, and how processes of speculation and judgment about things vast and mysterious might be natural to them (for instance, Benford 1984, 58–62). So it is in the main part of the story, centered on Nigel Walmsley—difficult, prickly, provocative, and generally right—and set on the *Lancer*, which is exploring a series of planetary bodies for traces of two different kinds of alien, one organic and the other machine based. The exploration takes on more and more urgency as its relevance to events unfolding on Earth becomes clearer. These events are part of a vast, unending conflict between machine-based and organic life and evolution, of which the scientists on the *Lancer* are finding traces wherever they go.

Meanwhile, events on Earth, while they have these huge ramifications, are narrated through the experiences of a castaway, Warren—on a raft, on an island, another island, a raft again. In Warren's part of the text, Benford explores the practical bases of science in technology and in human thoughtfulness about survival, and approaches his reservations about the group as compared to the individual in a very different context. The story of Nigel and the community of scientists on board the *Lancer* is emphatically social; we have "the wash of technical talk" (55), "a cascade of impressions" (63), and Benford adapts the form of the text to reflect this thronging of intelligent but very often anonymous voices. Castaway stories are stories about individuals alone in the face of nature and material circumstances. As it happens, Warren is never literally alone, and this is one of the ways in which Benford complicates and layers the castaway narrative, but Warren is a loner—an engineer, one who improvises, practical, not good with other people or comfortable with language, though in his adventures he is going to have to struggle with a whole series of codes and modes of communication.

On the *Lancer* the science is advanced (plasma physics, electromagnetic pulses), and the scientists often have to work at a distance, through instruments, probes, servo-operated substitutes for their bodies. This is not the whole picture, because Benford gives us sensuous evocations of the forces at work in vast, inhuman things—gases, currents, radio waves, chemical processes, plate tectonics, and interactions at the subatomic level. In addition, life on the *Lancer* has its material and bodily side: Nigel is part of a triangular relationship, with Nikka and also Carlotta, who becomes Carlos, as people on the long voyage start to experiment with remaking their selves. There is a contrast between the experience of Nigel and the other scientists and that of the loner Warren, struggling to improvise a sail for his raft, drinking from the bodies of the alien Swarmers he manages to kill with arrow and knife, and trying to decipher messages in a bottle, or anyway a container very like the traditional bottle, tossed to him by the alien Skimmers who are more friendly, but equally mysterious. ("Swarmers" and "Skimmers" are the names invented by Warren as he struggles to understand the aliens.)

Here in this area of the novel, we have technology in its origins in the struggle to survive (eating, drinking, keeping the sun off, getting the raft to navigate)—improvising, thinking out a problem, pushing yourself, going beyond what seems "natural" to your instinctual self. One example is the episode in which Warren realizes that he and Rosa, who have been together on the raft, must eat the Swarmers and drink their body fluids if they are to survive, though these creatures are alien and dangerous. Another is the episode in which he realizes that, having gained land after suffering on the raft, they must obey the Skimmers' enigmatic directions and not go ashore (Rosa disagrees and dies as a result). This last is typical of the way the novel complicates the castaway narrative. Usually someone who has had a grim time drifting on a raft would want to make the first possible landfall and get down to the business of survival there, but what is required of Warren is more complicated. In general terms we might expect this: a belated version of a narrative will be a complicated one. Something else is at work, however; Warren is only intermittently allowed the isolation of the castaway. The boundaries between him and a series of other agents and purposes that ultimately reach out to the stars are being continually penetrated, and that is why the story of his time as a castaway is so complicated.

The stylistic model is Hemingway: "Five times he went into the water and each time he had to push the fear away from him and swim as smoothly and quietly as he could until finally the fear came strongly and he could not do it anymore" (Benford 1984, 32). There are touches of *Robinson Crusoe* as well: "He kept track of the days by making a deep cut each morning in a tree limb. The ritual sawing became crucial, part of the struggle" (40).

When Warren is finally guided by the Skimmers to an island on which it is safe to land, he finds another castaway there already, Gijan. Gijan has some supplies and a gun, but he is not very enterprising or active. Not so Warren: "New facts, new problems. This island was just a bigger raft with more to take from but you had to learn the ways first" (158). He works out how to make fire, how to distill water, how to catch fish. Then he sets himself to decode the communications that the Skimmers continue to toss him. He realizes that they are using a salad of words from different languages (Japanese, English, German), and asks them to write to him in English only. They do, though the way they use language (strings of nouns, for instance) indicates a very different sense of being and becoming. Nonetheless he is eventually able to form their messages into a sequence, a cosmology followed by a narrative of how they were brought to Earth, and how their young were genetically modified. Their young are in fact the aggressive alien creatures Warren knows as the Swarmers. Engrossed in this decoding and translating, Warren has left the work of running the camp, distilling water, collecting coconuts, and so on to Gijan. He does the brain-work. It seems a revival of the Crusoe-Friday, European-native relationship: Warren has decided that Gijan is a fisherman from a Pacific island. Not so; Gijan reveals himself as a Chinese soldier, posted on the island to communicate with the Skimmers. He has failed in this, but Warren has succeeded, and the Chinese authorities can now make use of these advances. While Warren was absorbed in translating the Skimmers' story, Gijan for his part was off in the jungle contacting his superiors on a concealed radio.

Warren is taken to another island and imprisoned there. Eventually he escapes, and now he has to get back on his raft and head to sea. "Perhaps the Skimmers would speak only with humans who were alone," Warren thinks (239). Certainly they won't communicate with the Chinese, and their contact with Warren resumes only after he escapes. With their blaring acoustic signals to the Skimmers that just deafen them (as Warren empathetically realizes, dreaming of the Skimmers in his cell), the Chinese exemplify the same kind of bureaucratic clumsiness and lack of finesse that is corrupting the scientists on the *Lancer*. There is an alternative: technology in the form of a human manipulating the resources nature provides, thinking, improvising, in physical contact with the problem, but using his reason, not tradition or instinct. This is seen as valuable. It takes us to the material origins of technology in work, struggle, and using your head, the kind of thing that Defoe brings to life and that is still available in so grim a story as *Pincher Martin*.

But it is true that this work mainly enables Warren to survive, and perhaps to pass a test of fitness and intelligence. He certainly does not make his island into a little kingdom. There are no little kingdoms anymore: the task of the whole ramified narrative is to show the interconnections between what Warren is learning on his raft and what the *Lancer* expedition is learning nine light years away. Warren's task is not to subdue nature but to understand it and communicate with the Skimmers, whose status is itself complex, because they have language and even machines,[6] but are mysterious and beautiful. They are like dolphins or whales in their song, like game fish in their leaps. The human-alien contact is really achieved by the Skimmers, who have somehow mastered human language and writing; Warren responds to them, just as they guided him to the right island, though he was clever enough to make a raft that could sail there.

Can we read Warren's story in *Across the Sea of Suns* as a revision or critique of *Robinson Crusoe* and the castaway tradition, with a dash of Hemingway? Certainly Benford shows the value of Warren's toughness, thoughtfulness, and hard work; and then he shows that, loner though he is, Warren can't make an autonomous life or a little kingdom for himself. In *Across the Sea of Suns*, there seems to be an almost irresolvable antagonism between the loner—individualist, unprejudiced, difficult, yet able to listen to and understand nature (Warren, Nigel)—and the organized human group. In the latter the pursuit of knowledge is vitiated by calculations of power and by group-think, as with the Chinese in Warren's story and the "consensus" majority on the *Lancer* in Nigel's story. With both Warren and Nigel, Benford hints that a kind of emptiness of self may be a condition for perceptiveness about the nonhuman (306–7, 341): something very different from self-sufficiency.[7] The castaway narrative is always concerned with the pleasures and dangers of solitude, and Benford draws on this here. Yet the two strands of the text converge in this respect. The community of scientists on the *Lancer* begins to corrupt; its attitude to Nigel's theories becomes coarser, and it is manipulated by the bland Ted Landon almost to the point of endorsing his attempt to, in effect, murder Nigel by putting him into cryonic suspension.

There is a tension between the novel's project of showing us how the community of scientists does science from day to day, and the destined narrative outcome, which is the vindication of Nigel against the herd. Science, or simply careful thoughtfulness, can establish the truth; Nigel and Warren do succeed in this, though few acknowledge it. It seems more and more to be left to the loner. Meanwhile, Benford's positive valuation of the community is shifted to a different level: in posing the rich, struggling masses of evolving organic life against its antagonist, the patient, destructive machine-based life, which is precisely the vastly extended and perennial pattern that Nigel has discerned, Benford evokes the multiplicity, the throng of voices, of the former. It does seem that there are times when he is uncertain that human societies are really capable of carrying forward the cause of knowledge: loners like Nigel and Warren, yes, but otherwise the cause is better served by the alien Skimmers, and in some more general way by the multiplicity of organic life considered globally, or rather universally. There is a comparable shift in *Teranesia*, as the wonderful mind-like powers of the "São Paulo Protein" are revealed.

To come to the question about revision or critique: the castaway narrative has a role to play in the novel's complex rethinking of the nature and prospects of science. This has to do with belatedness, that is, with the implications of coming at a certain point in a developed tradition (both of sf and of stories about survival in the wilderness) and needing to review and strengthen that tradition. The outcome is an effect of layering and complication, as various possibilities are repeated and varied: encounters with many kinds of aliens, journeys on rafts and sojourns on islands, and variations on the theme of conflict between lone observers and politicized groups that are no longer able to observe clearly. There's nothing very remarkable about this effect in itself; stories retold tend to become more complicated and ingenious. What is remarkable is the intelligence of the recontextualizing (to use Hutcheon's term)—the range of the issues that the recontextualized castaway story is able to illuminate. Several of these are fundamental to the castaway story: the scope of practical reason (here, in the context of advanced science), and the contrasts between the loner and society.

Teranesia

Teranesia is set on a remote island, and involves several dramatic escapes from that island back to civilization, but it is not a novel about being cast away, nor a novel about the degeneration brought about by Western science on an island, though it is about a research station on an island and about processes of mutation in nature that have their frightening side. So it doesn't closely relate to or critique either *Robinson Crusoe* or *The Island of Dr. Moreau*, though it does converge with those novels in interesting ways. For instance, it makes use of the trope of naming the island that is often important in castaway narratives (Egan 1999, 3–4); and when Prabir's father fears the family may have to fend for itself in castaway fashion, he plants a garden, only for the home-grown yams to give Prabir diarrhea (16, 33). More important, general qualities of the castaway novel are present: the practicalities and limits of bodily work and activity; the dangers of aloneness (and, in this novel, the dangers of keeping secrets); and the dangers of possessing the island: "This is my island" . . . "You had no right to keep me out"—the child Prabir's rationalization for his primal crime in the forbidden butterfly house (34).

Teranesia tells of a scientist who is also a troubled soul. His trouble stems from his childhood on the island and is stirred up later in life when he sets out to visit it again. At the same time, however, *Teranesia* involves an exciting scientific quest that demands a different, dialogic narrative form, the exchange of reasons and hypotheses.[8] Prabir's capacity to reason and theorize in response to nature is stirred to its highest pitch by the scientific enigma of the São Paulo Protein, at the same time that his guilts and insecurities are so painfully revived that he several times attempts suicide. (What first comes to attention as a series of mutations is seen as a virus, then as a protein, the São Paulo Protein, SPP.) Both the protein and the guilt center on the island where Prabir grew up. The story takes someone doing science (mostly in collaboration with Martha Grant, his temporary partner on the trip back to the island) and helping to achieve a theory that explains a threatening, mind-blowing, and fundamental scientific problem, and at the same time traces how he is also on the verge of breakdown and needs to be rescued by a series of women from a series of emotional crises and physical dangers.

Teranesia resembles Benford's novel in that it investigates and dramatizes how the scientist's human subjectivity is involved in his work, which is part of his life anyway. Prabir is something of a mess, and the sources of this in his past are revisited. His past, in particular his relationship with his sister Madhusree, is then revised in the course of the narrative. Once, he rescued her, while coming to control the narrative of their shared past because he was older and became in effect her father; now she rescues him, as well as improvising a solution to the danger the SPP presents. The text begins with Prabir's naming the island Teranesia and ends with Madhusree renaming it Suresh island, after their family (16, 223). It begins with the child Prabir, monarch of all he surveys, climbing the peak at the center of the island, and ends with Madhusree saving the helpless Prabir by luring the virus out of his body into a different environment: "But once she offered it a path into a sheltered environment where it could feed and reproduce, cell by cell, without facing the same limits, a new feature would appear on the landscape of possibilities. A new peak, not as tall, but far closer" (248).

In Prabir and Madhusree's story, we can trace underlying story patterns, both oedipal and involving rescue and recovery of a lost one: Orpheus and Eurydice, Isis and Osiris, for example (Palmer 2005). Yet Prabir, for all his troubles, helps to solve the conundrum of the virus, and this part of the story is not shaped by underlying myths or repeated incidents (rescues, suicide attempts), but by exchanges with Martha, investigations of specimens of new mutations, and enthusiastic backgrounding by Egan concerning aspects of science at the time of the story.

The novel weighs the value of reason, both as it issues in practical improvisation, and as it issues in the testing and revising of hypotheses about the extraordinary and changing behavior of nature: the business of modern science. In this Egan is like Benford, in suggesting how nature can be understood by the use of reason, in the context of science, and also in suggesting that the structures and processes of nature are autonomous, and have no particular benign or malign relation to human purposes, to which they are indifferent and which they often dwarf. “Life is meaningless” is the novel’s last word (248), though in fact the behavior of the SPP is full of meanings to be speculated and reasoned out.

This is, at a deep level, a revision of the pictures both of science and of nature that run through the varied strands of castaway fiction that were discussed in Chapters 1 to 5. Humans can reason, and their reason can attain understanding. Reason goes beyond the practical improvisation that we see in novels about castaways from *Robinson Crusoe* to *Pincher Martin* and that figures as an element in Egan’s and Benford’s novels too. The exercise of reason opens a way for ordered interchange with others, though it was suggested that Benford was increasingly pessimistic about this in *Across the Sea of Suns*, and in *Teranesia* there is not only Prabir’s personal tendency to concealment, but also the factor of a corporatized science withholding knowledge.

Just as the castaway will tend to make a narrative and also to withhold it from publication,[9] so here there is an oscillation of aloneness and sociality, of the withholding of secrets and the exchange of information. Prabir’s traumatic past and his neurotic and sometimes shabby behavior in the present provide the narrative’s friction. Prabir and Madhusree are repeatedly helped or rescued by strangers, even by their egregious and much satirized postmodernist relatives Amita and Keith, who took the two children in after the deaths of their parents and their escape from the island, and Egan tells us about customs that can ensure the cooperation of Islamic and Christian neighbors in Indonesia (174). Prabir himself, however, is caught in a clumsy dance—he alone knows that it is on Teranesia that the secret of the SPP may be found, but as he works his way toward the island, he has to lie and conceal, because the island is the scene of his primal crime and guilt. Yet neither the clearing up of the puzzle of the SPP nor his recovery of health and sanity can happen without free communication.

Prabir is repeatedly rescued by a series of competent women: one of the scientists distracts the python that was drowning him; Martha thwarts his second suicide attempt; Madhusree frees him from terrorist imprisonment and finally saves his life. But the notion that nature might be gendered female is mocked in the person of the crackpot intellectual who sees nature as “The Unruly Woman” (114). Prabir and Madhusree are Indian, as were their scientist parents, who were also committed members of the IRA, the Indian Rationalists Association.[10] Prabir is probably named after the founder of the IRA (21). He is gay, and has acted as a parent to his sister, but his guilt about his past blocks his happiness in his relations with his sister and his partner. Indonesia is moving further into a complicated postimperial situation, with revolts and terrorisms bringing about the end of the Javanese empire (18) but perhaps replacing it with a conflict of contemporary globalized fundamentalisms such as that of the homophobic "Colonel Aslan." The Colonel is named for the deity of C. S. Lewis's Christian novels, but is "a muscular Papuan man in his thirties, apparently devoted to the Dallas Cowboys" (220). The unseen collaborators of Prabir and Martha in work on the virus are in São Paulo. The world of *Teranesia* has been given a good postcolonial (and feminist) shakeup, and when Prabir proclaims "This is my island," his proclamation can establish no possession, but only the foundation of a neurosis.

In novels of the Crusoe/Moreau tradition, nature is depicted either as passive, or as having in its depths some dangerous tendency to violence and degeneration—bestiality. Either nature is an assemblage of materials that the castaway or scientist can work on—whether this be Crusoe improvising and working, or Moreau cutting and molding the living flesh of animals—or its authentic violence lurks beneath a veneer of civilization. In the latter case, this nature is not exactly part of the island: it is imported, as Moreau imports the beasts that he works on; or it is "human nature," some element in the castaways that being cast away releases, as in *Lord of the Flies* or *The Beach*. Nature in Benford and Egan is an active source of energy and change that the humans have to set themselves to understand. And Egan goes further than this. The mysterious mutation-causing virus, whose activities originated on Prabir's island and were first studied by his parents, turns out to be mind-like in its purposiveness and transformative in its temporality—this in a novel that dramatizes how intensely humans can be drawn back into their unresolved pasts.

The virus, later redescribed as a protein, originated on Teranesia. In going back there to investigate it, Prabir is returning to the scene of his primal, oedipal crime, which itself involved the mutated butterflies that his parents were studying. The child Prabir was fitted with an implant to repel mosquitoes; but this was poisonous to the butterflies, so he was forbidden to enter the butterfly house. Yet one night he sneaked in, groped carefully in the dark, touched and killed a pupa. He told himself that this was his island and nowhere should be off limits to him (34). He followed this with a much more serious transgression, more directly oedipal, and involving (mis)communication. First he had "stolen his father's life" (19), then he had killed him. Chatting on the Internet, he obeyed his father's order never to disclose his identity, but he did this by borrowing his father's identity, and telling stories of his father's early life as if it were his own. When his chat-friend Eleanor warned him of dangerous political developments in Indonesia, his impersonation blundered: in the effort to reassure Eleanor, he signed off with a rebel slogan. Result—or so he guesses: the communication is intercepted, the island is mined from the air, and his father is seriously injured by one of the mines. Worse, in trying to rescue Prabir's father, while Prabir helps by balancing the ladder along which she crawls over the mined area, his mother is killed, and so is his father. These grim deaths are the nine-year-old Prabir's trauma, which his guilt will convert into a primal crime. Yet he did well in the aftermath, getting the infant, uncomprehending Madhusree into a small boat, and navigating across the sea to the nearest island.

Prabir and Madhusree end up in Canada. He becomes her father in effect, sacrificing his scientific ambitions for a dull job in a bank, uneasy in his relationship with his lover Felix, while Madhusree succeeds as a student of biology. Behind and in the past is the haunted island with the unburied remains of their parents. All this reemerges when reports of strange mutations reach the outside world, Madhusree wins the chance to go on an expedition to investigate, and Prabir decides to follow her, realizing that the butterflies his parents had studied were the first specimens of this now spreading mutation. He wants less to help study the mutation, however, than to prevent her reaching the island, scene of his guilt and his achievement, and yet also to protect her from the island.

There will be more human clumsiness and error, but the virus, later and better called the São Paulo Protein, introduces the narrative of scientific puzzle, which is from now on intertwined with that of Prabir's return to his past. The SPP's inventions are marvelous and eerily efficient: perfectly camouflaged fruit pigeons, a cockatoo with teeth, a carnivorous orchid embellished with an exact replica of a beetle on its lip by way of lure. All share the same gene. The wildlife on most earlier castaway islands existed to be used, eaten, or shot. The repertoire of goats, bananas, and coconuts was varied only by thrown-together collections of ostriches, apes, and so forth, none of them plausible in their locations, in *The Swiss Family Robinson* and *The Mysterious Island*. The topography was sometimes compelling, with its hidden grottoes or lagoons, but the wildlife was not. With these creatures in *Teranesia*, we at last meet interesting fauna and flora. The mutations that Prabir and Martha investigate suggest a mysteriously productive and energetic natural world. More important, the seemingly magical activity of the SPP breaks open time and logic and revises the relations of humans and nature.

The mutations seem so efficient as to be adaptive. But adaptations to what? There are now, for instance, thorny plants on Teranesia that did not exist when Prabir was there as a child, but there are no plant-eaters that would need to be discouraged by thorns. When Prabir and Martha reason and speculate, stretching the bounds of evolutionary theory as they do so, they cannot resist the conclusion that the adaptations are *anticipations*. Because the plants are thorny already, the plant-eaters that might have prompted the adaptation have not come into existence to do so; they have, as it were, been deterred. It's getting hard to avoid language that implies planning and intention; equally disconcerting, if these theorizings are correct, the SPP is ranging freely over future and past as it proliferates these mutations across species and orders. Not only does it anticipate the future, preempting threats that might happen, but it does so by reaching back into the past and reviving features discarded in earlier evolutionary circumstances, such as the teeth on the cockatoo. Humans remember the past and imagine or plan for the future; the SPP is mind-like in its operations, but not nearly so clumsy in putting them into material effect as, for instance, Prabir is in his behavior. Later the scientists modify this account: the SPP is not accessing the past so much as quantum possibilities that play out alternatives from which it can learn. This may weaken the analogy implied in the word *mind-like*, but not the impression that nature is leaving humans floundering in the wake of its smooth and dazzling inventiveness.

Yet it is humans who are coming to understand all this. Prabir and Martha and others work through a series of intelligent reassessments of the nature of evolution. In these reflections and tests they come to be living in a kind of charmed, ideal space of thought and reason.[11] *Teranesia* is set in a near future in which various advances in science and technology have become ordinary and commonplace, as often in sf, but more striking is the development in scientific culture. It's not just that at the crisis of the novel, while at sea in a small boat, Madhusree sets out to "synthesise growth factor blockers tailored to the receptors the cells are expressing" so as to stop the SPP's invasion of Prabir; it's that the challenge of this is airily dismissed, "It's a second-year lab project" (237). The characters to be taken seriously are women or men, gay or straight, Welsh or Indian, but all share intelligent articulacy about science—Prabir, Madhusree, Prabir's lover Felix, and Martha Grant, his temporary partner on the expedition to Indonesia. Serious people in this novel naturally discuss evolution the way serious people in our world discuss movies or politics.[12] Their conversations advance the solution of the scientific puzzle, while outside this charmed circle, utopian in its sophistication and seriousness, there are mostly postmodernist frauds (violently satirized by Egan), and New Age or theist cranks.

In classic castaway fiction, the story begins when the castaway arrives on the island and ends when he (or she or they) leaves. So it is, for instance, in *The Mysterious Island*, *The Island of Dr. Moreau*, *Lord of the Flies*, and *The Year of Grace*. This simplification is a condition for the fiction's resonance as a fable. By confining the casting away to an episode and mingling places and social settings, *Teranesia* and *Across the Sea of Suns* join with the capacious novel of social interrelatedness, with its greater provisionality. In this context the relations of humans and nature look very different. *Teranesia* is, however, open to the objection that the world of intelligent scientific exchange, the world of Prabir's neuroses and deceptions, and the world of postcolonial violence are coexistent in the text rather than interrelated.

Teranesia makes it clear that to pass from the other worlds that it depicts (those of personal neurosis and of postcolonial violence, in shorthand) to the utopian space of scientific discussion—the space in which the dazzling nature of the SPP's surpassing of time and logic can be contemplated—you have to move from secrets and lies to openness and exchange, and from aloneness to togetherness. It reinforces this by giving a metonymical function to various incidents in the adventure plot. These incidents can stand for larger issues.

For instance, at a certain point, Martha pushes on ahead of Prabir through the bush, and Prabir is attacked by a python while crossing a stream, and nearly drowned. Fortunately another female scientist happens along and rescues him (158–62). Martha feels guilty about having left him alone, Prabir is in an unsteady state, and now they meet up with the other scientists, including Madhusree, who is furious at the underhand and patronizing way in which her brother has followed her to Indonesia, having at first opposed her going. Prabir's response is to offer to take Martha to Teranesia, where he is sure the solution to the mystery of the SPP will be found; to do this is to betray Madhusree, who would also like to get to the island. He sets a condition, ironic in view of the deceptive way he is behaving: Martha must disclose whatever she finds out on Teranesia, though she has signed a contract of nondisclosure with the corporation that has supplied her boat and all her equipment. She complies, but at once tells the corporation what she is doing (170–71, 176). The corporation submits, for the sake of "some good P.R." These transactions serve as metonymy for broader values: open exchange not secrecy; go together not alone (later, when he is finally to visit the place on the island where his parents died, Prabir says, "I'd rather go alone" and Martha, "We'll go together [. . .] we won't get separated again" [197]).

Because she has refused to leave him alone, Martha is able to thwart Prabir's final suicide attempt. He is able to tell her what he did to his parents as a child. This doesn't quite heal him, however, because what needs to change is his relationship with Madhusree and his possession of the narrative of their childhood on Teranesia. At this point there is a change in the depiction of the SPP. It becomes menacing, eventually taking over Prabir's body and threatening his life. There is a danger here that this shift in the depiction of the SPP will confirm stereotypes regarding deadly and incurable diseases originating in the tropics

(AIDS, Kuru, Ebola fever). Egan handles this by having the terrorists (led by Colonel Aslan) who have captured Prabir, who combine sexual puritanism with homophobia, discover that the SPP is now in his blood. The discovery is scientifically valid, but the narrative allots it to the terrorists not the scientists. With this somewhat disappointing shift in the behavior of the SPP accomplished, the novel is ready to have Madhusree rescue Prabir from the terrorists, escape with him in an open boat (as he escaped with her long ago after their parents' deaths), and rescue him from the SPP by diverting it out of his body into an artificial environment where it can multiply freely. Human ingenuity and technology triumph, and the SPP has come to be seen as simple and constricted: "It had no purpose for anyone, no destiny. No journey in mind, no endpoint. It wanted nothing but itself. More of the same" (246).

It is significant that the story is played out on and through Prabir's almost invariably clumsy and helpless body: failing in his suicide attempts, breaking off an inept sexual advance to Martha (211–12), urinating in his pants (115), caught by a carnivorous plant (151), nearly drowned by a python, and finally taken over by the SPP. Nature certainly afflicts Prabir's body, even though its marvelous activities free his mind, and he displays none of the energetic workmanlike competence of earlier castaways, up to and including Warren of *Across the Sea of Suns*. But this sense that humans are still alienated from nature is, perhaps awkwardly, concentrated in the depiction of Prabir. *Teranesia* in its denouement rejoins the tradition's emphasis on the human ability to understand and improvise, and puts this in contrast to nature's relentless onward drive; in the earlier chapters of the novel, humans and nature are put into a more complicated and closer relationship, and in these chapters the revision of the castaway tradition is at its most radical.[13]

CONCLUSION

Living Phenomena

"Once it was only Nature that produced living phenomena," he concluded. "Now 'tis Reason." And the old sage plunged back into the chatter of his theistic admirers.[1]

ITALO CALVINO, *Il Barone Rampante*

There's a wise passage in Kenneth Clark's *Another Part of the Wood* in which he suggests that in criticism of art, "there must be some ritual, some telling of beads or reciting of sutras, which keeps one's attention fixed on the work till one's powers of appreciation revive" (Clark 1974, 151). He has a point, and I hope that this book has at least worked in Clarkian fashion so that the texts it has assembled and dwelt on now seem the more worth contemplating, rereading, or seeking out to read. Certainly I've found that they have increased in interest as they were read together, as a giant collective text. But where has this contemplation gotten us to—what themes can be elicited, without too much damage to the complexities, backtrackings, and diversions of this collective text as it unfolds in time and across languages?

The history of the castaway tale from *Robinson Crusoe* to the present falls roughly into three phases. It is a story of confidence proclaimed and exerted, then inexorably undermined by anxiety, and descending into violence and insanity, only to recover a degree of buoyancy in recent years. Confidence in the self and its power to work, improvise, survive, and settle gives way to anxiety about the self, its rights and powers, and about civilization. Stories engrossed in day-to-day practical reasoning are succeeded by expressions of the violence of unreason. Unease about the relations of human nature and animal nature, bestiality, displaces the confidence in reason. Thence, more tentatively, the value and the autonomy of nature are reasserted.

It's a chapter in the history of the West's thinking and feeling about itself and, necessarily, its others—subjects, servants, those who are different. It's a varied course of thinking, in the form of narrative, which is given clarity and often drastic or ironic edge by its reliance on revision: retelling a recognizable story pioneered by Defoe, and reusing, but varying and sometimes parodying, a series of images and tropes in a way that readers can easily grasp.

What makes this literary history fascinating is the startling contrast between initial buoyancy and confidence, and an encroaching and often extreme anxiety and rejection. That initial investment in practical reason and in the pleasures of making do gives the castaway tale an enormous and simple energy, so that the contest between this investment and what comes to threaten it is an engrossing and also a productive one—productive in imaginative terms and in terms of what it tells us about the vicissitudes of reason and of the colonial and imperial enterprise. The potential to express or be open to disquiet—to be open to an awareness of the limits of settlement and even of sanity—is built into some of the founding structures of the castaway tale. The elements making for friction and disturbance are present from the beginning. Nonetheless the changes that come over the castaway tale are radical ones; the texts discussed in Chapters 6 and 7 under the heading of Reconciliation suggest a revival of the earlier buoyancy, rather than firmly establishing it.

We can see *Robinson Crusoe* as a powerful and unusual literary experiment, one that sets a challenge for later revisions, as well as incorporating the potential for those later revisions to dramatize the dangers and insanities of the project of survival that becomes settlement or even domination. Defoe's novel suggests—indeed, affirms—that you make your life (your place, which is your life) by planning and working. Your life is not made for you by childhood or family; castaways have abandoned or lost all connection with home and parents. It's a project that relies on the resources of adulthood as Defoe conceives them: thinking, working, persisting, analyzing, making use of what is to hand—what can be salvaged from the wreck, the resources of the island, that is, the things and creatures of the island considered as resources. This is the vessel of Enlightenment Reason, made familiar and accessible by its domestic setting, but destined to venture into alien seas as it voyages on through the nineteenth and twentieth centuries, to times of disillusionment, doubt, violence. Later versions of the tale press the ambitions of this project to greater and even grandiose extents, until they collapse into violence and insanity, as can be seen from a series of fictions beginning with *The Mysterious Island* and *The Island of Dr. Moreau*, and culminating in *Lord of the Flies* and *The Wasp Factory*.

The castaway's island changes its quality, and we can trace the history of this, passing through a phase of abstraction, before nature begins to reassert itself as autonomous and hard to know or use in the phase of reconciliation, as we have labeled it. It was there to be worked on and used in *Robinson Crusoe*, but was present nonetheless in concrete immediacy. In later texts it tends to figure more as a blank space, an abstract field for experiment. Moreau imports the creatures on which he experiments, and he litters the island with the failures, or half-successes, of these experiments. The island has specific, sensuous reality for the bewildered Prentice, but not for Moreau. Pincher Martin tries to turn his rock into a kind of sign; the island in "The Terminal Beach" is abstracted and geometricized; in *The Invention of Morel* it has a technology-enabled fantasy superimposed on it, while the actual, flesh and blood Morel is long gone. Frank in *The Wasp Factory* makes his island the scene of ingenious murders and ritualized sites. In other texts the focus of the needs of survival and ambition of domination becomes the other castaways, as in *Lord of the Flies* and *The Beach*, or even the body of the castaway himself, as in Stephen King's "Survivor Type" and (with qualifications) *Concrete Island*. The megalomania of Moreau echoes in later texts in the form of a blind self-assertion and preoccupation with the self, for instance in Jack the leader of the savages in *Lord of the Flies*; in Pincher Martin; in much of Maitland's behavior on his island in *Concrete Island*. Eventually it becomes a kind of hollowing out of the self, in Frank in *The Wasp Factory* and Richard in *The Beach*: psychopathology without depth.

These are powerfully grim outcomes, and (keeping to this aspect of the modern history of castaway tales for the moment) it is difficult not to see them as reconsiderations of colonialism and imperialism. Colonialism and imperialism release energies and audacities, but survival becomes settlement and domination, the released energy becomes destructive, and the destruction turns inward. The intensifying grimness of this group of castaway tales tracks the darkening of feeling about imperialism, and then its failure. As Westerners retreat from empire, so, in several tales, the island comes with them, repatriated. It says something about the grim momentum of the modern castaway tale that recent post-apocalyptic novels such as Margaret Atwood's *Oryx and Crake* (2003) and Cormac McCarthy's *The Road* (2006) feature episodes in which a survivor, facing the end of humanity, behaves much as did castaways in more buoyant times.[2]

The situation of the castaway, alone on his island, invites a care for the self, and no doubt this allowable egocentricity is part of the attraction of the castaway tale. In later tales, however, this egocentricity can tip into madness and violence, or (as was discussed in Chapter 5) revision of the tale can bring Friday, originally the castaway's companion and servant, closer to the center of the tale, though he tends to haunt or to chasten the castaway without displacing him from the center of attention.

The movement from practical reason directly engaged with material things, to a more abstract and abstracting reason utilizing the island not as a set of material resources so much as a blank space, reflects the modern history of knowledge. As science and technology develop, knowledge gains power from its abstraction from the material things it works on. This is not the end of the story; that nature which was seen as resource or abstracted will reassert itself. Before touching on this, however, we need to sketch the changing relations of the castaway tale with the irrational and the unconscious.

Robinson Crusoe makes his life by working and reasoning, and this suggests that we should take seriously the way *Robinson Crusoe* excludes—or, better, simply lacks—the dimension of childhood and of irrational psychology, for all Robinson's occasional insecurities and guilts. If so, the irrational, and what has often been imagined as the primitive, comes flooding back into the picture, and not only in the form of a violence that gets out of control and a rationality become mere cunning and calculation. The landscape of *Concrete Island*, of *Pincher Martin*, of Tournier's *Vendredi*, of Spark's *Robinson* comes to reflect the body and the psyche of the castaway, or to figure as itself a body with hollows and secret places. This development, in turn, is no doubt a reflection of the broad dialectic of modernity and modernism, if the second is considered a reaction against as well as an expression of the first. The more power is gained by abstraction and utility, the more the countervailing powers of the unconscious assert themselves. The individual who behaved as if he were separate from nature and other people finds that his body and the body of nature resonate with each other, and that other people are apparitions (as in "The Terminal Beach," the text that reimagines its island in starkly abstract terms) or counterparts, as so often with Friday, or that all is imagined (*Pincher Martin*; "The Island of Doctor Death and Other Stories") or virtual (*The Invention of Morel*).

Here we need to pause in this summary. We have already had to simplify, because the island already has its elusive aspects in *Robinson Crusoe*, while the pleasures of making do that are so strong in *Robinson Crusoe* certainly do not vanish from later revisions of the castaway tale, even if they sometimes turn up in ironic contexts, as in *Pincher Martin* and *The Wasp Factory*.

There are, however, countervailing narrative moves, and movements of the imagination. Regarding the first: change the personnel in a tale that always gains intimacy and clarity because it involves so few characters, and a whole series of revisions and overturnings can follow. Make the castaway a woman; change the relations of Crusoe and Friday, or their equivalents; make the castaway an indigene or simply other than an Englishman or European. We noted in Chapter 5 a series of female castaways, and a series of revisions of Friday, and saw that these had far-reaching implications for the nature and status of language, in a form of tale in which language had been used to reinforce a confident, direct contact with and control of things. We noted in Chapter 6 how often recent castaway tales for children introduce both female and indigenous or non-Western castaways. In addition, Prabir in Egan's *Teranesia* and Pi in Martel's *Life of Pi* (the latter also an adolescent) are both culturally hybrid in ways that make one hesitate to use a crude term like *Westernized.*

One can change the nature of the island: in *Suzanne and the Pacific*, the island needs no cultivation, and the effort to survive by work and reasoning would itself be impractical. In *Foe* the island is barren and so is the work that Cruso and Friday devote to cultivating it; Susan Barton finds it dull and simple compared to the richness of Bahia; Cruso's rape of Susan issues in nothing—it is not so much a crime as something null—while, back in England, Susan's sex with Foe is productive. In Tournier's *Friday*, the organic richness of the island has begun to undermine Crusoe's attempts to order it even before Friday arrives, and Friday's relations with nature as well as his own naturalness work to complete Crusoe's transformation. It is in connection with *Friday* that we have to talk in terms of the unconscious as a source of connection and nourishment, rather than talking of the irrational and primitive as a source of violence, whether the violence comes from white men or savages or "beasts." In this and subsequent versions of the castaway tale, it's not a return of the repressed that is involved, so much as a release of nonrational powers that escape formulations of the irrational in terms of violence and the primitive. Not that the matter is simple: that which is explicit, indeed to my sense rather overexplicit, in Tournier is refined and reexamined in a series of later texts, while the imagination of violence has by no means run its course. Nonetheless the castaway tale is infiltrated by a more positive imagination of the natural.

We can approach this broader movement of the imagination by looking at the imagination of the sea in castaway tales. The sea has virtually no metaphorical power or resonance in early castaway tales. The castaways' ships are wrecked by it; the invaders' canoes pass over it easily. The sea hardly figures for Robinson Crusoe himself after he is wrecked. He doesn't even fish in it. It's the island that is all-encompassing; here and in many later tales, versions of the depth and mystery of the sea are incorporated in the topography of the island itself—islands within the island, caves, hollow places, and these places are often sources of insecurity and instability.

The sea reenters the castaway story when it turns toward violence and degeneration, but also when it begins to be infiltrated or haunted by the past. James Hamilton-Patterson offers some useful suggestions: "To go into space is in some sense to go forwards; to go down into the depths is at a psychic level to regress." "As always, the sea is really less connected with space than with time, as if there were a correlation between going deep and going back" (Hamilton-Patterson 2010, 253, 254). The castaway is wrecked at sea, struggles luckily to land, and there, on what becomes his island, he (or she or they) makes a settlement, progresses, by practical reason and hard work. His orientation is spatial; hence the map of the island, though the mapped space of the island tends in later texts to become unstable, kinetic, or subjectified—something that Prendick in *The Island of Dr. Moreau* and Ralph in *Lord of the Flies* experience intensely, the visual and stable giving way to the aural and unstable.[3] The deep connection of the sea with time past that Hamilton-Patterson traces would then seem to threaten this confident forward movement of the castaway tale as inaugurated by Defoe. Space becomes time, in a formula.[4]

Concrete Island conforms to the pattern we are beginning to sketch. The past begins to make its presence felt on the island—ruins, old bunkers—and so does the sea, not as what surrounds the island (concrete, culverts, and so forth) but as a suggestion of the waving grass on the island. The sea (the tide) invades and threatens the land in *The Invention of Morel*, a tale that is haunted by the past and its relics. In other texts, and these among the most violent, the sea is recognized and imagined, but in a way that is both tentative and striking, in the form of meditations and evocations at a distance from the sequence of the action, as if aside: the narrator's meditation on the sea that has received Simon's body in *Lord of the Flies* (170); in *The Wasp Factory*, Frank's meditation on the changes and the power of the sea, which comes after the final stunning revelation has shattered his defenses; the italicized passages on the sea in *Moreau's Other Island*, in this instance explicitly separate from the main body of the text.[5]

In these texts, the sea is an ambiguous presence, as it were kept at a (textual) distance, but its mysterious power, and its threat to the drive for order, is evoked. In the narratives discussed in Chapters 6 and 7, the sea is often imagined more directly and positively. We have the wisdom of the Vail (long-lived sea creatures) in Wilder's novels, or the guidance the dolphins give Karana in *Island of the Blue Dolphins* when she is in danger at sea. It is the power and autonomy of Nature that is expressed, however, not simply its benevolence; the bewildering aliens in *Across the Sea of Suns*, communicative in one phase, violent in another, can serve as an example. We have also Mau's confrontation with the god of death beneath the sea in *Nation*, and Coetzee's return to *The Tempest*'s imagery of death and transformation in the concluding undersea image of *Foe*.

Islands are inviting places to locate fictions because they can be seen as microcosms, but this in itself can encourage envisaging them as spaces for experiment, blank spaces. It's as if that valuation of nature which floods romantic poetry, and is to be found in the novel from Emily Brontë to D. H. Lawrence and beyond, has to be postponed or shut out while the castaway tale deals with the set of problems and forces that we just now summarized, the power of knowledge in separation from nature, the danger of domination of nature tipping into insanity, the release of the irrational and "primitive" in the castaways making the release of the unconscious slow to emerge. When it arrives, it does so in the context of a reconsideration of the relations of reason and nature, in sf, and in the context of ecologism, which can be considered, here, as a contemporary mutation of romanticism's valuation of nature. In each of these contexts, for instance in *Teranesia* as reconsideration of the relations of reason and nature, and in Wilder's *Second Nature* and *Signs of Life* as imagination of an elusive spirit in nature, or Diana Souhami's recent recentering of the Selkirk story on the island as a life form in itself, we are not so far from nature as romanticism imagined it.[6] Nature is an agent and as such something like us (we are part of nature) but larger and more complex than us.

The context is developments in the wider culture, powerful reconsiderations of gender, of race, of colonialism and its aftermath, and of nature in the continuing crisis of the ecosystem. We can also see in this recent phase of the castaway story an instance of the productivity of genre, considered as a machine, or a set of potentials, for turning cultural attitudes and intuitions into coherent narratives. Literature for children very often looks for ways to reassure its readers in the face of adult life in its daunting unknown-ness, and the castaway tale has always attracted writers for children because of its practicality, buoyancy, and connection to fantasies of seclusion and escape. The grim modern history of the castaway tale, for instance in the story of the boys in *Lord of the Flies*, might seem to put an end to all this, but the reconsiderations of race and gender abroad in contemporary culture can prompt revisions of the castaway tale and hence revive the castaway tale for children. The case of sf is more complex, because as science realizes more and more of (to put it amateurishly) the weirdness of nature, the discoveries react back on conceptions of reason and how to apply reason to nature; hence narratives of the elusive, shifting qualities of nature in *Teranesia* and *Across the Sea of Suns*. The dedication to reasoning out nature and reasoning out practical material problems, which is an important aspect of sf, persists in these novels and is refined in the presence of images of what nature is becoming as it shifts and changes.

Optimism about the state of the world and of culture is apt—perhaps too apt—to make the literary critic uneasy. If we turn to another medium altogether, television, we find that things are back to their gloomy norm. Series such as *Lost* and *Survivor*, both of them long running, and the second existing in multiple versions (a British *Survivor*, a New Zealand *Survivor*, and so on) express the popular contemporary conviction that humans stripped of culture, as happens when they are cast away, will show their real selves, and those real selves will be largely or totally competitive, ruthless, and devious. But (as the folktales have it) this is matter for another story that shall be told another time—or by someone else.

> "Robinson Crusoe wasn't so bad," he said. "A bit too bloody sane, but not so bad. Goodbye." (Gardam 1986, 117)

NOTES

Introduction

1. See, for instance, Edgar Allan Poe, *The Narrative of Arthur Gordon Pym of Nantucket* (1837), for the first; and William Cowper, "The Castaway" (1803), for the second.

2. See Martin Green 1990. Green gives detailed attention to the Enlightenment successors of *Robinson Crusoe*, which are passed over here because the focus of the present discussion is on the history of the genre from the twentieth century to the present. In Green's discussion there is a tension between the Robinson Crusoe story, a kind of adventure story, and the literary novel. For Green, too much attention to the values and attitudes of the literary novel (Conrad's is the case in point) is liable to distract us from a clear view of the values and attitudes of the Robinson Crusoe story. Hence, perhaps, he doesn't give much attention to the grimmer twentieth-century versions of the castaway tale, which play an important part in this book.

3. Modern examples, more or less ironic, include J. M. Barrie, *The Admirable Crichton* (1902), and Rose Macaulay, *Orphan Island* (1926).

4. For concrete blockhouses, see Ballard's "The Terminal Beach"; for space stations, Wolfe's "The Death of Doctor Island"; for freeways, Ballard's *Concrete Island*.

5. As many critics have suggested, the writing of a journal, the making of a record of the days as they pass (notches on a pole, for instance), and the exploration and naming of the island's topography are all interrelated, and all reflect the impulse to control and stabilize.

Chapter 1. The Sea Captain and the Perfect Mango

1. Indeed, Defoe follows the success of *Robinson Crusoe* with two sequels, *The Farther Adventures of Robinson Crusoe*, which gives a lot more detail on the population and settlement of Crusoe's island, and a volume of moral reflections; but because later readers and writers are scarcely acquainted with these sequels, they are not discussed here.

2. See, for instance, Zabus 2002.

3. See Hulme 1990, 16–34, and in particular 30: "So according to Locke humanity is defined by use of reason, and the exercise of reason demonstrated by improvement of land."

4. Thomas 2009, Chap. 3, "Work and Vocation," 78–109, at 93. The rest of the

work from which Thomas is quoting, however, *The Complete English Tradesman* (1725), suggests that the individual works not from love and delight but from insecurity, with bankruptcy a constant threat. Robinson Crusoe's situation on his island, with money irrelevant, releases this more simply positive feeling, though it is accompanied even here by a fear of undefined threats and of not doing enough to secure oneself against them.

5. Qtd. in Calvino 2003, 34. Also relevant is the connection Carlo Ginzburg draws between conjectural sciences such as archaeology and medicine, and the everyday practice of reasoning by hunters, farmers, cooks, and others; but when it comes to reading from some sign in the present to some occurrence in the past—the classic occasion for conjectural reasoning—Crusoe tends to falter, as the incident of the footprint on the beach shows. He is more successful when he progresses by reasoning out a process, by trial and error, as with his bread making. Conjectural reasoning on the basis of signs figures more in more recent texts, such as *Teranesia* (see Chap. 7). (See Ginzburg 1988, 81–118, and, for instance, 100–101.)

6. See the discussion in Green 1990, and in Chap. 2.

7. "Man Friday" is in Hope 1985. Hope echoes Keats's lines about Cortez's men when he saw the Pacific; Friday is "stunned with an incredible surmise" (line 152); in "On First Looking into Chapman's Homer," "all his men / Look'd at each other with a wild surmise" (12–13). And here, see Chap. 5, on Suzanne's equally subversive speculation about leaving a female handprint on Crusoe's island.

8. Verne 2005 (1865), 20: 303, 308. This is not a castaway narrative, though it includes a discussion of how much easier the lot of Pacific castaways is than that of Hatteras and his companions wintering in the far north; and the scene in which they salvage a few miserable remnants from their wrecked and burned ship surely alludes to the contrasting richness of Crusoe's salvage (10: 242). (Defoe's Robinson had also wondered whether the footprint on the beach was his own [202].)

9. See Chap. 4 here for discussion of Richard as castaway. This novel marks an extreme point in the castaway tradition because Richard is not only violent, he is *unserious*.

10. For instance, Ballantyne 1995, XXV: 270.

11. The lone survivor in King's story literally eats himself, limb by limb. He is a doctor (defrocked) and a heroin smuggler; he uses the heroin as anaesthetic and performs amputations on himself.

12. There is an excellent discussion of the passage enumerating the casualties by Michael Seidel, who sets it in the context of Crusoe's drive to write and record. Seidel 1991, 78–79.

13. Defoe 1987, 3: 23. (This is a reprint of the 1839 edition; the book was first published in 1726.) And, more pithily, Defoe's manifesto for his *Daily Post*: "just Accounts of Facts in plain Words" (qtd. in Shapiro 2000, 241, n.32).

14. Richetti, 38. Later he refers to "the symptoms of schizophrenia" (42). Relevant passages are that in which Crusoe's parrot speaks pathetically to him (*Robinson Crusoe*,

182), and his discussion of his "disturbed mind" (254), and of course his many struggles with his sinful condition and the purposes of Providence toward him. And see Fisher 1986, 295–96, on how Defoe handles Robinson's years of solitude and makes us believe he "remained fully articulate."

15. See Spacks 2006, especially 47.

16. Peter Hulme has discussed Western ambivalence about wanderers in relation to the story of Cain and to attitudes toward nomads—gypsies, hunter-gatherer peoples. If we look at settlers, including Crusoe on his island, we see one side of this mythical structure; if we look at Crusoe's overall restlessness, and further adventures, and at the eighteenth-century novel of adventure, we see another side. Hulme 1994, 196.

17. Linda Colley (2002, 63–64) feels that contemporary English people would not necessarily have made the connection between their vulnerability to becoming slaves in North Africa and their practice of enslaving Africans.

18. Thomas 1984, 25, 29, 40 (the older attitude); 122, 132, 170 (erosion of the barriers); 165–172, "the dethronement of man."

19. Watch: Book I, Chap. 2 (17 in Swift 1958); mole: Book II, Chap. 5 (89); fire: Book I, Chap. 5 (35). Claude Rawson (2004, 3–4) discusses Swift and Defoe. He suggests that Swift was always intensely aware of Defoe, whom he hated and saw as representing many modern evils. So he would never admit to reading him, but probably did read, especially, *Robinson Crusoe*: "It is more likely that Swift read it than Defoe's other fictions, and it has a teasing relationship with *Gulliver's Travels*."

20. This ending to Gulliver's story is alluded to at the end of *The Island of Dr. Moreau*, while Muriel Spark's *Robinson* in turn alludes to the ending of Wells's novel (1958, 186).

21. Qtd. in Seidel 1991, 34, from *The Works of Daniel Defoe*, ed. Howard Maynadier, New York and Boston: Brainard, 1903, 3: 4.

22. "Robinson Crusoe lost his reckoning in the monotony of his life and that bewildering dream of solitude, and was fain to have recourse to the notches in a piece of wood. What a diary was his! And how time must have spread its circuit around him, vast and pathless as the ocean!" (Hazlitt 1936 [1839], 54).

23. Seidel 1991, 98–99; *Robinson Crusoe*, 332, and also 354 (the reverse case—the Captain as Robinson's deliverer).

24. Giraudoux 1961 (1921), 4: 65. Giraudoux alludes to Bernardin de Saint-Pierre's melon, which was created to be eaten at the family table. (In turn, alluded to in Furet 1981, 91.)

25. McCarron (1996, 290) suggests that Pincher Martin's six days' labor creating his island likewise parodies the Genesis myth of creation.

26. See Halam 2001, 42, 118, 212.

27. Henry Kozicki sees the poem as anti-Crusoe in another sense, in its disillusioned picture of commercial society: "His is the obsolescence and tragedy of commercial man, symbol of a commercial age." His small business is ruined by the rise of

a rival port; he is injured in an industrial accident, and things get even worse when he embarks in a ship called *Good Fortune* (Kozicki 1979, 153; see also 151, n.4). Citations from "Enoch Arden" are from Tennyson 1953.

28. Rennie 1995, for instance, 66–75, 161, 197.

Chapter 2. *The Swiss Family Robinson* to *The Mysterious Island*

1. Johann Wyss, *The Swiss Family Robinson*, edited and introduced by John Seelye (Oxford: World's Classics/Oxford University Press, 1991). The first version, in German, was by Johann David Wyss and his son Johann Rudolf (1812); translated into English by William Godwin or his (second) wife, Mary Jane Clairmont, 1814, from a French translation by Isabelle de Montolieu, who then added a section about as long in its final form as that by the Wysses. Seelye has made changes to splice the two together; the break between the Wysses and Montolieu comes at about Chap. 37/38, or 285. Later editions in English involve cuts and other additions; the whole thing is a collective work.

2. Robert is cited in Tadié 1982, 10.

3. On Providence, see, for instance, the discussion of why the shark's mouth is not at the front of its head: so that some sea creatures can escape it and the stock is not too severely depleted (Wyss 1991, 8: 95).

Commentaries on the imperial collection of information on everything from geology to folktales range from the qualified (emphasizing the breadth of positivism and sheer appetite for information in the West in imperialism's heyday) to the unsparing (all is grist for an omnivorous imperial mill). See, for instance, Drayton 1998, 238–39, and Stafford 1999, 315.

4. Marryat in fact reacted against the errors he found in *The Swiss Family Robinson*, and set out to be more accurate in *Masterman Ready* (Hunt 1994, 56).

5. Marryat 1938, 19: 78–79. Coral islands also interested Darwin; see Marshall 1970, Chap. IV. Darwin will not make his entrance into the castaway narrative until *The Island of Dr. Moreau*; Mr. Seagrave's natural theology is that of the eighteenth century, of Paley for instance. (For more of Mr. Seagrave, see Marryat 1983, 35: 139.)

6. We find Jules Verne similarly optimistic in one passage from *The Adventures of Captain Hatteras*. Dr. Clawbonny theorizes grandly on the virtues of human settlement. We should consider no place "uninhabitable," he says, only "uninhabited." In fact, wherever humans settle, the land is made habitable: "So you must understand that it is man who makes the country habitable, by his presence, his habits, his industry, and even, I will say, by his breath. He gradually changes the exhalations of the ground and the atmospheric conditions, and he purifies things by the very act of breathing!" (Verne 2005, 16: 284).

A parallel in the history of settlement was the notion that "rain follows the plow," by which it was expected that cultivation of the arid Great Plains of the American West would be viable. (See Raban 1996.)

7. Marryat reflects the change of attitude to the convict colony, and arguably to emigration and settlement in general, which is still the subject of unease in *Robinson Crusoe*. Andrew Thompson (2005, 56–57) puts this change in the second half of the nineteenth century. James Belich puts it earlier, noting that "Before 1800, most Britons saw emigration as social excretion" and detailing what he calls "The Settler Transition" in Chap. 5 of his *Replenishing the Earth*, 2009. The remark about social excretion is at 145.

8. In *The Swiss Family Robinson*, all the children are boys and the society is explicitly "patriarchal." Even when they eventually meet Emily, another castaway, she at first bashfully or cautiously pretends to be male, "Sir Edward Montrose."

9. Martin 1990, 167; "Overloading is endemic in the Vernian universe."

10. The text frequently emphasizes this: the processes and designs on which the settlers successfully embark are often described as "simple," and accomplished "soon," or "swiftly"; for instance, 2, XI: 372; 2, XVI: 441; 2, XVIII: 467; 3, VII: 574 ("simple common sense"); 3, XV: 653; 3, XVII: 684. (Verne 2004, translated by Jordan Stump. Stump calls the orangutan Joop; other translations have "Jup.")

11. In the Wesleyan University Press edition of the novel (2001), William Butcher documents the various Robinsonades that Verne drew on, notably *The Swiss Family Robinson* and Fenimore Cooper's *The Crater* (1847), both of which tell of groups of castaways. In *The Crater*, the island that the settlers had ordered and colonized blows up and is destroyed, as in *The Mysterious Island* (Appendix A, 667–72). Paul Alkon and Andrew Martin both emphasize Verne's allusiveness as a writer (Alkon 2002, 77–79, discussing *20,000 Leagues Under the Sea*; Martin 1990, 30).

12. See the discussions of Wells's *The Island of Dr. Moreau* and Bioy Casares's *The Invention of Morel* that follow.

13. "Crusoe and his penned goats are outclassed, outdone, and ridiculed," remarks Michel Tournier (1988, 182). It has to be noted, however, that the original illustrations, by Ferat, give everything a darker and more heroic coloring: the settlers are gaunt and wiry, the woods thick, the rocky parts of the island very steep and haunted by clouds of seabirds. Loxley's statement that the illustrations in Verne are "in precisely the same representational mode" as those in the daily news (1990, 22) doesn't seem to apply in this case.

14. Butcher (1990, 49) argues from Verne's phrasing that Nab is placed on the same level as the party's dog, Top, and possibly below Joop.

15. See Thomas 1984, 130, 136 for a glimpse of the later, racist application of the argument, and also the views of Mac Nabb in Verne 1977 (1867–68), II, XVI, discussing Australian aborigines. Sir Oran Haut-Ton in *Melincourt* is Thomas Love Peacock's witty response to the Enlightenment discussion; references to Monboddo, Buffon, and Rousseau are posed against Oran's gentleness, rough way with malefactors, playing on the flute, and love of a drink: human enough even though he lacks the power of speech. See *Melincourt*, Chap. VI in Peacock 1963 (1817). The orangutan is the primate of choice

when the close relation of humans to apes is asserted (Monboddo and Peacock), denied (Coleridge), or exploited (Edgar Rice Burroughs) in the eighteenth and nineteenth centuries. Richard Holmes (2011, 322) quotes Coleridge on "the absurd notion of Man's having progressed from an Ouran Outang state." On Burroughs's *The Monster Men*, see Chap. 4 here.

16. And see Green 1990, 139: Ayrton as anti-Crusoe.

17. And see the conversation about castaways in *Les Enfants du Capitaine Grant*. Paganel says he could happily live "tout seul" as a castaway, and Lady Helena retorts: "L'homme est fait pour la sociétié, non pour l'isolement. La solitude ne peut engendre que le desespoir. [. . .] quand il se sent seul, loin de ses semblables, sans espérance de revoir son pays and ceux qu'il aime, que doit-il penser, que doit-il souffrir? Son îlot, c'est le monde entier. Toute l'humanité se renferme en lui, et, lorsque la mort arrive, mort effrayante dans cet abandon, il est là comme le dernier homme au dernier jour du monde" [Man was made for society, not for isolation. Solitude can only engender despair. [. . .] when a man feels himself alone, far from his fellows, without hope of seeing his country and those who love him again, what must he think, what must he suffer? His islet is the whole world. He is all humanity and, when death comes, a death terrifying in this abandonment, it is as if it comes to the last man on the last day of the world] (Verne 1977 [1867–68], II, III: 198).

18. Such a number eliminated, such a number left unaccounted for—this happens also in *Robinson Crusoe*, *Treasure Island*, arguably in *Moreau*, and in *Lord of the Flies*. The trope is both reprised and critiqued in the episode in *Suzanne and the Pacific* in which the dead sailors (seven German and ten British) are washed ashore from a sea battle, and Suzanne mourns them and reconstructs their homely lives from the contents of their pockets. The tenderness of this scene is one of the triumphs of Giraudoux's novel, and is in strong contrast to the depiction of violence between males in virtually all of the other texts discussed here.

19. See Verne 2001, xxxi, n.15 (Butcher's introduction). In J. M. Barrie's later parody of the Robinsonade, *The Admirable Crichton* (1904), we have electric light on the desert island.

20. Loxley (1990, 54–61) gives an interpretation of many of the settlers' activities (for instance, the big explosion that diverts the river) as masculinist; she notes moments of significant male tremor when Harbert, the boy they are trying to make into a man, is in danger of death. She comments in the following terms on the photographs of themselves they take shortly after Harbert recovers: "This then is the ultimate masculinist fantasy of autogenesis." (61) At some points in her discussion, Loxley's pedagogical ambitions are fully as relentless as she considers Verne's to be.

Chapter 3. *Moreau* and Its Progeny

1. See, for instance, Terry Eagleton's characterization: "Every formula or social arrangement must now be provisional and self-ironizing—so much ephemeral spume on the wave of the infinite—and the resultant cultural relativism threatens in Conrad, Kipling and others to pull the rug from beneath imperialist ideology, unmasking its fictional nature at just the moment it needed to absolutize itself" (Eagleton 1995, 15). Darwin (2013, 305) gives a more sober account of the intensified imperialist aggression and competition of the period.

2. Hunter (1983) gives many examples, from *Nostromo* (124, 132–34) and *The Secret Agent* (for instance, 157–60), in the context of a discussion of the possible influence on Conrad of a range of broadly post-Darwinian debates on the evolved or hereditary origins of ethics.

3. Blom (2008) offers a wide-ranging account: for instance, 59 (Mach); 79 (Rutherford); 89 (Musil); 278 (Virginia Woolf); 332 (Simmel).

4. In his seminar on *The Beast and the Sovereign* (published 2011), Derrida works between Robinson Crusoe and Heidegger, worrying at the distinction between human and animal, sovereign and beast, a distinction Heidegger theorizes in terms of the human capacity to apprehend the "as such" of beings. What this "as such" means had better be left to those with a firm understanding of Heidegger, but if there can be a comment on it in the very different form of the novel, then we can say that *The Island of Dr. Moreau* undermines a whole series of avatars of the "as such." Later castaway fictions return persistently to the question of the beast, the beastliness of humans, humans becoming beast or being misrecognised as beast (Simon in *Lord of the Flies*) or recognizing equality with beasts (Pi and the tiger Richard Parker in *Life of Pi*).

5. See Thomas 1984, especially Chap. III, Pt. iii ("The Narrowing Gap," 121–36) and Chap. IV, Pt. iii ("The Dethronement of Man," 165–80). It's the growing humanity of attitudes to animals that is Thomas's main interest; Wells enters this long discussion in the West at the moment when the dark underside of social Darwinism is interacting with imperialism, and inhumanity is the result.

6. As Frank McConnell says (1981, 91). Michael Fried: "*The Island of Dr Moreau* must be one of the most unpleasant books to read in world literature" (1994, 101).

7. Thence we will have the "taste of blood" that is a motif in the regression of the beast people later in the novel. Earlier narratives allude to cannibalism (Caliban) or have the protagonist witness it (*Robinson Crusoe*; *The Coral Island*). Wells goes for it, though at the same time, as usual in the novel, blurring the categories, because we are not sure whether the beast people are of the same kind as each other. There is a full discussion of carnivores and blood eaters in Wells in Kemp 1982.

It is usually "savages" who are imagined to practice cannibalism, so they can be defined by this, as "the cannibals." But Westerners can resort to it also. There is a significant episode in Poe's *The Narrative of A. Gordon Pym of Nantucket* (1837): the survivors on a drifting hulk eat one of their number, after agonizing debate; but this was unnecessary, because shortly after, the hulk turns turtle and its bottom is found to be covered with edible barnacles. Poe's narrative is offering a catalogue of horrors, many of them committed by Negroes or natives—mutiny, massacre, treachery—and it seems that cannibalism has to find a place.

8. Roger Bozzetto (1993) gives an excellent account of the various generic levels of the text (adventure story, fable, island myth, and so on), but in doing so, I think he lends clarity to a text that is successfully destabilizing to its reader, as the experience that he underwent was for the narrator. There is a sense in which commentary on the novel can be too clear: by this clarity we are rescued from Prendick's panic confusion, which is vital to the novel's effect. See also Atwood 2005, 390.

9. Swift 1958 (1726), Book IV, Chap. X: 230.

10. The best discussion of the element of parody in *Moreau* is Parrinder's. Bergonzi has a good summary and list of target texts: "*The Island of Dr Moreau* is composed of extremely literary materials." Shippey sees the novel as a kind of attack on canonical literature—a point that is compatible with Bergonzi's. Showalter also emphasises the novel's literariness, though from a broader viewpoint: "The psychological, literary, social and intellectual sources of *The Island of Dr Moreau* are enormously complex, and this story deserves to be read in the company of Kafka, Conrad, Camus, and Coetzee." Parrinder 1970; Bergonzi 1961, 100; Shippey 2005, 21; Showalter 1992, 77.

11. Here Moreau's ancestor is Prospero. Bergonzi (1961, 100) calls *Moreau* a "demonic parody" of *The Tempest*.

12. Wells gives a clear statement of the idea in his story "The Lord of the Dynamos": "And Azumi-zi was practically a savage still; the veneer of civilization lay no deeper than his slop suit, his bruises, and the coal grime on his face and hands" (Wells 1987, 287). In a discussion of the notion of the alien as it applies to Wells's fiction, John Reed shows, however, that Wells increasingly felt that the alienating force within humans was less their drive to animality than their drive to subordinate matter/flesh to mind/spirit. From this point of view, *Moreau* shows how each kind of alienation can be horrifying, and that the beast people and Moreau are two aspects of a single deformation (Reed 1987).

13. Le Guin 1973, 8: 74. See the discussion of the issue in de Waal 2006.

14. By this time the potential humanness of the orangutan, which had been the subject of speculation in the eighteenth century, and is perhaps behind the depiction of Jup in *The Mysterious Island*, has clearly become savagery. The orangutan is human in exhibiting the same lust as other humans in *The Monster Men*, or in brutal violence, as in Emmanuel Frémiet's sculpture, "Orangutan Strangling a Native of Borneo" (1895) in the Museum of Natural History in Paris (illustrated Schultze 1970, 181).

15. Relevant passages are at 7, 159, 195 in Wright 1928. Brian Stableford (1983) has

discussed *The Island of Captain Sparrow* in the context of Wright's oeuvre as a whole. He argues that characters in Wright commonly turn to nature as preferable to a corrupted industrial society; nature is tough and harsh, but not the source of degeneration. H. de Vere Stacpoole's *The Blue Lagoon* (1908) presents a similarly idyllic view of nature, which teaches the castaway cousins the delights of sex. Here the "nature" that shapes Em and Dick is kept separate from that of the indigenes who have visited the island and left signs of grim violence behind, but are never encountered by the rather Aryan-seeming pair the story deals with.

16. Bioy Casares's later collection, *La Trama Celeste* (1948), includes another variation on *Moreau*, "The Future Kings." It's an inversion, in that the equivalents of the beast people are working on and subduing the equivalents of Moreau.

17. *Robinson Crusoe*, 144; *The Mysterious Island* 2, XV: 423.

18. This heading comes from Aldiss's introduction to the Everyman *Moreau*, 1993, xxxiv.

19. Ruddick (1993, 178) says it is better seen as an homage to *Frankenstein* than as an homage to *Moreau*; perhaps so, but there are a lot of resemblances to Wells's novel.

20. Overy 2009 (published in Britain as *The Morbid Age*), especially Chap. 5; Baldwin is quoted on 176. Edward Bond is quoted in Sinfield 1983, 98. Shauffer (2006, 66) sums up, "The idea that the beast inheres in us supports the idea that 'civilization' is something of a veneer."

21. Everett 1986, 110. By contrast, John Bayley, in the same volume, sees the novel as "placing wholly actual and authentic children in an uncreated and unimagined background" (Bayley 1986, 133).

22. See the skeptical account of the endings of this and other Golding novels in James Gindin 1962, Chap. 12, especially 198.

23. Norman Page 224, contrasted to 93. This is a powerful moment in Peter Brook's film (1963): Percival tentatively touches the officer, and then when he is asked his name, his lips move and he can't make a sound.

24. The extinction of Jack's inner life might be signified indirectly by Ralph's lapses, in which his mind simply goes blank (156, 181): perhaps we are to guess that this process has gone a lot further in Jack.

25. Yet there are moments of happiness, and of what might be called pastoral, for example 60; but they are ambiguous: "Eyes shining, mouths open, triumphant, they savoured the right of domination. They were lifted up: were friends" (27).

26. A good example is the passage in which Jack, Ralph, and Simon climb the peak early in the novel (21–27); this passage includes classic castaway moments: "We ought to draw a map" (Ralph, 24); "This belongs to us" (Ralph, 26, when they view the whole extent of it from the peak). Others include the exploration of what will become Castle Rock (112–17), then trekking back along the shore of the island.

27. See the critical discussion in Keegan 1993, 94–103.

28. See Chap. 16, "Spring, Sacred and Profane" in P. Conrad 1999, 381–99; the connection with fascism is discussed at 390–91.

29. "He asked for it," says Piggy of Simon's death (173). He won't let Ralph name it as murder, though Ralph does name it—just as Jack won't name the action ("In the silence that followed each savage flinched away from his individual memory" [177]).

30. Barbara Everett discusses this aspect of the novel: "The 'childishness' of Ralph and Piggy, Simon and Jack gives their history a dimension of mock-heroic or grave burlesque. The horror of the political side of the action, which needs no stress here, is both sharpened and lightened, made personal and strange, by being played out by little boys" (1986, 123). She concludes, "The children's innocence diminishes the 'adulthood' their corruption is helplessly in love with" (123). Eloquent as this is, it perhaps settles the novel into too calm an equilibrium.

31. Stone throwing has happened earlier too (64–65), also involving the sinister Roger.

Chapter 4. Successors of *Moreau*

1. Such as the island in Conrad's *Victory*, or that in Ion L. Idriess's *Madman's Island* (1938), on which the castaways were prospecting for tin.

2. See the recent play dealing with the depopulation of the Chagos Islands to make room for a Cold War military base. Its title: *A Few Man Fridays* (by Adrian Jackson, London, 2012). Hashima is the stunningly stark island of abandoned mine works that featured in a scene from the film *Skyfall* (2012).

3. Stephen Boyd's words (1988; for example, 55). Boyd sees the enema that Martin improvises at one point as "a rather appropriate punishment"—"sodomising himself" (54). He also comments that "On the world of the rock these earthly goods and comforts are profoundly unsatisfying" (53): so much for food and drink. For a more recent example of the same kind of response, see McCarron 1996, 289, writing of Martin's "egotistical and perverse refusal to die."

4. Pritchett 1991, 614. Gindin (1962, 202) is also skeptical: "the novel ends by supplying its own parody." In the United States, the novel was published as *The Two Deaths of Christopher Martin* (1957).

5. Compare *Concrete Island*, where the injured and marooned Maitland speaks his name out loud, "as a self-identification signal" (4: 30).

6. Pincher is confined to reading the inscription on his identity disc (5: 76).

7. Castaway narratives are not the only intertexts to *Pincher Martin*. Golding's novel alludes to Prometheus and Lear, as well as *Pincher Martin, O.D. A Story of the Inner Life of the Royal Navy* by "Taffrail" (1916). See Page 1985, 101–11. Page comments that Golding's novels are like "counterblasts or rejoinders" to earlier texts. The "source" is like a speech in a debate with which Golding takes passionate or ironic issue (101).

8. Changing uses of "pre-" suggest the percolation through contemporary culture of unease about the relations of present and future. My very aged aunt recently suffered a serious fall and her doctor told us this was a "preterminal event."

9. Parrinder (1992, 193–204) discusses the significances of beaches in Ballard's fiction as places that mark epochal transitions, as happened, for instance, when life crawled up out of the sea. No doubt this is alluded to in the story's title, as well as Nevil Shute's *On the Beach* (1957); but in fact the story turns away from the beach, into the labyrinthine interior of the island.

10. In his discussion of Ballard ("Alone among the murder machines"), David Punter comments on features of his style: "Thus the unlubricated style, the piling of paragraphs, the refusal of inward inspection become themselves parodic equivalents for the deadly masculinization of the planet" (Punter 1985, 27). This helps to explain the poignant presences of Traven's wife and child in "The Terminal Beach," if they are that which is denied by "masculinization."

11. This happens in Chap. 20, "The Naming of the Island." Miranda teaches Caliban language, also with negative results. (Shakespeare 1968, I, 2: 353–65.)

12. See, for instance, Brigg 1985, 69–74. Often a surrender to the sun is involved, for instance at the end of *The Drowned World* (1962) and "News from the Sun" in *Myths of the Near Future* (1999), and in another sense in *Empire of the Sun* (1984). In this Ballard joins a broad strand of solar worship in modernist culture, along with Tournier (as will be seen in Chap. 5), Bataille, and D. H. Lawrence.

13. All this is also true to the experience—the neurological phenomenon—of having a broken leg. See Sacks 1984.

14. Several stories in the later *War Fever* (1990) develop the trope of a space vastly bigger inside than outside: "Report on a Newly Discovered Space Station"; "The Enormous Space."

15. An intense concern with security is, however, also to be found in *Robinson Crusoe*. Seidel sees the overcoming of this obsession as Crusoe's achievement in the novel; he becomes able to leave his island.

16. See, for instance, Rudyard Kipling's reminiscence: "When my father sent me a *Robinson Crusoe* [. . .] I set up in business alone as a trader with savages [. . .] in a mildewy basement room where I stood my solitary confinements. My apparatus was a coconut shell strung on a real cord, a tin trunk, and a piece of packing-case which kept off any other world. Thus fenced about, everything inside the fence was quite real, but mixed with the smell of damp cupboards. If the bit of board fell, I had to begin the magic all over again. I have learned since from children who play much alone that this rule of 'beginning again in a pretend game' is not uncommon. The magic, you see, lies in the ring or fence that you take refuge in" (Kipling 1937, 9–10). A ritual is devised, and a confined space for fantasy is thereby made "real."

17. Nairn 1993, 128.

18. This happened while Frank's mother was giving birth to Paul, whom Frank would later murder: nothing subtle about the family dynamics here, and Frank himself underlines the connection of Paul and Saul.

19. Banks returns to what can easily be read as oedipal themes in several of his sf novels, including *Against a Dark Background* (1993) and *Use of Weapons* (1992). The latter is closest to *The Wasp Factory*, in giving importance to a primal crime and to the main character's sensational discovery of his true (mis)identity, but again the psychology seems schematic—like a parody of a collection of clues to be interpreted in Freudian terms.

20. Mister Duck dies near the beginning of the novel (that is, "Mister Duck he dead"); he quotes "The horror" as the descent into violence intensifies beyond Richard's affectless game-playing. The latter doesn't understand: "*What horror?*" (419).

21. I owe this point to Riquet 2010.

22. Later, when things begin to fall apart, some of the community want to take the corpse of Sten to the mainland and inform his parents—but they don't (310). At the very end, those who get away from the beach to the mainland telephone their parents: "The last thing I want to do is lapse into sentimentality at this stage, but we were all crying by the time we'd hung up" (438).

23. In their history of the beach in Western culture, Lena Lençek and Gideon Bosker devote their last chapters to the failure of what they have depicted as a quest for "paradise": the more people strive to make the beach an alternative to the mess and crowdedness of the city from which they are escaping to the beach, the more the mess and crowdedness follows them. Their comment on the 1960s is relevant to the situation of Garland's backpackers: "During the years of the Vietnam War and the 1970s, the beach was "primitivized"—returned to an imagined state of nature where mostly single young adults came for spiritual reinvigoration, and to escape the discordant realities and false needs of a world whose center would no longer hold (Lençek and Bosker 1998, 248). The failure of this quest is easy to trace and is inscribed in *The Beach*: Bali as a place to drink, Goa as a place to take Ecstasy.

24. I was prompted to this view by Palitzsch 2010.

25. The second more effectively than the first. Rebecca Duncan notes that the central episode on the lifeboat "features very little religious or spiritual insight," though there are plenty of invocations of gods or God (Duncan 2008). The film (directed by Ang Lee, 2012) works harder at the spiritual, aided by magnificent images of the vast ocean and tiny boat; we have less of Pi's practical reasoning.

26. "How I Wrote *Life of Pi*" and *Life of Pi*, 317. Yet Martel underlines another relevant aspect of the matter when he remarks in his later novel *Beatrice and Virgil*, "We are cynical about our own species, but less so about animals, especially wild ones. We might not shelter them from habitat destruction, but we do tend to shelter them from excessive irony" (Martel 2010, 29–30).

27. An anecdote that Martel apparently substituted for the fact that Richard Parker was the name of a shipwreck survivor who was a victim of cannibalism (Duncan 2008). Philip Hoare (2014, 48) mentions that the cabin boy in Poe's *Arthur Gordon Pym* who is about to become a victim of cannibalism is also named Richard Parker.

28. Richard Parker, 87, 97; Orange Juice, 111.

29. Martel read "castaway and disaster stories" when researching the novel (http://www.powells.com/fromtheauthor/martel.html); possibly, however, he refers to stories about sailors drifting after shipwreck, such as the narratives of the wreck of the whale ship *Essex*, to which he refers on 189.

30. Duncan (2008) maintains that this "prequel" "disrupts a logical chronology of events." Perhaps this judgment follows from her decision to read the novel as a survivor narrative; otherwise, it seems logical to start a novel called *Life of Pi* with the main character's early life.

31. Animals contented in zoos (16–19); his father's lesson about the ferocity of animals (31–39); rhinos and goats (26); the circus trainer as alpha male (43–44).

32. Flying fish (183); dorado (185: "Killing it was no problem"); young sharks (221); turtle, (200–202). The sequence, which traces Pi's increasing willingness to kill and eat whatever he can get hold of, begins with his moment of compunction about the animal fat in the biscuits that are among the lifeboat's stores, continues through the passages just cited, and circles back to the biscuits: "By the time the last of the biscuits had disappeared, anything was good to eat, no matter the taste. I could put anything in my mouth, chew it, and swallow it—delicious, foul or plain—so long as it wasn't salty" (213). The anticlimactic rhythm of the novel kicks in a page or so later: "After just a few weeks my body began to deteriorate" (214).

33. For instance, the work of Frans de Waal. See also Derrida's questioning of Heidegger's notion that animals, unlike humans, don't have "world," his reaching for what they do have in common, and his circlings around notions of power as crucial in this regard (Derrida 2011). In giving us the relations of Pi and Richard Parker, Martel is working with a broad and exploratory definition of power.

Chapter 5. Always Another Island

1. The heading comes from Bishop, "Crusoe in England," lines 8–10, in *Geography III* (1976).

2. "If a man is bored, excite him; if a woman is bored, hold her close." "In exchange for advice so useful for her, Australia sent for me." The novel was translated on its first appearance, but this translation is not readily available. The present discussion uses the French text (Paris: Grasset, 1961).

3. "The owl, which used to leave the hold each evening, greeted by 'owl' in all the languages of the globe, and flit round the ship."

4. The other relevant episode is the death earlier in the novel of Marie-Sévère, one of Suzanne's friends.

5. "like the request stops of the trams, in Paris"

6. "This island, which has become something which mingles with my soul."

7. This happens in *Robinson Crusoe* too (238); it's the prelude to the wreck of the Spanish ship whose survivors end up eventually on Crusoe's island.

8. There is an interesting discussion of Giraudoux's indirect and independent treatment of World War I in Winter 2006, 127–32. Winter discusses *La Guerre de Troie N'aura Pas Lieu* (1935), finding in it an irony that brings Giraudoux closer to English writing about the war than to that of his compatriots.

9. Tournier simply has "dix-neuf jours" (235). *Vendredi ou les Limbes du Pacifique* (*Friday or the Limbo of the Pacific*) was first published in 1967, and published in a revised version in 1972. Tournier further rewrote his novel in a version for children, *Vendredi ou la Vie Sauvage* (1977). Tournier often writes versions of older texts or stories, and often recycles his own work. In this discussion, the first reference in each case is to Norman Denny's translation (1969, published as *Friday or the Other Island*) and the second to the revised French edition of 1972. It seemed better to refer to Tournier's revision even though Denny translated the first version; differences have been noted. *Vendredi ou La Vie Sauvage* is briefly discussed in what follows.

10. Actually, Jeudi in Tournier's original: "C'est je jour de Jupitre, dieu du Ciel. C'est aussi le dimanche des enfants" ["It's the day of Jupiter, god of the sky. It's also the Sunday of children"], but Dimanche in his later version for children because according to Robinson it is "le jour des fêtes, des rires et des jeux" ["The day of parties, laughter and play"] (126). Many of Denny's changes have to do with names; for instance, the ship that eventually calls at the island is the Heron in Denny, and the Whitebird (already English) in Tournier.

11. See, for instance, Dunmore 1965.

12. *The Wind Spirit* (*Le Vent Paraclet*) 1968, 161, 190.

13. In *La Vie Sauvage* it is Friday who makes a canoe, his skill and efficiency contrasted to Robinson's ineptitude as a boat builder. (Philip Boucher comments on how Friday seems to lose all his native skills once he is rescued and converted in *Robinson Crusoe*: "Never once in the novel is Friday depicted as using his 'native' skills. It is Crusoe who teaches the Carib to build a barbeque pit!" [Boucher 1992, 127].)

14. See Gascoigne 1996, 56–68, for an account of Robinson's metamorphosis. He sees Robinson as needing to emancipate himself from an authoritarian male patriarchy into which he has swerved by way of reaction against his own weak father, who is in contrast to Robinson's loving and strong mother. He downplays Friday's role in the process.

15. In his autobiography Tournier discusses the topic of a dedication of *Friday*; the novel should have been dedicated to the immigrant population of France, "those silent

masses of Fridays shipped to Europe from the third world" (Tournier 1998, 197). The dedication was not made, and perhaps would not have fitted the novel's interest in Friday as he affects Robinson. Tournier delivers on his feelings about immigrants and his interest in anthropology with *The Golden Droplet*, and its sympathetic main character, Idris (*La Goutte d'Or*, 1985; *The Golden Droplet*, 1987).

16. "To construct, organize, order"; "regularized, mastered"

17. For the leech, see 47/47; for the rats, 22/24. (Most of this is omitted from *La Vie Sauvage*.)

18. Roger Shattuck (1984, 21) gives a more sympathetic account, commenting that "Tournier gives appropriate space to Crusoe's sexuality" and noting that Tournier sometimes "explores the limits of plausibility and fantasy."

19. See also his treatment of the injured vulture he is tending: he chews maggots to make a mush before feeding it to the bird. (We already know that Robinson finds vultures repulsive.) 154/172; 26/29.

20. See the cited edition of *La Vie Sauvage*, which includes critical commentary, at 181.

21. 19–21 (Robinson's labor and failure with *L'Evasion*), compared with 58–59 (Friday's efficient construction of a pirogue); 48 (complications of the cultivation of rice) compared with, for instance, 78–80 and 111 (Friday's sophisticated cuisine, and how he makes the Aeolian harp). For Friday, the transformation of Andoar is release into a new life ("Andoar va voler," "Andoar va chanter" [105, 111]), so this is more than play.

22. "Squeezed, all three of them, under a mass of rock, Robinson, Friday, and the kid Anda, all eyes, watched this terrible spectacle, and listened, all ears, to the singing which seemed, at the same time, to fall from the stars and to climb from the depth of the earth."

"Meanwhile, Friday was using a knife to cut the inside parts that were still stuck to the shell. Suddenly, the tortoise rolled on its side; leaving its shell on the ground. It got back on its feet and set off galloping toward the sea, followed by Tenn, running behind barking. Then it plunged into the waves.

'It's made a mistake,' said Friday calmly, 'By tomorrow crabs will have eaten it.'"

23. The term is used by Don DeLillo of the character Karen in *Mao II* (1991, 119).

24. There's a further play on words, as Fernández Cubas notes in an interview: "un año de desgracia," meaning misfortune (Beilin 2004, 137).

25. But as Fernández Cubas notes in an interview, Daniel forgets to include *Robinson Crusoe* in his list of the adventure novels that marked his childhood (Beilin 2004, 133). For Daniel's list, see 30.

26. "There was never in the world such an intelligent creature as his companion."

27. "I had passed from poor and shipwrecked to cruel, voracious and starving."

28. "He can go absolutely anywhere on the island, except into the gloomy, lifeless wood, where nothing can make him go. The wood is his god."

29. "De esclavo a dama de compañía, de náufrago a Sherezade . . . La verdad, no podía dejar de sonreír ante mi ascenso" [From slave to lady companion, from shipwrecked sailor to Scheherazade . . . It's true, I couldn't refrain from smiling at my elevation] (137).

30. "The fathomless mysteries of the laws of flotation."

31. These are the facts that Fernández Cubas read in a brief story in a newspaper: the germ of her novel (Beilin 2004, 133).

32. "Simple and inoffensive as a child."

33. "The old man looked at me with an expression that was impossible to define."

34. In his review of Gunter Grass's *Crabwalk*, J. M. Coetzee notes that the subject of the novel "is not the sinking of the *Gustloff* but the need to write, and the coming to be written of, the story of the sinking of the *Gustloff*." (Coetzee 2008, 142) The *Wilhelm Gustloff* was sunk by a Russian submarine late in World War II and perhaps as many as 10,000 people died, including many children: an atrocity in which the victims were German and thus arguably hard for a German to make into a novel. Coetzee as a white male writer can be seen as tackling another set of difficulties in writing about Susan and Friday.

35. Critics are often suspicious on this point; see, for instance, Victoria Carchidi: "Certainly, as Edward Said suggests, it is presumptuous to write the story of another; inevitably that tale will be shaped to reflect the aims and goals of those who write it" (Carchidi 1993, 81), or Gayatri Chakravorty Spivak: "I confess to a certain unease reading a man's text about a woman" (Spivak 1991, 159).

36. Cruso is more irrational about cannibals than was Robinson in Defoe. He tends to imagine them everywhere, and there is no equivalent in *Foe* to Robinson's meditation on what cannibalism might mean to those who practice it.

37. But contrast Carchidi's sense that "Barton" is rapacious and imprisons Friday, and Coetzee "sexist" and "racist," dwelling on Barton's body. Carchidi doesn't refer to the passage about the tribe that communicates with its tongue, or mention Susan's attempt to return Friday to Africa; she says that she "sleeps with" Cruso (Carchidi 1993, especially 82–85).

38. In *Concrete Island* Maitland gets Proctor to carry him about on his back. See Ballard 1974, 19: 143.

39. Jean-Paul Engélibert says that the narrator here must be seen as the reader; he doesn't offer evidence for this idea (Engélibert 1996, 276).

40. For instance, Head 1997, 116; and Attwell 1993, 114: Susan and Foe "lie in a casual embrace signifying, perhaps, the de facto, unspoken collusion of the male tradition with its unauthorized female counterpart."

41. And could there be yet another allusion, this time to Foucault's phrase, referring to sexuality, "the fragment of darkness that we each carry within us" (Foucault 1990, 69)?

42. Bishop 1976 and Walcott 1986.

Chapter 6. Recent Children's Novels

1. "For children" is a summarizing term here; *Kensuke's Kingdom*, for instance, is a novel for young adults.

2. For the image of the crab, see *Nation*, 2: 56.

3. The adaptation of Defoe's familiar figures is completed in the sequel, *Zia*. A report by a white sailor who has been to Karana's island gives us the footprints:

> "But you saw her with your own eyes?"
>
> "Saw her and her footsteps, too."
>
> "It could not be a man that you saw?"
>
> "Men don't look like women even on that island. No, I saw her and her footsteps." (O'Dell 1976, 4: 22)

4. See also Fisher 1986, 314–16.

5. Clare Bradford (2009, 293) notes that Australian fiction for children had begun in the 1960s to modify these attitudes. She mentions Southall's *Hill's End* (1962) and *Ash Road* (1965) and novels by Colin Thiele and Reginald Ottley as "project[ing] onto the natural environment a sense of unease about the shallowness of European knowledge and habitation, through novels in which children struggle for survival in an indifferent or hostile landscape."

6. The ruined colony perhaps reflects the failed attempts to establish a British outpost on the Coburg Peninsula, in the present Northern Territory—there were in fact three failed attempts: Fort Dundas, Fort Wellington, and Port Essington. The last (1831–49) left ruins that still exist, and a vivid account by T. H. Huxley during the voyage of the *Rattlesnake*. See McCalman 2010, 191–94.

7. Clute and Grant 1997, 173, 704. Both entries are by Clute; the phrase comes from Tolkien.

Chapter 7. Recent Science Fiction Novels

1. Karen Burnham (2014, 29) has him as Indonesian, with Indian parents, born on an island in Indonesia, living in Canada.

2. "The konos came from their camp at midday and offered singing for all, anti-stress therapy in smaller groups" (70). Žižek (2001, 1) claims that the psychotherapeutic practice of "western Buddhism" is the "hegemonic ideology par excellence of late capitalism."

3. See "Hard SF" in Clute and Nicholls 1993, 542; the articles "On Hard Science Fiction" edited by Samuelson 1993, 145–240; and Burnham 2014, 18–19 (on "radical hard SF").

4. "There is probably no more fundamental theme in science fiction than the alien" (Benford 1987, 13). Wilder's Rhomary novels perhaps give too amiable a picture of the

alien; this is redressed in the episode in *Second Nature* concerning the powerful and sinister shape-changers, whose role in the overall narrative is, however, obscure.

5. Fredric Jameson (1987, 241–47, 243) has commented on this "transformation" of science in the context of hard sf.

6. At one point Warren sees the Skimmers gathered at something on the seabed that he recognizes as alien, yet as a machine: "There is a logic to a piece of equipment that comes out of the job it has to do and he felt that this machine was well shaped" (164). The novel's vast scope and its suggestion that humans do advance in knowledge, in spite of their deficiencies as social, political animals, depend on this assumption that the universe has an underlying structure and uniformity. (Benford's brisk dismissal of postmodernist and other theories is at 194.)

7. The person in quest of or in contact with aliens becomes alienated from himself and other humans: this is how Samuelson sees it (1978, 5–19).

8. On these double aspects of the novel, see also Blackford 2005, 448: "the vision of a universe that offers no privileged place or role for humanity, and is indifferent to our actions and needs—but is open to rational investigation."

9. Examples include *The Island of Dr. Moreau* (Prendick's nephew is dubious about the reliability of the text he is publishing); Spark's *Robinson*; *Dr. Franklin's Island*; and *Kensuke's Kingdom*.

10. An actual organization, as Egan emphasizes in an author's note.

11. As Burnham points out (2014, 62, 121), this idealism is taken further in Egan's more recent novels set in the far future, where the practice of science is unhindered by political or economic interests and disputes.

12. Prabir's father's realization that he wants to be a scientist is narrated on 21–22. This is the discovery of a vocation, in a novel that is frequently scornful of theism.

13. A recently published castaway novel in the genre of hard sf is Andy Weir's *The Martian* (2013). *The Martian* features a sustained series of practical improvisations, all of them based on carefully detailed science. Unlike earlier castaways such as Crusoe, this castaway knows and details the relevant science, but, like earlier castaways, he deals with ordinary things (rocks as ballast; sugar as ingredient in an explosive; potatoes as food source). The traditional castaway novel's emphasis on practical reason is thus updated and reinforced. The novel is mainly narrated by the castaway, Mark Watney, and in the buoyant, buttonholing style of much hard sf with, in this case, lots of jokes and disclaimers of sophistication. The castaway is utterly alone, but Earth is in contact (but not always communication) with him. His improvisations and solutions to problems and emergencies are soundly based in science but often involve risky transgressions of rules and procedures (explosions; discarding safety equipment), and, being a buoyant and jokey person, Watney takes these risks with a certain glee. The result is a revision of the relations between the loner and the collective of scientists that we noted as relevant to Benford and Egan. The bureaucrats at NASA and the crew of the spaceship

that will rescue Watney find themselves also, against their will, adopting his risky recourses.

Conclusion: Living Phenomena

1. Calvino 1998, 214. *Il Barone Rampante* was first published in 1957. "The old sage" is Voltaire.

2. Very relevant here is Michael Crummey's *Sweetland* (first published 2014), the story of an aging man who turns himself into a castaway on his island (named after his family) when the rest of his community has been moved to the mainland of Newfoundland. The novel traces his tough, stubborn making do, the encroachment of hallucination, and his eventual death, and all this is done with solid sensuous vividness.

3. See, for instance, *The Island of Dr. Moreau*, 12: 116, and *Lord of the Flies*, 212.

4. The sea has a very different, rich presence in *The Tempest*, where it is accompanied by a very different presence of the past, given that Prospero's project is to redress this past and that the play begins with an extended account of his past sufferings, explaining the bitterness and desire for revenge that he will spend the rest of the play overcoming.

5. See Chap. 3, 65; Chap. 4, 86; Chap. 3, 60.

6. *Selkirk's Island* (2002). Souhami's book is not fiction; it is an account of the life of Alexander Selkirk, whose sojourn on Juan Fernandez Island is thought to have influenced *Robinson Crusoe*; but it is definitely a reimagining of Selkirk's story in light of the contemporary valuation of the natural. Selkirk is softened and nurtured by nature; see, for instance, 17–19, 99–100, 94 ("He became the island's man"), and 104 ("It was as if The Island claimed him with its secrets, its essential existence, made him a part of its rhythms, turned him fleetingly into more than he was").

BIBLIOGRAPHY

Aldiss, Brian. 1982. *Moreau's Other Island*. London: Triad Granada (1980).

———. 1993. Introduction to H. G. Wells, *The Island of Dr. Moreau*. London: Everyman.

Alkon, Paul K. 2002. *Science Fiction Before 1900*. New York and London: Routledge.

Atwood, Margaret. 2005. "Ten Ways of Looking at *The Island of Doctor Moreau*." In *Writing with Intent: Essays, Reviews, Personal Prose 1983–2005*, 386–398. New York: Carroll and Graf.

Bachelard, Gaston. 1969. *The Poetics of Space*. Translated by Maria Jolas. Boston: Beacon Press.

Ballantyne, R. M. 1995. *The Coral Island*. London: Penguin (1858).

Ballard, J. G. 1966. "The Terminal Beach" (1964), In *The Terminal Beach*, 136–57. Harmondsworth: Penguin.

———. 1974. *Concrete Island*. New York: Farrar, Straus and Giroux (1973).

———. 1990. *War Fever*. London: Collins.

———. 1999. "Myths of the Near Future" (1982). In *Myths of the Near Future*. London: Vintage.

Banks, Iain. 1990. *The Wasp Factory*. London: Abacus (1984).

Banks, Iain M. 1988. *Consider Phlebas*. London: Orbit (1987).

Barth, John. 1968. "Anonymiad." In *Lost in the Funhouse: Fiction for Print, Tape, Live Voice*, 168–201. Garden City, NY: Doubleday.

Bayertz, Kurt. 1990. "Biology and Beauty: Science and Aesthetics in *Fin-de-Siècle* Germany." In *Fin de Siècle and its Legacy*, edited by Mikulàs Teich and Roy Porter, 278–95. Cambridge: Cambridge University Press.

Bayley, John. 1986. "The Impersonality of William Golding: Some Implications and Comparisons." In *William Golding: The Man and his Books*, edited by John Carey, 126–37. London and Boston: Faber and Faber.

Beilin, Katarzyna Olga. 2004. *Conversaciones literarios con novelistas contempáraneos*. Woodbridge, Suffolk: Tamesis.

Belich, James. 2009. *Replenishing the Earth: The Settler Revolution and the Rise of the Anglo-World, 1783–1939*. Oxford: Oxford University Press.

Benford, Gregory. 1984. *Across the Sea of Suns*. New York: Timescape (Simon and Schuster).

———. 1984b. "Is There a Technological Fix for the Human Condition?" *Vector* 119: 5–15.

———. 1987. "Effing the Ineffable." In *Aliens: The Anthropology of Science Fiction*, edited by George Slusser and Eric S. Rabkin, 13–25. Carbondale and Edwardsville: Southern Illinois University Press.

Bergonzi, Bernard. 1961. *The Early H G Wells: A Study of the Scientific Romances*. Toronto: University of Toronto Press.

Birkerts, Sven. 1987. *An Artificial Wilderness: Essays on Twentieth-Century Literature*. New York: William Morrow.

Bishop, Elizabeth. 1976. "Crusoe in England." In *Geography III*, 9–18. New York: Farrar, Straus and Giroux.

Blackford, Russell. 2005. "Greg Egan." In *A Companion to Science Fiction*, edited by David Seed, 441–51. Oxford: Blackwell.

Blom, Philipp. 2008. *The Vertigo Years: Europe, 1900–1913*. New York: Basic Books.

Boucher, Philip P. 1992. *Cannibal Encounters: Europeans and Island Caribs, 1492–1763*. Baltimore and London: Johns Hopkins University Press.

Boyd, S. J. 1990. *The Novels of William Golding*. Hemel Hempstead: Harvester.

Boyle, Danny, director. 2000. *The Beach*.

Bozzetto, Roger. 1993. "Moreau's Tragi-Farcical Island." *Science Fiction Studies* 59, Vol. 20, Pt. 1: 34–44.

Bradford, Clare. 2009. "Australian Children's Literature." In *The Cambridge History of Australian Literature*, edited by Peter Pierce, 282–302. Melbourne: Cambridge University Press.

Brantlinger, Patrick. 1988. *Rule of Darkness: British Literature and Imperialism, 1830–1914*. Ithaca and London: Cornell University Press.

Brigg, Peter. 1985. *J G Ballard*. Mercer Island, WA: Starmont House.

Brook, Peter, director. 1963. *Lord of the Flies*.

Burnham, Karen. 2014. *Greg Egan*. Urbana, Chicago and Springfield: University of Illinois Press.

Burroughs, Edgar Rice. 1913. *The Monster Men*. New York: Ace (nd; first published 1913 as *A Man Without a Soul*).

Butcher, William. 1990. *Verne's Journey to the Centre of the Self: Space and Time in the Voyages Extraordinaires*. Basingstoke and London: Macmillan.

Calvino, Italo. 1998. *Baron in the Trees*. In *Our Ancestors*, translated by Archibald Colquhoun, 73–284. London: Vintage (1957).

———. 2003. *Hermit in Paris*. Translated by Martin McLaughlin. New York: Pantheon Books.

Carchidi, Victoria. 1993. "At Sea on a Desert Island: Defoe, Tournier and Coetzee." In *Literature and Quest*, edited by Christine Arkinstall, 75–88. Amsterdam and Atlanta: Rodopi.

Casares, Adolfo Bioy. 1964. *The Invention of Morel and Other Stories* (from *La Trama Celeste*). Translated by Ruth L. C. Simms. Austin: University of Texas Press (*The Invention of Morel* first published 1940).

Clark, Kenneth. 1974. *Another Part of the Wood*. London: John Murray.
Clute, John, and Peter Nicholls. 1993. *The Encyclopedia of Science Fiction*. London: Orbit.
Clute, John, and John Grant. 1997. *The Encyclopedia of Fantasy*. London: Orbit.
Coetzee, J. M. 1987. *Foe*. London: Penguin (1986).
———. 1999. Introduction to Daniel Defoe, *Robinson Crusoe*. Oxford: World's Classics.
———. 2001. *Stranger Shores: Essays 1986–1999*. London: Secker and Warburg.
Cohen, Margaret. 2006. "The Chronotopes of the Sea." In *The Novel*, Vol. 2: *Forms and Themes*, edited by Franco Moretti, 647–66. Princeton and Oxford: Princeton University Press.
Colley, Linda. 2002. *Captives*. New York: Pantheon Books.
Conrad, Joseph. 1963. *Nostromo: A Tale of the Seaboard*. Harmondsworth: Penguin (1904).
———. 1963b. *Victory: An Island Tale*. Harmondsworth: Penguin (1915).
———. 1973. *Heart of Darkness*. Harmondsworth: Penguin (1902).
Conrad, Peter. 1998. *Modern Times, Modern Places*. London: Thames and Hudson.
Couégnas, Daniel. 2006. "Forms of Popular Narrative in France and England: 1700–1900." In *The Novel*, Vol. 1: *History, Geography, and Culture*, edited by Franco Moretti, 313–35. Princeton and Oxford: Princeton University Press.
Crummey, Michael. 2015. *Sweetland*. London: Corsair (2014).
Csicsery-Ronay, Istvan. 2003. "Science Fiction and Empire." *Science Fiction Studies* 90, Vol. 30, Pt. 2: 231–45.
———. 2005. "Science Fiction/Criticism." In *A Companion to Science Fiction*, edited by David Seed, 43–59. Oxford: Blackwell.
Darwin, John. 2012. *Unfinished Empire: The Global Expansion of Britain*. London: Penguin.
Davis, Lennard J. 1983. *Factual Fictions: The Origins of the English Novel*. New York: Columbia University Press.
Defoe, Daniel. 1945. *The Farther Adventures of Robinson Crusoe*. In *Robinson Crusoe*, edited by Guy Peacock, 223–427. London: Dent (1719).
———. 1987. *The Life and Adventures of Robinson Crusoe*. London: Hamlyn/World's Classics (1719).
———. 1987b. *The Complete English Tradesman*. Gloucester: Alan Sutton (reprint of the 1839 edition; the book was first published in 1726).
DeLillo, Don. 1991. *Mao II*. London: Jonathan Cape.
Derrida, Jacques. 2011. *The Beast and the Sovereign*, Vol. II. Translated by Geoffrey Bennington. Chicago: University of Chicago Press.
de Waal, Frans (with comments by Robert Wright, Christine M. Korsgaard, Philip Kitcher, and Peter Singer). 2006. *Primates and Philosophers: How Morality Evolved*. Princeton and Oxford: Princeton University Press.
Donald, Tania. 2000. *Island Dystopia*. PhD diss., La Trobe University.
Drayton, Richard. 1998. "Knowledge and Empire." In *The Oxford History of the British Empire*, Vol. II, edited by P. J. Marshall, 231–52. Oxford: Oxford University Press.

Duncan, Rebecca. 2008. "*Life of Pi* as Postmodern Survivor Narrative." *Mosaic* (Winnipeg) 41, No. 2 (accessed at Proquest).
Dunmore, John. 1965. *French Explorers in the Pacific*, Vol. I: *The Eighteenth Century*. Oxford: Clarendon Press.
Eagleton, Terry. 1995. "The Flight to the Real." In *Cultural Politics at the Fin de Siècle*, edited by Sally Ledger and Scott McCracken. Cambridge: Cambridge University Press.
Egan, Greg. 1999. *Teranesia*. London: Victor Gollancz.
Engélibert, Jean-Paul. 1996. "Daniel Defoe as Character: Subversion of the Myths of Robinson Crusoe and of the Author." In *Robinson Crusoe: Myths and Metamorphoses*, edited by Lieve Spaas and Brian Stimpson, 267–81. London: Macmillan.
Everett, Barbara. 1986. "Golding's Pity." In *William Golding: The Man and his Books*, edited by John Carey, 110–25. London and Boston: Faber and Faber.
Feeney, Dennis. 2008. "How Virgil Did It." *Times Literary Supplement*, Feb. 15.
Fernández Cubas, Cristina. 1985. *El Año de Gracia* [*The Year of Grace*]. Barcelona: Tusquets.
Fisher, Margery. 1986. *The Bright Face of Danger*. London: Hodder and Stoughton.
Fitzgerald, Robert, translator. 1998. *The Odyssey of Homer*. New York: Farrar, Straus and Giroux.
Foucault, Michel. 1985. *The History of Sexuality*, Vol. I: *Introduction*. Translated by Robert Hurley. New York: Vintage.
Fried, Michael. 1994. "Impressionist Monsters: *The Island of Dr. Moreau*." In *Frankenstein, Creation and Monstrosity*, edited by Stephen Bann, 95–112. London: Reaktion.
Furet, François. 1981. *Interpreting the French Revolution*. Translated by Elborg Forster. Cambridge, New York and Paris: Cambridge University Press.
Gardam, Jane. 1986. *Crusoe's Daughter*. London: Abacus (1985).
Garland, Alex. 1997. *The Beach*. London: Penguin (1996).
Gascoigne, David. 1996. *Michel Tournier*. Oxford and Washington, DC: Berg.
Gindin, James. 1962. *Postwar British Fiction: New Accents and Attitudes*. Berkeley and Los Angeles: University of California Press.
Ginzburg, Carlo. 1988. "Morelli, Freud, and Sherlock Holmes: Clues and Scientific Method." In *The Sign of Three: Dupin, Holmes, Pierce*, edited by Umberto Eco and Thomas A. Sebeok, 81–118. Bloomington and Indianapolis: Indiana University Press.
Giraudoux, Jean. 1961. *Suzanne et le Pacifique*. Paris: Grasset (1921).
Golding, William. 1956. *Pincher Martin*. London: Faber (published in the United States as *The Two Lives of Christopher Martin*).
———. 1988. *Lord of the Flies*. London and Boston: Faber (1954).
Green, Martin. 1990. *The Robinson Crusoe Story*. University Park and London: Pennsylvania State University Press.

———. 1991. *Seven Types of Adventure Tale: An Etiology of a Major Genre*. University Park: Pennsylvania State University Press.

Greenblatt, Stephen J. 1976. "Learning to Curse: Aspects of Linguistic Colonialism in the Sixteenth Century." In *First Images of America: The Impact of the New World on the Old*, Vol. II, edited by Fredi Chiappelli, 561–80. Berkeley: University of California Press.

Halam, Ann (Gwyneth Jones). 2001. *Dr. Franklin's Island*. London: Ted Smart (Orion).

Hamilton-Patterson, James. 2010. "Seven-Tenths: The Sea and its Thresholds." In *The Penguin Book of the Ocean*, edited by James Bradley, 250–57. Camberwell: Penguin.

Hawkins, Harriet. 1995. *Strange Attractors: Literature, Culture and Chaos Theory*. New York and London: Prentice Hall and Harvester Wheatsheaf.

Hazlitt, William. 1936. *Sketches and Essays*. London: Oxford University Press (World's Classics).

Head, Dominic. 1997. *J M Coetzee*. Cambridge: Cambridge University Press.

Hoare, Philip. 2014. "Castaway José Salvador Alvarenga." *Guardian Weekly*, Feb. 14–20.

Holmes, Richard. 2011. *The Age of Wonder*. London: HarperPress.

Hope, A. D. 1985. "Man Friday." In *The Age of Reason*. Carlton: Melbourne University Press.

Hulme, Peter. 1990. "The Spontaneous Hand of Nature: Savagery, Colonialism, and the Enlightenment." In *The Enlightenment and its Shadows*, edited by Peter Hulme and Ludmilla Jordanova, 16–34. London and New York: Routledge.

———. 1994. "European Ethnography and the Caribbean." In *Implicit Understanding*, edited by Stuart B. Schwartz, 157–200. Cambridge: Cambridge University Press.

Hunt, Peter. 1994. *An Introduction to Children's Literature*. Oxford: Oxford University Press (Opus).

Hunter, Allan. 1983. *Joseph Conrad and the Ethics of Darwinism*. London and Canberra: Croom Helm.

Hutcheon, Linda. 1985. *A Theory of Parody: The Teachings of Twentieth-Century Art Forms*. New York and London: Methuen.

Idriess, Ion L. 1938. *Madman's Island*. Sydney: Angus and Robertson.

Jameson, Fredric. 1987. "Shifting Contexts of Science-Fiction Theory." *Science Fiction Studies* 42, Vol. 14, Pt. 2: 241–47.

———. 1991. *Postmodernism, or The Cultural Logic of Late Capitalism*. Durham: Duke University Press.

Keating, Peter. 1989. *The Haunted Study: A Social History of the English Novel, 1875–1914*. London: Secker and Warburg.

Keegan, John. 1993. *A History of Warfare*. New York: Alfred A. Knopf.

Kemp, Peter. 1982. *H. G. Wells and the Culminating Ape: Biological Themes and Imaginative Obsessions*. London: Macmillan.

King, Stephen. 1986. "Survivor Type." In *Skeleton Crew*, 429–51. London and Sydney: Futura (1982).

Kipling, Rudyard. 1937. *Something of Myself*. London: Macmillan.
Kozicki, Henry. 1979. *Tennyson and Clio: History in the Major Poems*. Baltimore and London: Johns Hopkins University Press.
Lee, Ang, director. 2012. *Life of Pi*.
Le Guin, Ursula K. 1973. *The Left Hand of Darkness*. Frogmore: Granada (1969).
Lençek, Lena, and Gideon Bosker. 1998. *The Beach: The History of Paradise on Earth*. New York: Viking Penguin.
Loxley, Diana. 1990. *Problematic Shores: The Literature of Islands*. London: Macmillan.
Luckhurst, Roger. 1997. *The Angle Between Two Walls: The Fiction of J. G. Ballard*. Liverpool: Liverpool University Press.
McCalman, Iain. 2010. *Darwin's Armada*. London: Pocket Books (Simon and Schuster).
McCarron, Kevin. 1996. "In Contemplation of My Deliverance: *Robinson Crusoe* and *Pincher Martin*." In *Robinson Crusoe Myths and Metamorphoses*, edited by Lieve Spaas and Brian Stimpson, 285–93. London: Macmillan.
McConnell, Frank. 1981. *The Science Fiction of H. G. Wells*. New York: Oxford University Press.
MacDonald, Dwight, editor. 1960. *Parodies: An Anthology from Chaucer to Beerbohm—And After*. New York: Random House.
Marryat, Captain Frederick. 1938. *Masterman Ready or The Wreck of the "Pacific."* London: Juvenile Productions Ltd. (1841).
Marshall, A. J. 1970. *Darwin and Huxley in Australia*. Sydney: Hodder and Stoughton.
Marshall, P. J., and Glyndwr Williams. 1982. *The Great Map of Mankind: British Perceptions of the World in the Age of Enlightenment*. London: Dent.
Martel, Yann. 2002. *Life of Pi*. Edinburgh: Canongate (2001).
———. 2010. *Beatrice and Virgil*. Melbourne: Text Publishing.
———. Nd. "How I Wrote *Life of Pi*." www.powells.com/fromtheauthor/martel.html.
Martin, Andrew. 1990. *The Mask of the Prophet: The Extraordinary Fictions of Jules Verne*. Oxford: Clarendon Press.
Moretti, Franco. 1983. *Signs Taken for Wonders: Essays in the Sociology of Literary Forms*. Translated by Susan Fletcher, David Forgacs, and David Miller. London: New Left Books.
Morpurgo, Michael. 2005. *Kensuke's Kingdom*. Illustrated by Michael Foreman. London: Egmont (1999).
Nairn, Thom. 1993. "Iain Banks and the Fiction Factory." In *The Scottish Novel Since the Seventies*, edited by Gavin Wallace and Randall Stevenson, 127–35. Edinburgh: Edinburgh University Press.
O'Dell, Scott. 1960. *Island of the Blue Dolphins*. New York: Houghton Mifflin (Dell Yearling).
———. 1976. *Zia*. New York: Yearling (Dell).
Overy, Richard. 2009. *The Twilight Years*. New York: Viking.

Page, Norman. 1985. "Golding's Sources." In *William Golding: Novels, 1954–67*, edited by Norman Page, 101–11. London: Macmillan.
Palitzsch, Francesca. 2010. "Managing Wilderness: Insular Topographies, Outcast Identities and Cultural Representation." Paper presented at conference on Coast and Sea at Christian-Albrechts University, Kiel.
Palmer, Christopher. 2005. "The Teeth of the New Cockatoo: Mutation and Trauma in Greg Egan's *Teranesia*." In *World Weavers*, edited by Wong Kin Yuen, Gary Westfahl, and Amy Kit-sze Chan, 205–14. Hong Kong: Hong Kong University Press.
Parrinder, Patrick. 1970. *H. G. Wells*. Edinburgh: Oliver and Boyd.
———. 1992. "Landscapes of British Science Fiction." In *Styles of Creation*, edited by George Slusser and Eric S. Rabkin, 193–204. Athens and London: University of Georgia Press.
Pasternak, Boris. 2002. *Doctor Zhivago*. Translated by Max Hayward and Manya Harari. London: Vintage (1958).
Peacock, Thomas Love. 1963. *Melincourt*. In *The Novels of Thomas Love Peacock*, Vol. 1, edited by David Garnett, 91–343. London: Rupert Hart-Davis (1817).
Philmus, R. M. 1981. "The Satiric Ambivalence of *The Island of Doctor Moreau*." *Science Fiction Studies* 8: 2–11.
———. 1990. "Textual Authority: The Strange Case of *The Island of Doctor Moreau*." *Science Fiction Studies* 50, Vol. 17, Pt. 1: 64–70.
Poe, Edgar Allan. 1975. *The Narrative of Arthur Gordon Pym of Nantucket*. Harmondsworth: Penguin (1837).
Pritchett, V. S. 1991. "Pain and William Golding." In *The Complete Essays*. London: Chatto and Windus.
Pratchett, Terry. 2009. *Nation*. London: Corgi (Random House) (2008).
Punter, David. 1985. "J. G. Ballard: Alone among the Murder Machines." In *The Hidden Script: Writing and the Unconscious*, 9–27. London and Boston: Routledge and Kegan Paul.
Raban, Jonathan. 1996. *Bad Land: An American Romance*. New York: Pantheon Books.
Rawson, Claude. 2004. "Behind the Tub." *Times Literary Supplement*, Sept. 10, 3–4.
Reed, John R. 1987. "H. G. Wells' Familiar Aliens." In *Aliens: The Anthropology of SF*, edited by George S. Slusser and Gary Westfahl, 145–56. Carbondale and Edwardsville: Southern Illinois University Press.
Rennie, Neil. 1995. *Far-Fetched Facts: The Literature of Travel and the Idea of the South Seas*. Oxford: Clarendon Press.
Richetti, John J. 1975. *Defoe's Narratives: Situations and Structures*. Oxford: Clarendon Press.
Riquet, Johannes. 2010. Paper on *Treasure Island* and *The Beach* presented at conference on Coast and Sea at Christian-Albrechts University, Kiel.

Robert, Marthe. 1980. *Origins of the Novel*. Translated by Sacha Rabinovitch. Brighton: Harvester Press.

Rogers, Pat. 1979. *Robinson Crusoe*. London: Allen and Unwin.

Ruddick, Nicholas. 1993. *Ultimate Island: On the Nature of British Science Fiction*. Westport and London: Greenwood Press.

Sacks, Oliver. 1984. *A Leg to Stand On*. New York: Summit Books.

Samuelson, David N. 1978. "From Aliens to Alienation: Gregory Benford's Variations on a Theme." *Foundation*, Sept. 14, 1978, 5–19.

———, editor. 1993. "On Hard Science Fiction." *Science Fiction Studies* 60, Vol. 20, Pt. 2: 145–240.

Saxton, A. 1996. In *Robinson Crusoe: Myths and Metamorphoses*, edited by Lieve Spaas and Brian Stimpson. London: Macmillan.

Schultze, Jürgen. 1970. *Art of Nineteenth-Century Europe*. New York: Harry N. Abrams.

Seidel, Michael. 1986. *Exile and the Narrative Imagination*. New Haven and London: Yale University Press.

———. 1991. *Robinson Crusoe: Island Myths and the Novel*. Boston: Twayne.

Shakespeare, William. 1968. *The Tempest*. Edited by Anne Righter. Harmondsworth: Penguin (1611).

Shapiro, Barbara. 2000. *A Culture of Fact: England, 1550–1720*. Ithaca and London: Cornell University Press.

Shattuck, Roger. 1984. "Locating Michel Tournier." In *The Innocent Eye: On Modern Literature and the Arts*, 205–18. New York: Farrar, Straus and Giroux.

Shauffer, Brian W. 2006. *Reading the Novel in English 1950–2000*. Oxford: Blackwell.

Shippey, Tom. 2005. "Hard Reading: The Challenges of Science Fiction." In *A Companion to Science Fiction*, edited by David Seed, 11–26. Oxford: Blackwell.

Showalter, Elaine. 1992. "The Apocalyptic Fables of H. G. Wells." In *Fin de Siècle/Fin du Globe: Fears and Fantasies of the Late Nineteenth Century*, edited by John Stokes, 69–84. London: Macmillan.

Sinfield, Alan, editor. 1983. *Society and Literature 1945–1970*. London: Methuen.

Slusser, George, and Eric S. Rabkin, editors. 1986. *Hard Science Fiction*. Carbondale and Edwardsville: Southern Illinois University Press.

Souhami, Diana. 2002. *Selkirk's Island*. London: Phoenix.

Southall, Ivan. 1967. *To the Wild Sky*. Illustrated by Jennifer Tuckwell. Sydney: Angus and Robertson.

Spacks, Patricia Meyer. 2006. *Novel Beginnings: Experiments in Eighteenth-Century English Fiction*. New Haven and London: Yale University Press.

Spark, Muriel. 1958. *Robinson: A Novel*. London: Macmillan.

Spivak, Gayatri Chakravorty. 1991. "Theory in the Margin: Coetzee's Foe reading Defoe's Crusoe/Roxana." In *Consequences of Theory*, edited by Jonathan Arac and Barbara Johnson, 154–80. Baltimore and London: Johns Hopkins University Press.

Stableford, Brian. 1983. "Against the New Gods: the Speculative Fiction of S. Fowler Wright." *Foundation* 29, 10–52.

Stacpoole, Henry de Vere. 1960. *The Blue Lagoon*. London: Four Square Books (1908).

Stafford, Robert A. 1999. "Scientific Exploration and Empire." In *The Oxford History of the British Empire*, Vol. III, edited by Andrew Porter, 294–319. Oxford: Oxford University Press.

Stevenson, Robert Louis. 1987. *Treasure Island*. London: Oxford World's Classics (1883).

Sutherland, James. 1975. "On *Robinson Crusoe*." In *Robinson Crusoe*, edited by Michael Shinagel, 379–93. New York: Norton.

Swift, Jonathan. 1958. *Gulliver's Travels*. Edited by Ricardo Quintana. New York: Modern Library College Editions (1726).

Tadié, Jean-Yves. 1982. *Le Roman d'Aventures*. Paris: Presses Universitaires de France.

Tennyson, Alfred Lord. 1953. "Enoch Arden." In *Poetical Works*, 117–29. London: Oxford University Press (1864).

Thomas, Keith. 1984. *Man and the Natural World: Changing Attitudes in England 1500–1800*. Harmondsworth: Penguin.

———. 2009. *The Ends of Life: Roads to Fulfillment in Early Modern England*. Oxford: Oxford University Press.

Thompson, Andrew. 2005. *The Empire Strikes Back?* Harlow: Pearson Longman.

Tournier, Michel. 1969. *Friday or The Other Island*. Translated by Norman Denny. London: Collins.

———. 1972. *Vendredi ou Les Limbes du Pacifique*. Paris: Gallimard (1967, revised 1972).

———. 1987. *The Golden Droplet*. Translated by Barbara Wright. London: Collins (*La Goutte d'Or*, 1985).

———. 1998. *The Wind Spirit: An Autobiography*. Translated by Arthur Goldhammer. Boston: Beacon Press (*Le Vent Paraclet*, 1977).

———. 2005. *Vendredi ou La Vie Sauvage*. Additional material by Nicholas Veysman and Isabelle Varloteaux. Paris: Folioplus (1977).

Verne, Jules. 1977. *Les Enfants du Capitaine Grant*. Paris: Hachette (1867–68).

———. 2001. *The Mysterious Island*. Translated by Sidney Kravitz, edited by Arthur B. Evans, introduction and critical material by William Butcher. Middletown, CT: Wesleyan University Press.

———. 2004. *The Mysterious Island*. Translated by Jordan Stump. New York: Modern Library (1875).

———. 2005. *The Adventures of Captain Hatteras*. Translated and introduced by William Butcher. Oxford: World's Classics (1865).

Walcott, Derek. 1986. "The Castaway and Other Poems." In *Collected Poems 1948–1984*. London: Faber (1965).

Watt, Ian. 1987. *The Rise of the Novel*. London: Hogarth Press.

Waugh, Evelyn. 1951. *A Handful of Dust*. London: Penguin (1934).
Weir, Andy. 2014. *The Martian*. New York: Del Rey (2013).
Wells, H. G. 1975. *The War of the Worlds*. London: Pan (1898).
———. 1982. *The Island of Dr. Moreau*. In *H. G. Wells*, 76–159. New York: Octopus (1896).
———. 1987. "Aepynornis Island" (1894) and "The Lord of the Dynamos" (1894). In *The Complete Short Stories of H G Wells*, 260–72 and 284–93. London: A & C Black.
Wilder, Cherry. 1986. *Second Nature*. London: Allen and Unwin.
———. 1996. *Signs of Life*. New York: Tor/Tom Doherty.
Winter, Jay. 2006. *Remembering War*. New Haven and London: Yale University Press.
Wolfe, Gary K. 1989. "Science Fiction as Criticism as Fiction." *Extrapolation* Vol. 30, No. 4: 380–87.
Wolfe, Gene. 1980. *The Island of Doctor Death and Other Stories and Other Stories*. New York: Pocket Books.
Wright, S. Fowler. 1928. *The Island of Captain Sparrow*. London: Victor Gollancz.
Wyss, Johann. 1991. *The Swiss Family Robinson*. Edited and introduced by John Seelye. Oxford: World's Classics/Oxford University Press (see 1901n1 for further details on the authorship of the English version).
Zabus, Chantal. 2002. *Tempests After Shakespeare*. New York: Palgrave.
Žižek, Slavoj. 2001. "From Western Marxism to Western Buddhism." *Cabinet* 2 (cabinetmagazine.org/issues/2/western.php).
Zemeckis, Roger, director. 2000. *Cast Away*.

INDEX

For further material on texts by Crummey, King, Spark, Stevenson, and Weir, see the website for *Castaway Tales*, at http://chrispalmercastaway.com/.

Books, stories, and poems are indexed under the name of their author.

THE WESLEYAN
EARLY CLASSICS OF
SCIENCE FICTION
SERIES

General Editor Arthur B. Evans

The Centenarian
Honoré de Balzac

We Modern People: Science Fiction and the Making of Russian Modernity
Anindita Banerjee

Cosmos Latinos: An Anthology of Science Fiction from Latin America and Spain
Andrea L. Bell and Yolanda Molina-Gavilán, eds.

The Coming Race
Edward Bulwer-Lytton

Imagining Mars: A Literary History
Robert Crossley

Caesar's Column: A Story of the Twentieth Century
Ignatius Donnelly

Vintage Visions: Essays on Early Science Fiction
Arthur B. Evans, ed.

Subterranean Worlds: A Critical Anthology
Peter Fitting, ed.

Lumen
Camille Flammarion

The Time Ship: A Chrononautical Journey
Enrique Gaspar

The Last Man
Jean-Baptiste Cousin de Grainville

The Emergence of Latin American Science Fiction
Rachel Haywood Ferreira

The Battle of the Sexes in Science Fiction
Justine Larbalestier

The Yellow Wave: A Romance of the Asiatic Invasion of Australia
Kenneth Mackay

The Moon Pool
A. Merritt

Castaway Tales: From Robinson Crusoe to Life of Pi
Christopher Palmer

Colonialism and the Emergence of Science Fiction
John Rieder

The Twentieth Century
Albert Robida

Three Science Fiction Novellas: From Prehistory to the End of Mankind
J.-H. Rosny aîné

The Black Mirror and Other Stories: An Anthology of Science Fiction from Germany and Austria
Franz Rottensteiner, ed., and Mike Mitchell, tr.

The Fire in the Stone: Prehistoric Fiction from Charles Darwin to Jean M. Auel
Nicholas Ruddick

The World as It Shall Be
Emile Souvestre

Star Maker
Olaf Stapledon

The Begum's Millions
Jules Verne

Five Weeks in a Balloon
Jules Verne

Invasion of the Sea
Jules Verne

The Kip Brothers
Jules Verne

The Mighty Orinoco
Jules Verne

The Mysterious Island
Jules Verne

Travel Scholarships
Jules Verne

H. G. Wells: Traversing Time
W. Warren Wagar

Star Begotten
H. G. Wells

Deluge
Sydney Fowler Wright

Sisters of Tomorrow: The First Women of Science Fiction
Lisa Yaszek and Patrick B. Sharp, eds.

CHRISTOPHER PALMER is a former associate professor of English at La Trobe University in Melbourne, Australia. He is the author of the book *Philip K. Dick: Exhilaration and Terror of the Postmodern*, and his essays have appeared in *Science Fiction Studies* and *Extrapolation*. The author's website is chrispalmercastaway.com.